READINGS ON AUDIENCE AND TEXTUAL MATERIALITY

THE HISTORY OF THE BOOK

Series Editor: Ann R. Hawkins

TITLES IN THIS SERIES

1 Conservatism and the Quarterly Review: A Critical Analysis
Jonathan Cutmore (ed.)

2 Contributors to the Quarterly Review: A History, 1809–1825
Jonathan Cutmore

3 Wilkie Collins's American Tour, 1873–1874
Susan R. Hanes

4 William Blake and the Art of Engraving
Mei-Ying Sung

5 Charles Lamb, Elia and the London Magazine: Metropolitan Muse
Simon P. Hull

6 Reading in History: New Methodologies from the Anglo-American Tradition
Bonnie Gunzenhauser (ed.)

7 Middle-Class Writing in Late Medieval London
Malcolm Richardson

FORTHCOMING TITLES

Elizabeth Inchbald's Reputation: A Publishing and Reception History
Ben P. Robertson

READINGS ON AUDIENCE AND TEXTUAL MATERIALITY

EDITED BY

Graham Allen, Carrie Griffin and Mary O'Connell

Routledge
Taylor & Francis Group

LONDON AND NEW YORK

First published 2011 by Pickering & Chatto (Publishers) Limited

Published 2016 by Routledge
2 Park Square, Milton Park, Abingdon, Oxfordshire OX14 4RN
711 Third Avenue, New York, NY 10017, USA

First issued in paperback 2015

Routledge is an imprint of the Taylor & Francis Group, an informa business

BRITISH LIBRARY CATALOGUING IN PUBLICATION DATA

Readings on audience and textual materiality. – (The history of the book)
1. Books and reading – History. 2. Books – Format – Psychological aspects.
3. Books – Format – History.
I. Series II. Allen, Graham, 1963- III. Griffin, Carrie. IV. O'Connell, Mary.
002'.09-dc22

ISBN-13: 978-1-138-66448-7 (pbk)
ISBN-13: 978-1-8489-3159-6 (hbk)

Typeset by Pickering & Chatto (Publishers) Limited

CONTENTS

Acknowledgements   vii

List of Contributors   ix

List of Figures   xiii

Introduction   1

1 The Memory and Impact of Oral Performance: Shaping the
Understanding of Late Medieval Readers – *John J. Thompson*   9

2 Print, Miscellaneity and the Reader in Robert Herrick's *Hesperides*
– *Ruth Connolly*   23

3 Searching for Spectators: From *Istoria* to History Painting
– *Liam Lenihan*   37

4 Returning to the Text of *Frankenstein* – *Graham Allen*   51

5 'Casualty', Mrs Shelley and Seditious Libel: Cleansing Britain's Most
Corrupt Poet of Error – *Nora Crook*   61

6 Writing Textual Materiality: Charles Clark, his Books and his Bookplate
Poem – *Carrie Griffin and Mary O'Connell*   75

7 Charles Dickens's Readers and the Material Circulation of the Text
– *Robert McParland*   89

8 Victorian Pantomime Libretti and the Reading Audience
– *Jill A. Sullivan*   107

9 Material Modernism and Yeats – *Alex Davis*   119

10 Changing Audiences: The Case of the Penguin *Ulysses*
– *Alistair McCleery*   131

11 The Sound of Literature: Secondary School Teaching on Reading
Aloud and Silent Reading, 1880–1940 – *Ton van Kalmthout*   143

12 Intermediality: Experiencing the Virtual Text – *Órla Murphy*   155

Notes   163

Works Cited   197

Index   217

ACKNOWLEDGEMENTS

Collections of essays never come into existence without collaboration and cooperation. The editors wish to unreservedly acknowledge the contribution of Siobhán Collins to this volume of essays and to the conferences from which it emerges. Siobhán is a founding member of *Making Books, Shaping Readers* and, at an earlier stage, was part of the editorial team of this book, and we thank her wholeheartedly for her input and expertise. Credit is also due to our publishers, Pickering and Chatto, and especially to Mark Pollard, Publishing Director at Pickering and Chatto, along with series editor Ann Hawkins, and Stephina Clarke, copy editor, for their trust in and assistance with this project. We thank also the external reader, whose comments and suggestions guided us in refining the focus and concerns of this book. We were, too, fortunate to have the keen eye of Liam Lenihan, who provided invaluable feedback on our introductory remarks. We are, of course, grateful to our essayists: they are a remarkable group of scholars, unfailingly professional, good humoured and generous, and exceedingly patient. We feel privileged that they chose our conferences and our volume as the places in which they would share their work with the wider scholarly community. We especially thank those who acted as keynote speakers at our meetings: Nora Crook, Alistair McCleery and John Thompson, and also Bill Bell, keynote speaker at our first conference, whose paper was promised elsewhere.

The conferences from which this book emerges were held at University College Cork's School of English under the auspices of the *Making Books, Shaping Readers* project. We acknowledge the excellent contributions of the speakers and delegates at each conference: together they cultivated a collegial and friendly atmosphere which initiated discussion, exchange and the creation of new ventures. The support received from the School of English was key to the success of both conferences, and we sincerely thank Colbert Kearney and Anne Fitzgerald for their generosity and advice, along with our colleagues in the School for continuing to provide a supportive and friendly environment in which to work. The conferences received financial assistance from the School of English, the College of Arts, Celtic Studies and Social Science at University College Cork; the Association for Manuscripts and Archives in Research Collections and Fáilte Ireland.

As well as supporting the conferences, the College of Arts, Social Sciences and Celtic Studies at University College Cork generously supported this book with a grant from their publication fund.

We acknowledge the continued support of and collaboration with the Boole Library, University College Cork, in particular that of John Fitzgerald, Elaine Charwat, Crónán Ó Doibhlin and Julian Walton. We would like to extend special gratitude to Tom Dunne who has been unfailingly supportive of the ideas and concepts that helped to make this book a reality, as well as having supported us in numerous practical ways.

Many others helped with both conferences and this book project in important ways. We owe great debts of gratitude to: Loretta Brady, Carmel Murphy, Brian Oh-Aounghusa, David Ryan, Keith Crook, and Wilifred Raussert; and to all of the participants, speakers and chairpersons at both meetings. Last, but not least, we thank our families and friends for their constant love and support.

LIST OF CONTRIBUTORS

Graham Allen is the author of *Harold Bloom: A Poetics of Conflict* (1994), *Intertextuality* (2000), *Roland Barthes* (2003), *Mary Shelley* (2008), *Frankenstein: A Readers Guide* (2008) and co-editor of *The Salt Companion to Harold Bloom* (2007). He is the author of numerous articles on Romanticism and literary and cultural theory. He is currently Professor of English at the School of English, University College Cork, and Distinguished Visiting Fellow of the London Graduate School. He is also the winner of the Listowel Poetry Prize (2010).

Ruth Connolly completed a PhD at University College Cork and is now a lecturer in seventeenth-century literature at Newcastle University, UK. She has recently co-edited the collection *Community and Conviviality in the Work of Robert Herrick* (2011) with Tom Cain, and is also co-editor (with Cain) of *Robert Herrick: The Complete Poetry*, forthcoming with Oxford University Press in 2011–12.

Nora Crook is Emerita Professor of English at Anglia Ruskin University, Cambridge. Jamaican by birth and education, she has lived in England since 1959 since arriving there to study English Literature at Cambridge. After a career that involved specialist teaching of reading at primary school level and adult literacy work, she joined the staff at Cambridgeshire College of Arts and Technology, forerunner to Anglia Ruskin. Among her numerous publications on Romantic and nineteenth-century topics are monographs on Shelley and Kipling. The greater part of her scholarly work has been editorial. She has transcribed and edited two volumes (one with Timothy Webb) of Shelley's notebooks at the Bodleian Library for *The Bodleian Shelley Manuscripts* (1986–97), and general-edited twelve volumes of Mary Shelley's works (1996, 2002), for which project she was also volume editor for *Frankenstein* and *Valperga*. She retired in 2003 and subsequently became a visiting professor at Ferris Women's University, Yokohama (2005–6). She is currently a co-general editor, with Donald Reiman and Neil Fraistat, of the multi-volume *Complete Poetry of Percy Bysshe Shelley* (2000–), with particular responsibility for the volumes containing Shelley's posthumous poetry.

Alex Davis is Professor of English at University College Cork. He has published widely on Anglophone poetry from the 1890s to the present day. He is the author of *A Broken Line: Denis Devlin and Irish Poetic Modernism* (2000); co-author, with John Goodby, Andrew Hadfield and Eve Patten, of *Irish Studies: The Essential Glossary* (2003); and co-editor of three collections of essays on modernist poetry: with Lee M. Jenkins, *The Cambridge Companion to Modernist Poetry* (2007) and *Locations of Literary Modernism: Region and Nation in British and American Modernist Poetry* (2000); and, with Patricia Coughlan, *Modernism and Ireland: The Poetry of the 1930s* (1995).

Carrie Griffin received her doctorate from University College Cork in 2006, where she taught medieval and Renaissance literature part-time, and full-time 2006–7. She is currently IRCHSS Government of Ireland CARA Postdoctoral Mobility Fellow at the School of English and Drama, Queen Mary University of London, and she was previously National University of Ireland Postdoctoral Fellow at the School of English, University College Cork. Her edition of the Middle English *Wise Book of Philosophy and Astronomy* will be published in 2011, and she is currently working on a monograph that investigates material and semantic strategies for the ordering and representing of information in manuscript and print, *c.* 1450–1660. She is a coordinator of the *Forum for Medieval and Renaissance Studies in Ireland*, a contributor to the *Year's Work in English Studies*, and she has published several articles on book and manuscript history. Along with Mary O'Connell, she was the recipient of The Bibliographical Society's Antiquarian Booksellers Association Award (2010), bestowed for their work on Charles Clark (1806–80).

Liam Lenihan has recently completed the National University of Ireland Centennial Postdoctoral Fellowship in Irish Studies as part of the School of English and Department of History of Art, University College Cork. He is currently completing a monograph on the writings of the Irish neoclassical artist James Barry which details Barry's relationship with contemporary artists and authors such as Joshua Reynolds and William Blake. His research interests include nineteenth- and twentieth-century aesthetics and artistic practice, eighteenth-century literature and philosophy; in particular Jonathan Swift, Edmund Burke, Mary Wollstonecraft and William Godwin. He currently teaches eighteenth-century literature at the School of English, University College Cork and is working on a new project which aims to describe the ideas behind the generic shift from history painting to landscape art.

Alistair McCleery is Professor of Literature and Culture and Director of the Scottish Centre for the Book at Edinburgh Napier University. He has published widely on Scottish and Irish literature, particularly on Neil Gunn and James Joyce. He is co-author of *An Introduction to Book History* (2005) and *The*

Book History Reader (second edition, 2006). He was co-editor and contributor to *The History of the Book in Scotland 1880–1980* published by Edinburgh University Press in 2007. His most recent books include *In Search of a Hero: Looking for Allen Lane* (2006), two editions of Neil Gunn's essays, *Landscape and Light* (2009) and *Belief in Ourselves* (2010), and the co-edited *An Honest Trade: Bookselling in Scotland* (2009). He has contributed chapters to *The Book in Germany* (2010) as well as the forthcoming (2010) *Scottish Comics: A Celebration* and *The Influence of D. F. McKenzie*. His current work includes the history of twentieth-century reading and the history of libraries in Scotland.

Robert McParland is Associate Professor and chair of English at Felician College. He edited the collection *Music and Literary Modernism* (2006) and is the author of *Charles Dickens's American Audience* (2010) and *Writing about Joseph Conrad* (2010). Along with research in book history and reception, he often writes about music and literature.

Órla Murphy is a member of the teaching and research team in the School of English at University College Cork. She lectures to undergraduate and postgraduate students about theories of textual transmission from the earliest oral poems in the English language through to the discipline of digital humanities and innovative scholarship in new media. Her research focus is on the digitization of cultural heritage artefacts and generating new models for research, teaching and learning. She is particularly concerned with building a fundamental e-literacy at all levels of scholarly practice and with engaging in international, standards driven, best practice for collaborative research and teaching communities across the university.

Mary O'Connell received her PhD from University College Cork in 2009. She currently teaches eighteenth- and nineteenth-century literature in the School of English, University College Cork. She is the author of various articles on Byron and book history and is currently working on a monograph on the relationship between authors and their publishers in the Romantic period. Along with Carrie Griffin, she was the recipient of The Bibliographical Society's Antiquarian Booksellers Association Award (2010), bestowed for their work on Charles Clark (1806–80).

Jill Sullivan recently completed postdoctoral research at the University of Exeter on the AHRC-funded project 'Moving and Projected-Image Entertainment in the South-West 1820–1914'. Her research interests lie within the field of nineteenth-century theatre and popular entertainments, with a particular interest in the development and expression of regional identity through theatre and other visual and performance genres. Her book, *The Politics of Pantomime: Regional Identity in the Theatre 1860–1900*, is due to be published in Spring 2011 and she is a contributor to *Victorian Pantomime: A Critical Reader* (Autumn 2010).

John J. Thompson is Professor of English Textual Cultures in the School of English at Queen's University Belfast. He has been director of two major AHRC-funded projects at Queen's, the first dealing with the so-called 'English Brut tradition' and how a national history was imagined in England through the late medieval and early modern period; the second (in collaboration with the University of St Andrews) deals with affective renderings of vernacular lives of Christ in the same period. His current research explores the textual 'afterlife' of medieval literature through to the modern period, a continuation of his collaborative interests that includes his participation in a series of scoping workshops funded by the Royal Society of Edinburgh and organized in conjunction with colleagues at the University of St Andrews, the University of Glasgow, and the University of Dublin, Trinity College.

Ton van Kalmthout is a senior researcher at the Huygens Institute of the Royal Netherlands Academy of Arts and Sciences in The Hague. He obtained his doctoral degree for his thesis entitled *Muzentempels, Multidisciplinaire kunstkringen in Nederland tussen 1880 en 1914* [Temples of the Muses, Multi-disciplinary art clubs in the Netherlands from 1880 to 1914] (1998). His research interests and his publications lie in the field of the transmission of literature in the nineteenth and twentieth centuries, including the history of philology and literary education, cultural sociability and the reception of foreign literature in a national context. He is an editor of the *Tijdschrift voor Nederlandse Taal- en Letterkunde* (Journal of Netherlandic Linguistics and Literary Studies).

LIST OF FIGURES

Figure 3.1: James Barry, *Elysium and Tartarus*, first published 1792,
    etching and engraving (black ink), 41 x 92.4 cm   46
Figure 6.1: Clark's Bookplate   81
Figure 9.1: Advertisement in *Beltaine*, 2 (February 1900)   127
Figure 11.1: Some experiments using notation from C. L. Merkel,
    Physiologie der menschlichen Sprache (*physiologische Laletik*),
    (Leipzig: Otto Wigand, 1866), pp. 412–28   147

INTRODUCTION

Graham Allen, Carrie Griffin and Mary O'Connell

> once we acknowledge that the physical book as a whole is a rich complex of signs, each of which has its own human history and all of which unite to *create* the 'finished' book as a palpably articulated 'text' (to *form* it, not *de*-form it), then we enter an entirely new, more positive and, for me at least, more exciting phase of textual criticism.[1]

By the time you read these opening lines you have already formed an impression of this book and perhaps established certain fundamental truths about it. These will most likely be challenged or confirmed as you read, but the point remains that you have established them using some textual and some non-textual signifiers. You encounter thresholds with each book you come across: the cover, the picture: what is inscribed on the outside of the volume either in text or in image. These signifiers lead you to conclusions about genre, audience, relevance and scope, and those conclusions are altered, or confirmed or dismissed, upon delving further into the object.[2] In other words, you have first encountered the material form of the book: you have first *read* that materiality, and you read that materiality every time you come into contact with a physical text. This text has a physical reality. The physical, material nature of the text can change (you may be reading this, for instance, on a computer screen), but the materiality of the text always contributes to its meaning. According to Jerome McGann, this is the case 'whether we are aware of such matters when we make our meanings or whether we are not'.[3] The essays in this volume describe this process.

Readings on Audience and Textual Materiality is concerned with the importance and impact of materiality on the reader(s) and audience(s) of texts. It assesses how material concerns contribute to the structure and life of a text (taken broadly); and how materiality and physicality, to varying extents, influence and establish readings, readers and publics. In other words, it attempts to identify the variant ways in which readers read a text and how those readings are constructed by the way a text is represented physically. At a more theoretical level, the purpose and achievement of the essays in this volume is difficult to articulate: it is at once simple and complex, simple in the sense that most historians of the book, along with textual critics and social theorists, will accept that the physical form of a text both contributes to meaning and influences reception, interpretation and attitudes. It is complex because there is no one established precedent with which to describe and theorize that influence. This complexity is not a negative, however, and is largely due, we argue, to the fact that the concept of materiality is a protean one. Yet it is possible, through what are essentially interdisciplinary approaches combining critical analysis, textual and bibliographical studies, historical and theoretical studies, and a concern with the 'literalism of imagination', to imagine, recover and exemplify the cultural significance of the material form of a text.[4]

This collection proceeds with the assumption that the linguistic and material meanings of a text are fundamentally and inextricably linked. Such an approach aligns this volume with the latest scholarly enquiry in the field of book history. On the first page of the recently published *A Companion to the History of the Book* the editors Simon Eliot and Jonathan Rose state that 'readers can read the same book in a variety of ways, with important consequences'.[5] Following Wolfgang Iser and Stanley Fish,[6] this assertion gives priority to the reader's interaction with the text. The essays in this volume show that this interaction takes place not just in relation to linguistic, but also to bibliographical codes, and specifically in relation to the materiality of the text. Thus they consciously follow McGann's attempt to 'sketch a materialist hermeneutics', and his insistence on the necessity of 'grounding literary scholarship in a ... study of material texts'.[7] The phrase we use in the title is 'textual materiality'; taking the term 'text' broadly, to signify anything that can be read and thus interpreted, or to which meaning can be ascribed. Our approach demands the following: 1) a text is read in conjunction with its physical form or forms; 2) a text, and/or its paratexts, embody and can be read for evidence of awareness of the meaning of that physicality; 3) the relationship between the text and the physical form constitutes meaning; and 4) the physical form, or the articulation of that relationship between the physical and the intellectual, contributes to the understanding and attitudes of its readership and audiences to a greater or lesser extent. This basic framework, coupled with the interdisciplinary thrust of the essays herein, aligns us closely both with the sociological concept of material culture, and with the now emerged and established – but still institutionally diverse – discipline of the history of the book.[8] Our approach bridges these two important critical concepts in twenty-first-century literary, socio-cultural and historical studies. In the first instance, material culture recognizes that two normally-opposed concepts – the physical and the intellectual – must be understood not only as mutually informative, but that the 'material dimension is ... fundamental to understanding culture'.[9] Like the history of the book, then, it is interdisciplinary, or 'undisciplined', which implies lack of restriction as well as challenges in definition.[10] Material culture arises out of a variety of disciplines, and the concept of materiality is 'heterogeneous and ambiguous', with attempts at definition being 'entangled with deep metaphorical roots and cultural connotations'.[11] Where we, as students of textual materiality, relate to material culture as a sociological, political and theoretical approach is that we recognize text (again, in its broadest sense) as both object and cultural artefact, as something that responds to investigations that consider power, symbolism, identity and gender as well as to critical and social theories like Marxism, Structuralism and Feminism. In this respect a book cover can be read as gendered or an inscribed stone can be interpreted as a symbol of patriarchal and masculine power structures.

Our concern with textual materiality diverges from material culture because we argue that the linguistic and intellectual content of a text has a physical reality and, as such, contributes to the meaning of its own physicality, whereas theories of material culture frequently and implicitly accept that the object's meaning is largely constructed by the changing world around it. Rather than relating ideas, concepts and theories to an object, textual materiality insists on the symbiosis of the intellectual and the physical, so that a text cannot be fully understood without its physical aspect, nor can the physical be understood and appreciated without the meaning given by the intellectual. Textual materiality, in our sense, views an object in terms of its contribution to the meaning it conveys or which is ascribed to it. It maintains that meaning already exists in the conjunction of the linguistic and bibliographical codes of a text.

Yet this distinction presumes a simple notion of textual materiality, whereas our sense of it is nuanced, more so in its relation to the increasingly influential discipline of book history. Robert Darnton's now-famous and influential essay 'What is the History of Books?' was concerned to define a discipline, to establish a set of principles by which book historians might proceed, and to curb what he envisages as its potential to 'interdisciplinarity run riot'.[12] His 'Communications Circuit'[13] proposes a framework with which historians of the book can interrogate or describe their chosen object, agent or system, be it the bookseller, the publisher, the press, the reader or the papermaker. Darnton's work, rightly so, has been heavily influential on book history, but as a discipline (and by extension something that needed to be defined in order to exist and evolve) it remains concerned, generally speaking, with the strictly historical, commercial and sociological. It is also strongly indebted to an eighteenth century model of textual production; for example it would be difficult to apply to a study of oral or manuscript culture. Book historians have frequently argued against the limitations of Darnton's circuit (see especially Adams and Barker);[14] however the influence of his model is surely indicative of the need to establish common ground in a field that, in Darnton's own words, is often 'less like a field than a tropical rainforest'.[15] You can read an essay in this book on anything from pantomime libretti, the Penguin edition of *Ulysses*, an eccentric Victorian printer, the manuscript of *Frankenstein*, or even the practice of reading aloud in Dutch secondary schools. In this respect, the volume might appear to be the physical embodiment of Darnton's tropical rainforest. In fact, all of the essays have something in common: in their different ways they explore how the materiality of the text (whether it is in the form of a manuscript, painting, textbook, (con)text or bookplate) contributes to the reader's experience and the production of meaning.

With this as the unifying principle of the book, it should be clear that while we recognize the needful aspects to the study of book cultures outlined by Darnton, we propose that these concerns can be allied to the study of meaning and ideas in order to extend the possibilities of book history to interpretive activity. Rather than acknowledging disciplinary and historical divisions, we have allowed powerful unifiers – the acknowledgement that the materiality of a text signifies and, moreover, insists upon a set of audiences or responses (whether successfully or not is a matter for another work) – to highlight connections and tangents. Moreover, we identify the concern with textual materiality not as distinct from but an important, and frequently inarticulated, aspect of the approaches that constitute the history of the book; that is, inherent to and implicit in the study of bibliographic codes and agents of production and dissemination, and central to considerations of commercial success (or failure), reconceptions, and new media.

Readings of textual materiality restore the potential for interpretive rather than enumerative or analytical activity to all aspects of Darnton's network of connections. They do so in moving away from some of the constraints implicit in the term 'history' and, also, importantly, in their basic concern with the signifier. Moreover, the term 'textual' allows for a broader and more inclusive set of criteria that does not exclude 'book'; rather, it imagines the book in the wider sense (codex, scroll, digital) and extends parameters to include anything that is inscribed or to which meaning can be ascribed; an artwork is a 'text' in the sense that it can be read and thus interpreted. Reading materiality and form as part of – not just a vehicle for – the art or text, invites fresh perspectives on the creation, transmission, presentation, reception and comprehension of the text or art to emerge.

The essays in this collection present a number of practical demonstrations of the manner in which the various disciplinary theories and practices around book history and textual materiality can shape and direct literary criticism. The overall aim is not to return to an old-fashioned intentionalist criticism, in which a hypothetical author imagines his or her audience's responses. Rather, the works here attempt to draw a closer relation than has arguably thus far been achieved between literary criticism and the various historical and sociological modes of book history and the study of textual materiality. The text remains the object of analysis, therefore, but now it is a text which, within its own generic and figurative structures, affects the possibilities of its reception. This approach does not present itself as an alternative and rival to existent theoretical methodologies, silently assimilating established approaches in the manner Derrida has described discussing the emergence of New Historicism in the United States of America.[16] These essays make use of a good amount of the various theoretical paradigms associated with book history, reader response and reader reception theory, cultural studies, bibliography and textual criticism, but they do so in ways that are oriented towards an examination of how textual structures respond to previous acts of reading and an attempt to figure future acts of reading.

There can be a tendency, in some work which is produced under the umbrella of book history, to rely on historical and sociological models which are designed to show broad commercial trends in production and consumption. Richard Altick's exhaustive sociological study, *The English Common Reader* described the forces which led to the formation of the mass reading public.[17] As Jonathan Rose reminds us, Altick's social, economic and cultural history helped to establish many of the basic principles of what would eventually become book history. Rose himself (along with Janice Radway) has continued the scholarship of Altick, making important contributions to the history of reading.[18] Rose argues that the possibility of a history of reading audiences, one which revealed the 'interactions of specific readers and texts' could potentially help us move beyond the debate of 'whether the reader writes the text or the text manipulates the reader'.[19] With increased access to diaries, letters, publishers' records, library registers, and resources such as the *Reading Experience Database*[20] it is now possible to reconstruct the experience of actual readers (as in McParland's comprehensive essay on American readers' reception of Charles Dickens). Whether it will ever be possible to reconstruct the experience of a mass reading audience is doubtful. In his monumental study, *The Reading Nation in the Romantic Period*, William St Clair alerts us to the dangers of such an enterprise, stating that 'such reports [records of individual reading] ... can never be, at best, anything beyond a tiny, randomly surviving, and perhaps highly unrepresentative, sample of the far larger total acts of reception which were never even turned into words in the mind of the reader let alone recorded in writing'.[21] St Clair's quantitative study of what books were actually read during the Romantic period is a compelling account of the production and distribution of texts, challenging us to understand how knowledge was diffused during this period. Whilst approaches such as Altick's, Rose's and St Clair's are crucial, they work at a level far above that of the text. It would be something of mistake, however, to assume that anything that does work at the level of the text is a return to the intentional fallacy or is just another example of a dehistoricized, professionalized poststructuralism. The text exists in relation to its potential reader(s), as Fish argues. What each of these essays singularly demonstrates is the peculiarities involved in readings which attempt to reflect upon the text's call to, or imagining of, its own readership, realized in the material. There is no single or stable methodology and/or vocabulary available for such a double reflection (the reader attempting to read how the text seeks to produce and influence reading). What is clear is that readings which do make this attempt can revivify the art of literary interpretation and analysis; each of the essays here succeeds brilliantly in manifesting this critical, rich and rewarding exploration, and in embracing the fluid boundaries both suggested and presented by material culture and book history.

This method of critical analysis and interrogation of form utilized in the essays here is not new: the work of Jerome McGann, and in particular his *Black Riders: The Visible Language of Modernism*, recognizes the encoding of meaning in the material presentation of verse, specifically. He argues that since poetry 'descends to us through an early tradition of recitation and performance, poets set a high value on the integration of medium and message'.[22] McGann is not alone in his insistence on the relationship between materiality and meaning; D. F. McKenzie, Philip Gaskell, David Pearson and Anthony Rota have all argued that material form affects how we read texts.[23] The essays in this volume extend that very concept – the interrelatedness of physicality and meaning – to consider not just the physical reality of texts but the various forms that physicality takes and, frequently, what surrounds and frames the text: the bibliographic codes, strategies of presentation, frontispieces and book covers, statements on text and how those statements are physically rendered, and perspectives on para-, hyper- and meta-text. They consider works of art as text and texts as works of art; they not only articulate but they theorize the relationship of the words on the page with what physically frames them, and to the varied audiences that encounter them; and they find evidence for the shaping and re-formation of audiences by the materiality of the text. That sense of the *audience* requires a broad perspective, but for us it represents an anchor concern: a critical component of the framework and ideology of this volume and, even in its variance, a key, powerful thread that is common to each of the pieces here presented. It is not just allied, but is central, to our perspectives on the significance of the material text. Materiality, by definition, both demands and requires an audience; and that audience can confirm, create, change or reject meaning. An audience – in all of its incarnations – obviously involves and implies the reader, but widens the concept of both reader and reading to include viewers and listeners who receive texts in ways that are other than the conventional reading model. The contributors to this book, then, are audiences as well as readers, providing readings on the material, and their work places the audience at the centre of receptions of the material text.

The meetings which produced this volume had a salient scholarly concern with the significance of the materiality of the text, shared between students of different literary historical periods, and the two conferences explored the interconnectedness particular to work conducted across disciplines and time frames in book history and material concerns.[24] These essays reflect those dialogues and discussions. Whilst most of the essays here are naturally concerned with the period from 1700 onwards, which saw the rise of the mass audience, the inclusion of work from earlier periods reinforces the fact that where there is a text, there is always an audience, though evidence for the existence of that audience is variable. What this also allows are intersections and interplays between perspectives on earlier and later material texts: a resonance exists across literary historical periods centring on the material and its relationship to the audience. Audiences (discussed here in fine detail by Jill Sullivan, in particular), however, are not simply passive recipients: most frequently, they are political, instructive, demanding, authoritative, involved and conscious. An audience can be a bookseller, a collector, a publisher. It can be a pantomime crowd, encountering and experiencing text at various, significant levels. An audience is author. An audience can be both author and reader: Carrie Griffin and Mary O'Connell demonstrate how Charles Clark inscribes his experience of the material book into a bookplate poem, which itself courts and demands a public. Audiences are layered and complex, none more so than the readers, consumers and anticipated public for the 1969 Penguin *Ulysses*, expertly described here by Alistair McCleery. Frequently, the evidence of an audience is embedded in a text; the first- and second-readers of Mary Shelley's *Frankenstein* – Mary and Percy – fill pages with their responses to a text and to each others responses, a complexity that is navigated by Graham Allen. Other papers look to the text in a holistic manner to find evidence of materiality and audience articulated in various ways, such as Ruth Connolly's superbly detailed analysis of Robert Herrick's self-fashioning and shaping of audiences in his poetical collection *Hesperides*, and Alex Davis's compelling journey through the rich landscape of material modernism, and its relation to and influence on William Butler Yeats. Van Kalmthout's essay offers a sociological perspective on material guides to reading in *fin-de-siècle* Holland, imagining the effect of surviving printed instruction on the apparently unrecoverable act of reading. John Thompson's study expertly articulates the rich complexity of the visual, material, textual and cultural landscape of the later Middle Ages, advocating and exemplifying close, detailed reading that, taken together, map and plot that landscape. Liam Lenihan looks at the manner by which painters search for spectators for history painting, in particular that of James Barry and Henry Fuseli, in a nuanced paper that challenges and deepens our sense of reception amongst eighteenth-century audiences. Nora Crook's comprehensive insight into the history of editing and reading P. B. Shelley demonstrates the necessity for authoritative versions of the Romantic poet in an astonishingly detailed essay.

Órla Murphy's timely and precise paper extends the scope of this book, considering the impact of the screen on the material text, and imagining the life of the material text in the future. She alerts us to the rapid and constant developments that affect textual production and consumption, and taken in relation to the volume as a whole, highlights that the changes we are now experiencing are at once specific and cyclical. Questions about the materiality of the text have recently been brought to the fore with the imminent launch of the Amazon Kindle e-book reader in the United Kingdom. The *Independent* newspaper recently published two articles engaging with this debate. The first detailed the foundation of a company dedicated solely to publishing e-books.[25] With digital books outselling hardbacks on amazon.com by three to two and most predictions stating that sales of e-books will be between 25–50 per cent of the market within ten years, the establishment of such a company would seem a prescient move. An article by a publisher in the same paper implicitly dismissed the idea, describing the e-book as 'parasitical' on 'physical' (the implication being 'real') books. A few days later saw the publication of a piece entitled 'You can't tell a book by its cover' which discussed the potential impact of the e-reader and our continued 'emotional attachment to the traditional book format.'[26] It is difficult to discount the idea of having an 'emotional attachment' to the physicality of certain books. David Lodge's evocative description of his reading of Joyce is a fine example of the articulation not just of the emotion, but the impact of the material:

> I read *Ulysses* in the Penguin edition because that is what my students use, but I still have the Bodley head edition, protected by a tattered and faded green dust jacket … [J]ust to handle the old Bodley Head edition was to feel a shiver of premonitory pleasure, a sense that this was no ordinary novel, but a magic book.[27]

The sense of wonder holding the 'magic book' is strongly related to the materiality of the book. The tattered cover signifies the countless readings; the imminent pleasure of re-reading. What the history of the book shows, and what any study of the materiality of the text demonstrates, is that the book has always changed form. Clay tablets, stone, vellum, paper; the electronic screen is simply the next, and in all probability not the last incarnation on this list. History has proven that our attachment to texts will not diminish on account of changing materiality; the text will always find some form.

1 THE MEMORY AND IMPACT OF ORAL PERFORMANCE: SHAPING THE UNDERSTANDING OF LATE MEDIEVAL READERS

John J. Thompson

The late medieval period in book history is characterized by two remarkable developments in terms of the production and dissemination of vernacular literature, both of which continued to have a profound impact on the processes of making books and shaping readers in Britain long after the period. These developments were, first, a perceptible shift from memory to written record: at a varying pace right across the literary and bureaucratic cultures of Western Europe, there continued in this period a seemingly irresistible movement away from a predominantly oral-based culture of wisdom, instruction, entertainment and information gathering, in the direction of a culture dominated by the material text.[1] Across a period extending hundreds of years, there was a shift in medieval European attitudes away from large-scale (one hesitates to say popular) participation in an oral culture based on consensus and folk wisdom, passed on by tradition and word of mouth, to, broadly speaking, a text-based book culture and archive-based documentary record. The cultural attitudes of literary audiences had to adjust to take on the business of reading a text as well as hearing it delivered orally.[2] Secondly, following on from that first perceptible shift, the late medieval period in the west witnessed the beginnings of the movement from script to print.[3] This was a movement away from a manuscript culture where texts were often written to order, either as part of an obligation-based system or as a bespoke trade towards the new technological miracle of printing for profit. When the printing trade was introduced and established in the early capitalist cultures of the west, it allowed for multiple copies of a single text to be released simultaneously and relatively cheaply to large numbers of readers. By the late fifteenth century, books were becoming commodities for everyday use and they were being produced in quantity and sold at a price that the growing and voracious market for cheap reading material could sustain. As a result, by the end of the fifteenth century in England and right across continental Europe, the idea that medieval readers were 'shaped' solely by a largely clerical and highly-educated reading elite, dominated by the *literati* and their books, is forced to yield some ground to the notion of the pragmatically literate vernacular reader and the mercantile instincts associated with large-scale metropolitan literary production based on the supply and demand principles of early capitalism.[4]

Although the *grand récit* approach prefers its history with clean edges, one would have to say that the two hugely important cultural and technological developments alluded to in the previous paragraph were not in any sense complete by the time when traditional surveys of English literary history tell us that 'the Medieval', with its tried and tested old ways, had given way to 'the Renaissance' and the shock of the renovated new.[5] Indeed, there is a sense in which the shifts from speech to writing and from pen to moveable type and keyboard will never be complete or absolute, even in societies that pride themselves on higher literacy and educational achievement for more people than ever before and 'popular' written culture seems dominated by the electronic text and the much-anticipated demise of the book as codex. Technology always advances faster than our ability to realize its full potential, of course, so, in this paper, I want to examine and test the presumed impact of the cultural and technological developments I have outlined above on our understanding of English vernacular manuscript culture and late medieval reading experience.

Preliminaries

Geoffrey Chaucer offers us perhaps the best example of a fourteenth-century experimental English writer fully aware of the fictional potential of documenting these changing times for contemporary writers and audiences. The *Canterbury Tales* narrative frame is a storytelling contest, the rules of which are set up by the host of a London suburban tavern before the pilgrim company of 'sondry folk' depart on their way to Canterbury.[6] As someone who usually deployed verse for his fiction, Chaucer demonstrates all the skills of an accomplished European short story writer, matching an acute sense of the placement and juxtaposition of textual details, generic conventions and narrative traditions, with a superb awareness of comic timing. Such mastery of the narrative forms and techniques he found in both written and oral sources is presumably one of the main reasons why modern scriptwriters have found Chaucer's greatest fictional work so readily adaptable for translation to both the large and small screen.[7]

The various narrative qualities in Chaucer's writing have often been commented on, of course, but they come together nicely for my present purposes in the passage known as 'The Miller's Prologue' – the link between 'The Knight's

Tale' and 'The Miller's Tale' in fragment one of the *Canterbury Tales*. For hundreds of years, Chaucer's audiences and critics have been entertained in this passage by their vicarious experience of a dispute between the drunken Miller and the choleric Reeve over the nature and relevance to the Reeve's version of reality (the fictional assumption here being that the Reeve *could* have a version of reality). Written in a colloquial documentary style worthy of the voyeuristic tendencies of contemporary reality television, Chaucer 'the creator' finally intervenes with an *apologia* to the 'gentil' audience members for the undignified and churlish exchange we have just witnessed.[8] Chaucer's preferred narrative technique here is the equivalent of the apologetic television voiceover since, in order to address his audience directly, he has had to create, first of all, the fiction that we are actually witnessing a dispute, or, perhaps more accurately, the performance of a dispute in real time, and then destroy that fiction by reminding us that we are holding a material artefact – a book – and one that he has created for us as a book of tales. His words shape our reading experience since they are a reminder – a completely unnecessary reminder, in most cases – that we are not the 'gentil wight' being addressed and that we are neither pilgrims nor hearers, but merely readers of a book:

> And therefore every gentil wight I preye,
> For Goddes love, demeth nat that I seye
> Of yvel entente, but for I moot reherce
> Hir tales alle, be they better or werse,
> Or elles falsen som of my mateere.
> And therefore, whoso list it nat yheere,
> *Turne over the leef and chese another tale*
> (ll. 3171–7; emphasis mine)

Only Chaucer's readers, it would seem, can destroy the delicate fictional tapestry he has created for their vicarious pleasure by taking offence at this point in his work. But to do so would also make us similar, in some important respects, to the Reeve. Chaucer reminds us of this by playing fast and loose in this passage with the rules that bind together oral and written fiction, narrative authority, and documentary reality. Far more crucially, for my purposes in this paper, 'The Miller's Prologue' as a whole demonstrates that such self-conscious japery is only possible because of Chaucer's acute awareness of the unstable nature of the relationship between his audience and the spoken and written word, and the widely-differing experiences of reading and performance that might be found in the vernacular manuscript culture to which he belongs.

There are many other reminders of different worlds of oral performance and aural understanding now almost completely lost to twenty-first-century readers of Chaucer's fiction. In the dream poems and *Troilus and Criseyde*, for example, Chaucer permits us to imagine vicariously that we are hearers, not readers.

Through his elaborately-contrived fictions of the 'I' voice, he shapes readerly experience in this manner by adopting the persona of the puzzled courtly narrator, someone who is intimate with us but obviously also disturbed by love; as such, he is sometimes sleepless, often bookish, and implicitly comes across to us as a failure in love, and he usually also betrays to us that, as a love poet, he has not fully comprehended the subtlety and complexity of the love experience described. By these quasi-dramatic narrative techniques Chaucer grants us temporary insight into what it would have been like to attend a reading: to have Chaucer present to read his poetry for us, perhaps as a performance at court, or to have his stories performed at some elevated social gathering where poetry really mattered, such as at a *puy*, for example, with Chaucer available at our side as a commentator on the issues raised for debate.[9] The jury remains out as to whether or not these kinds of intimate courtly readings or wider public performances took place in late fourteenth-century London in the changing socio-literary milieu in which Chaucer's poetry was written and first enjoyed. In any event, his bravura performance as the English poet-narrator of *fin amor* flatters one into thinking that the experience of human love chronicled in his verse offers something more than just an opportunity for a private reading experience.[10]

The snatches of lyric occasionally integrated in Chaucer's fiction permit another world of oral performance to intrude momentarily on the reader's imagination. 'Ful loude he soong "Com hider, love, to me!"' we are told of the Pardoner, followed immediately by the information that 'this Somonour bar to hym a stif burdoun'.[11] Apart from the obvious sexual connotations, the Summoner's 'stiff burden' probably refers either to the hearty chorus or refrain he sang, or, if we go back to the original French meaning of the word, it may indicate the recurring bass part of a song that once had accompanying music.[12] We shall never know for sure, of course, since no other trace of the Pardoner's song has ever been found, and, after all, we are dealing with a fiction. Nevertheless, the Pardoner/Summoner episode serves as a useful reminder that the written forms in which much Middle English lyric poetry has survived cannot always do justice to the casual or occasional manner in which such texts were often originally composed, performed and disseminated.[13] Chaucer's integration of lyric snatches into his fiction – for example, in *Troilus and Criseyde*, the *Parliament of Fowls*, and in some of his minor verse, as well as in the *Canterbury Tales* – points to his exploitation of a now largely unfamiliar world of both courtly and popular secular music and song, existing beyond the book, that his earliest readers would have been in a far better position than the modern private reader to appreciate and contextualize. There is a variety of different kinds of short verse of this kind, the original utility of which has largely fallen from sight but that falls into this category. Examples include short pieces that were originally deployed on special occasions such as musical performances or at public recitations (sometimes also deployed within other fictions to indicate such a performance mode), or snatches of secular verse used as sermon prompts or sung with liturgical settings, or impromptu performances of such verse in a range of domestic settings, or in the classroom, on pilgrimage, at church, or occasional verse presented as polite forms of personal petition, for epitaphs or memorials, or on gravestones, in celebration of anniversaries or special events, as gifts or love tokens, as broadsides posted on doors and walls, or funerary verse to adorn a tomb, or inscriptions painted or carved on wood, stone, tile or glass.[14] Some of the extant English metrical romances are often keen to announce to their readers that they too were once recited by minstrels in a tavern setting, so we might also want to include here short verse texts that were often declaimed as part of street drama or as the 'popular' literature of crossroads, squares and taverns.[15]

Codicology and Micro-Study

Faced with the challenge of examining how book production and reader experience was shaped by such a spectacular oral, aural and visual literary culture in Chaucer's day, one might well ask how it might be possible to link a discussion of English manuscript culture to the general themes of this chapter and the book of essays as a whole. Fortunately, various quasi-scientific approaches have been taken to some key book production issues raised by English pre-print culture that offer the promise, in the medium to long term, of far more ambitious and all-embracing studies of that phenomenon than anything that I can attempt here. Such studies proceed through careful palaeographical identification of fourteenth and fifteenth-century English copyists and the precise description of their individual handwriting, for example, or through close linguistic analyses of the written dialects used by individual copyists in the period before English spelling was standardized, thus providing a possible means of localising and comparing a shared network of English scribal associations and activities.[16]

Over the past half century or so, the value of codicological method – the study of the archaeology of the medieval book – has also been demonstrated. It combines traditional forms of textual scholarship with palaeographical and dialectological evidence in various small-scale studies – *petits récits* – that promise, ultimately, to advance our understanding of how English book production in the late medieval period can be mapped onto a much larger and more comprehensive book history. Faced with a similar challenge to scholars of the modern book – the challenge, that is, to construct critical structures and ideological frameworks that will somehow make it possible to map writing evidence on to larger and more familiar patterns of reception and reading – medievalists must always, surely, resort to individual case study. That is because, generally speaking, they are forced to focus, far more exclusively than scholars of the later period, on the evidence revealing that each book (or cluster of books) they study represents in the final analysis an individual handmade artefact (or set of artefacts) that will always carry meanings greater than simply the written texts it contains. In other words, medievalists must consider each medieval manuscript as *sui generis* – a specific event – and one that will always require mapping as an individual event onto the material culture of its day.[17] Regardless of how comprehensive their study sets out to be, it must always be nuanced enough to take account of individual provenance issues and later histories, to appreciate the potential complexity and multilayered experience of reading a book that may have been produced to order, or bought second-hand, or received as a gift, or borrowed, or stolen, or received into ownership, but, perhaps, never read at all. For the period just before, during and after the introduction of printing, they must also learn to appreciate both the impact of the availability of written texts in greater numbers than ever before, yet also the literary and codicological implications of the shift into writing of a literature that was still readily associated with oral performance and aural understanding. Admittedly, most of these are important issues for later book scholars as well, but, for later periods of English book history, one at least has the opportunity to examine much larger patterns in the consumption of printed books, or to locate the experience of the 'common reader' through examining various manifestations of mass production techniques, such as the extent of print runs or circulation figures, or advances in literacy and legislation.[18]

From Memory to Written Verse

There are many individual cases – in the short works by John Lydgate or Thomas Hoccleve and related short pieces by Chaucer, for example, or in the multitudes of other anonymous religious, didactic or courtly items that were sometimes copied alongside their works – where convincing reference is made to the original occasion for which a poem was first written. From such cases, it is clear that, at their presumed point of origin, many such items may have enjoyed a far more perilous and ephemeral existence 'beyond the book', before reaching the relative safety of a scribal copy in a manuscript setting.[19] Such material was often anthologized in the fifteenth-century period – by its author, in the case of the Hoccleve holograph manuscripts – as well as in clusters, sometimes as an originally discrete part of more miscellaneous collections that, in turn, belonged to larger networks of interrelated manuscripts and exemplars shared by different scribes.[20] Items sometimes were recopied in these fifteenth-century books in different forms and for different purposes. Certain Middle English lyrics are particularly interesting in this respect. They sometimes survive as filler material at the end of booklets, or they have been jotted down in margins, sometimes perhaps from memory. Sometimes, too, it is evident that they have been copied at a much later date than the other material they are now preserved alongside, but with which they have no apparent connection. Perhaps they are jotted down singly or in groups in a planned way, or perhaps simply in spaces left unfilled when the gatherings making up larger books were finally assembled. Authors and copyists seeking to 'shape' the reader's experience of their work in some more meaningful way may sometimes have gone in search of specific kinds of exemplary material from a variety of different sources in order to create anew, or rework, the types of material on commonplace religious and didactic themes found in different versions in broadly similar styles of miscellaneous collections. Although there is much thematic overlap and repetition between these books (and sometimes also overlap with the early printed versions of the same or similar short items), one can readily see that the late medieval reading experience was far richer, more varied and unpredictable than the usually mundane appearance of these mostly plain and cheaply-produced manuscripts and prints might initially suggest.[21]

Making Books and Shaping Readers for 'Erthe upon Erthe'

It is salutary to turn from these necessarily generalized comments to chart the progress of some short Middle English verse in transit through the centuries and across both oral and written media. The material in question can all be associated with a range of different versions of 'Erthe upon Erthe', a set of interlinked verse writings that, in their totality, can hardly be considered a single poem in any accepted sense of the word, at least not if we think of a poem as generally having some stability as an integral text and representing the work of a single author.[22] Several of the 'Erthe' texts have been expanded in various ways but a number preserve the same or similar stanza forms and rhyme schemes, with sufficient textual similarities to each other in the sections of verse they have in common, to suggest that some earlier shared source has occasionally been cannibalized several times over at an early stage in the process of picking up on the admonitory theme of *memento homo quod cinis es et in cinerem reverteris*.[23] Fifteenth-century copyists exhibited widely-differing skills of organization and memory in copying out their 'Erthe' versions; however, it is fair to say that in many of the extant versions, the cumulative reinforcement of a religious commonplace through wordplay, centred on the riddling repetition of the word 'erthe', has the potential to encourage readers to commit their version of the text to memory. There was doubtless also some level of interpretative pleasure for most readers in the working out of the cautionary reminder that we are ordinary mortals, all made of earth; that we pay too much attention to material things, the earthly; that when we die we are buried in a grave, surrounded by earth, and that, in death, our body will return to earth as the substance from which it originally emerged and to which it rightly belongs.

The extant manuscript copies offer major editorial challenges if they are simply to be considered contaminated versions of a poem derived ultimately from a single written source. Hilda M. R. Murray, the modern editor of the material for the *Early English Text Society*, characterizes 'Erthe' as a poem extant in two main versions, A and B.[24] She sees A as the earlier version, extant in just two trilingual manuscripts, both dating from the first decades of the fourteenth century. Within the Harley 2253 MS held at the British Library, London, a collection from the Welsh border country, 'Erthe upon Erthe' survives on fol. 59v as an item of just four lines, preceded by five lines of French verse, beginning 'Charnel amour est folie' (fleshly love is folly), with the opening line of the short French and English items marked by a simple capital letter and a paraph mark but no other indication, such as an *incipit* or heading, that they necessarily have to be read as separate items.[25] Both sets of verse follow on closely from the last lines of the previous item, a lament in French verse on the death of Simon de Monfort which ends with a simple 'amen'. Although the arrangement has sometimes confused modern scholars, there seems a certain logic to this arrangement. It is certainly not inconsistent with the view that the Harley 2253 copyist may well have carefully chosen to follow his lament for one of the most remarkable figures in the baronial uprising during Henry III's reign with a transcription of two snatches of verse – one in French and one in Middle English – both dealing with the folly of putting one's trust in earthly things.[26]

I think one can also quite readily demonstrate the general effect that the process of relying on one's memory has had on the textual transmission of the so-called A version of 'Erthe' by setting the Harley 2253 version side by side the opening lines in the only other A text, now within the Harley 913 MS held at the British Library London. The comparable lines read as follows:

Erþe toc of erþe erþe wiþ woh,	Whan erþ haþ erþ iwonne wiþ wow,
Erþe oþer erþe to þe erþe droh,	þan erþ mai of erþ nim hir inow.
Erþe leyde erþe in erþene þroh,	Erþ vp erþ falliþ fol frow
Þo heuede erþe of erþe erþe ynoh	Erþ toward erþ delful him drow
(Harley 2253, ll. 1–4)	(Harley 913, ll. 1–4)

One would naturally expect the word play on 'erthe' to act as a mnemonic here, but, apart from preserving the same basic rhyme ending of oh/ow, the texts exhibit significant divergence from each other.[27] This feature is consistent with the view that the 'Erthe' verses were sometimes memorized rather than written down. The A-text of 'Erthe' in Harley 2253 now reads like a memorial epigraph for Simon de Monfort. Indeed, Murray has described how other short versions of 'Erthe' material (but not the lines preserved in Harley 2253) are found scribbled down as sixteenth-century scribal commonplaces on the *memento mori* theme, or carved on memorials and on grave stones, or presented as mural inscriptions.[28] The material vestiges of all this handiwork offers convincing evidence that, because of the dexterity of its relatively simple wordplay, 'Erthe' survived in the popular imagination from the late medieval period through to the nineteenth century.

The 'Erthe' text in MS Harley 913 is much more substantial and of quite a different order than the text in Harley 2253. Harley 913 is a trilingual manuscript collection, compiled in Ireland (Kildare and Waterford have been variously offered as possible places of origin) but it is also important to note that it preserves a cluster of Middle English material known to have been derived from the same general south-west Midlands area as the roughly contemporary Harley 2253 collection.[29] This includes the 'Erthe' material on fols 62r–63v (comprising seven eight-line stanzas with alternating six-line stanzas of a rhyming Latin parallel version using *terra*, *vesta* and *humus* in place of the English wordplay on 'erthe'), and also the short lyric on the miseries of bodily failure in old age that originally preceded it in the collection before the manuscript suffered some disarrangement, *viz.*, the text beginning 'Elde makiþ me geld'.[30] The Harley 913 copyist's alternating English and Latin versions of the 'Erthe' material, and his habit of glossing some of the English words in this pairing of mortality items, may suggest a reworking of vernacular material that might have seemed in some sense 'foreign' to his intended readers.[31] The dialect evidence implies that both the 'Elde' verse and the 'Erthe' item were probably brought into Ireland with a new wave of English settlers from the Welsh borders, well versed in the leisure time and professional literary interests of trilingual preacher poets.

That the 'Erthe' material may well have been readily assimilated into other verse on commonplace moral and didactic mortality themes is also indicated by the absorption of a brief echo of the tradition in another gloomy Harley 913 item, ostensibly on contemporary ills, that now survives uniquely in this manuscript. This is the item beginning 'Whose þenchith vp þis carful lif' (Harley 913, fols 44v–47v, 52r–v). Lines 153–6 of the poem read,

> What erþ haþ erþ igette
> And of erþe so haþ inovʒ,
> Whan he is þer in istekke,
> Wo is him þat was in wouʒ!

Furthermore, there are much more extensive verbal reminiscences in this item, at lines 157–68, and again at 193–6, shared with another neighbouring verse item, also uniquely surviving in Harley 913, that deals with similar mortality themes. This is the text beginning 'þe grace of godde and holi chirche' (fols 16r–20r, at lines 161–72 and 185–8). Interestingly, this latest mortality lyric bills itself as a little sermon in its last lines and imagines a future for itself as a privileged work, for delivery in a congregational setting:

Alle þat beþ icommin here
Fort to hire þis sarmun,
Loke þat ʒe nab no were,
For seue ʒerʒe habbiþ to pardoun (ll. 237–40).

'þe grace of godde and holi chirche' is one of several items uniquely surviving in Harley 913 that have been characterized by modern scholars as 'preaching poems'.[32] As such, one wonders quite what role the task of frequently reciting the English verse clusters now preserved in written form in the manuscript may once have played in the textual prehistory of this material. Often that material can be related to the themes and preoccupations of the English verse in the fourteenth-century Franciscan instructional treatise known as the *Fasciculus Morum*.[33] Indeed, one could, without much difficulty, extend the current enquiry to encompass the relationship of Bernardine and Franciscan treatments of mortality themes in other similar vernacular items in parallel trilingual manuscript collections compiled at around the same time as Harley 913 and Harley 2253. Several of these have often been characterized as 'friars' collections', yet are perhaps better considered on their own terms as more varied productions that merely have in common the feature that they preserve in written form vestiges of the vernacular repertoire of itinerant preachers, often written down in these books for the delectation of new vernacular readers.[34]

The endurance of such mortality themes in Middle English literary treatments is perhaps one of the most remarkable features shared by a number of later extant manuscripts containing 'Erthe' material alongside other admonitory and didactic pieces. These versions often became part of larger instructional strategies designed to encourage the active participation of fifteenth-century readers in a religious culture that, at all times, urged participants to move beyond the material realities of their lives and hear, see and contemplate the reality of their own mortality. The 'Erthe' version on fol. 170r, within the B.15.39 MS held at Trinity College, Cambridge, is followed by a rubric that makes explicit the attitude of mindreaders are expected to bring to the material following, for which the 'Erthe' version has perhaps acted as an opening rhetorical salvo. This rubric urges that 'a man þat wilneþ for to profite in þe wey of perfeccioun & souvereinli to plese God, he must studie bisili for to haue þese maters in his herte þat folewiþ here aftir'.[35]

The same general impression of the necessity of 'busy study' is generated by some of the material accompanying the mid-fifteenth-century 'Erthe' version, now extant with accompanying illustration on fols 67r–68v in Cambridge University Library, MS Ii.4.9.[36] On fol. 68v, the 'Erthe' text is followed immediately by the image of a fashionably-dressed young man with his right hand resting on the hilt of his sword; he stands on an earth mound, below which a skeleton lies in his grave. Without doubt, the image is meant to reinforce for readers the message of the preceding item and locate it within a biblical context: the young man's banner preserves the words *Festina tempus et memento finis* ('Hasten the time and remember the end'; *Sirach* 36:10), whereas the skeleton's words offer readers the advice: *In omni opera memorare nouissima et in eternum non peccabis* ('In all works remember your end and you shall never sin'; *Sirach* 7:40).

The illustration in MS Ii.4.9 fairly obviously belongs to the 'Dance of Death' pictorial tradition and it is fascinating that two later London manuscripts that preserve unillustrated 'Erthe' versions can be associated with visual markers of the same tradition in a specifically metropolitan setting. The 'Erthe' material written in sixteen quatrains, on fols 207v–208r in MS 354 at Balliol College, Oxford, survives in an early sixteenth-century 'commonplace book', compiled in a long and narrow account-book format by the London grocer Richard Hill.[37] The poem includes a lengthy extrapolation detailing the mortality of the Nine Worthies, and of William the Conqueror and Henry I (ll. 25–40). The narrator next addresses his imagined audience directly, in preaching mode, as follows:

> Now ye folk þat be here, ye may not long endure,
> But þat ye shall torn to erth, I do you ensure;
> & yf ye lyst of þe trewth to se a playn fugure,
> Go to seynt Powlis, & see þer the portratowre (ll. 45–8).

The reference is to the well-documented existence of paintings in a cloister called Pardon Churchyard, on the north side of old St Paul's. In 1598, John Stow reports in his *Survey of London* that 'John Carpenter, town clerk of London, in the reign of Henry V, caused with great expense to be curiously painted upon board, about the north cloister of Paule's, a monument of Death leading all estates, with the speeches of death and answer of every state. This cloister was pulled down 1549'.[38] Stow also indicates that the work was produced in imitation of a similar Parisian commission, at St Innocent's cloister (painted between 1424 and 1425 in the biggest cemetery in the city with accompanying verse that is sometimes credited to Jean Gerson). Of the St Paul's commission he states further that 'the metres or poesy of this dance were translated out of French into English by John Lidgate, monk of Bury', repeating the information 'and with the picture of death leading all estates, painted about the cloister, at the special request and in the dispence of Jenken Carpenter, in the reign of Henry the sixt'.

The John Carpenter commission has been described in a near-contemporary Middle English verse item, written to celebrate the event. Accompanying the St Paul's dance of death imagery, we are told, was Lydgate's poem known as 'Dance Machabre', now also extant in a number of fifteenth-century manuscripts and early prints.[39] One of these manuscript copies is MS R.3.21, Trinity College, Cambridge, owned by Roger Thorney, mercer of London, where the poem is introduced on fol. 278v as follows: 'this Daunce of machabre is ... translated by Dan John lydgate monke of Bury out of Frensshe in to englyssh whiche now is callyd the Daunce of Paulys. & these wordes payntted in þe cloystar at þe dispensys & request of Jankyn Carpynter'.[40] The manuscript also contains a seven-quatrain 'Erthe' version on fol. 33v where the penultimate stanza makes another immediate and direct address to its readers. It reads:

> Lo erthe opon erthe considere well thow may
> How erthe commeth to erthe nakyd alway.
> Why shuld erthe than opon erthe go stout and gay
> Seth erthe in-to erthe shall passe in a pore array? (ll. 21–4)

In common with several other unillustrated 'Erthe' versions, the informed London reader of these lines is asked to imagine with the mind's eye a not dissimilar scene to the painted image of the gallant and the skeleton in the grave that adorns the 'Erthe' version in MS Ii.4.9. Or, perhaps, when they proceeded to read 'this Daunce of Machabre' later in the same collection, their inner eye was drawn irresistibly by its rubric to a remembrance of the images of those 'stout and gay' personages that John Carpenter ensured, with John Lydgate's help, had once adorned St Paul's.

The materiality of its survival in various written forms reveals the unusual degree of shape-shifting that the 'Erthe' poems have had to endure in their convoluted textual histories. According to this account, the reminiscences of an oral literary culture and the intensely visual representations of the reader's own mortality that are brought to mind by the Middle English texts must have had a profound effect on how the imagined fifteenth-century reading experience was itself 'shaped'. In such a context, private reading can no longer be imagined as a solitary activity, divorced from everyday life. Instead, in these usually rather drably-presented homemade books, it seems embedded in a much wider cultural experience. The manuscript culture of the age that I have described in this essay seems to have been part of a much larger matrix of everyday family life, domestic and social relationships – and the memory of relationships enjoyed in the past as well as in the present time. Such a matrix encompassed both the work of the preachers, poets and copyists who have gone before the reader, and the activities of leading municipal and ecclesiastical benefactors who sometimes also doubled as the literary patrons or agents and secretaries who encouraged the deployment of Middle English as a frontline literary language in many different English cultural settings. It was through such efforts that late medieval reading and listening audiences were entertained by and instructed in socio-historical and religio-didactic home truths of one kind or another.

Our twenty-first-century understanding of English vernacular literary habits in the period obviously has to be constructed from the surviving remnants of what may once have been a truly kaleidoscopic array of writing talent. If we take John Lydgate's poetical output as representative of one branch of that living stream, then the Middle English verse being produced in quantity in the fifteenth century was often derived from episodes in English history, or from edifying stories derived from a more remote biblical and classical past, with perhaps an implicit contemporary application for readers and hearers to find and apply. The books containing such material were therefore describing for their first English readers – sometimes in vigorous or confusing detail – not only how the world is but also how the imagined daily lives of devout Christians and loyal citizens might be improved by living well, according to the acceptable moral and ethical standards exhibited by the items in their manuscript collections. Some English listeners and readers may have fallen by the wayside at this point, but many more must surely have heeded such good advice, or, at least, paid lip service to that urgent call in the one-volume libraries that presumably played some important part in their daily lives.

2 PRINT, MISCELLANEITY AND THE READER IN ROBERT HERRICK'S *HESPERIDES*

Ruth Connolly

The origins, organization and printing of *Hesperides* represent a striking and still under-examined moment in the history of authorship: one of the earliest attempts by a poet to supply a 'perfected' version of his lifework in a volume especially created for that purpose.[1] *Hesperides* is an exemplary representative of the author-identified poetic collection. Its contents are gathered by Herrick and put into print during his own lifetime and its title, the *Works of Robert Herrick, Esq*, declares Herrick's privileged position in relation to his own poems. *Hesperides* demonstrably follows the path laid down by Ben Jonson's *Works*, which blazed a troubled trail for such authorial self-advertisement, and this reading is reinforced by Herrick's characterization of print as a medium uniquely equipped to perpetuate his legacy. In his poem 'To Julia', he explicitly links notions of print to ideas of possession and perfection:

> Julia, if I chance to die
> Ere I print my poetry;
> I most humbly thee desire
> To commit it to the fire:
> Better 'twere my book were dead,
> Then to live not perfected.[2]

'Perfected' is not simply a promise that these are Herrick's final versions of his poems but also puns on the printing practice of reiteration, or 'perfecting', the process of printing the second form of type on the reverse of already printed sheets.[3] Elsewhere, Herrick deploys more printing puns to illustrate how he expects his book to ensure his own (and his friends') perpetuation across the centuries:

> Look into my Book and therein see
> Life endlesse sign'd to thee and me.

We o're the tombes, and Fates shall flye;
While other generations dye.[4]

In this poem, the signatures of the book, the coffin of the printing press and the printer's fly, the boy employed to pull the sheets off a busy printing press, are all implicated in the process of literary immortality.[5] But for every poem which radiates this assurance there are others that foresee the volume's imminent destruction and the poet's with it, as vulnerable paper yields to the hands of tradesmen and the unappreciative masses.[6]

Nor is this liability to fragmentation confined to the materials of his book. The whole collection lacks a unifying principle, an omission which caused T. S. Eliot to categorize Herrick's work as 'minor' in its lack of any 'pervasive purpose'.[7] More recently John Creaser has accurately described *Hesperides* as a 'loose baggy monster' of 1402 poems, 'most of them very brief, extremely diverse not only in subject matter but also in the views expressed'.[8] This reading of the collection has never been comprehensively refuted, although studies that examine Herrick's debt to classical authors have demonstrated that a greater degree of unity exists within the collection than might be supposed at first glance, and this stress on the collection's inherent disorder is well-placed.[9] However, the reasons for this disorder, even the idea that they might be deliberate, have been lost through an overwhelming if understandable emphasis on *Hesperides* as a collection which perpetuates the poet. Eliot's remarks, for example, are driven by the expectation that a collection of poems and, more pertinently, a self-proclaimed 'works', should be structured in a way that supports a coherent narrative of poetic and personal development.[10] My argument here is that *Hesperides* should instead be read as a work in which disorder respects an alternative source of poetic authority – the reader. Herrick's arrangement of his poems shapes his book into a verse miscellany and embeds it within the socio-literary networks from which his verse emerged.[11] It is the failure to make this connection to manuscript composition and circulation which has caused *Hesperides* to be treated as a collection characterized by Herrick's lack of judicious discrimination between his best poems, but when interpreted within an account of the volume's attitude to its readers and Herrick's own immersion in manuscript culture, the collection appears in a very different light.

Herrick, whose work is invariably read in its printed form, is a very inexperienced print poet, who apparently did not contemplate print publication until the beginning of the 1640s.[12] He began composing poetry in the 1610s, perhaps even earlier, and he writes within a series of contexts – literary coteries, university colleges, urban clubs and rural households – where the manuscript transmission of poetry was the norm.[13] Most (though certainly not all) of *Hes-*

perides's poetry is written for and in these milieus, although it should be stressed that evidence for its circulation is confined to relatively few poems. Nonetheless, manuscript contexts of circulation account for the characteristic occasionality of Herrick's poetry. Occasionality is a mode of literary communication that develops from writing in manuscript for small groups of readers. As an umbrella term, it 'identifies poetry as a response to, and the product of, a specific devotional, social or political moment' and its poems as the shared property of a coterie environment.[14] The meanings of occasional poems can be difficult to disentangle from the situation and medium in which and the audience for whom they were written. This is because the manuscript medium and the occasion for writing work together to forge a generic register for this poetry which is intimate, sociable and reflective of the shared geographies, politics and identities of both the poet and his or her audience. Occasional poetry flourishes in relatively closed institutional environments such as universities, Inns of Court, and large households and its typical confinement to manuscript demonstrates both its reliance on a particular context for its meaning and a desire to use this poetry to sustain exclusive social bonds. The most significant influence on its construction is its intended addressee, whose response to the poem is necessary either to complete its meaning or begin a dialogue. This kind of poetry is, in Wendy Wall's phrase, 'socially embedded'; better read as individual expressions of a common concern than as a route to an authorial subjectivity, not least because its openness to re-appropriation by its readers.[15] If the poem enters wider circulation, readers copying the poem into their own miscellanies may scrupulously transcribe the accompanying title or they may attach a new one which speaks to their own occasions, re-contextualizing the poem in the framework of their own interests or redeploying its sentiments in the service of their own ends. Removing this poetry from these contexts can mean losing significant, even critical, dimensions of its meanings, and a shift into print can represent the most far reaching of these removals, tamping the verse with the authority of the poet rather than the audience.[16]

Herrick's refusal to embed his collected printed poetry in any kind of sustained personal, thematic or chronological narrative is an acknowledgement of this loss and an attempt to compensate for it by translating his poems into the print marketplace in a form which keeps their occasionality to the forefront. Herrick's arrangement of his poems is a negotiation between his and his audience's authority, which results in the creation of a hybrid genre, the single-author printed miscellany. This hybridity, combined with the socio-political context of the volume's publication at the end of the civil wars, creates a book constructed around the tension between two opposing yet mutually constitutive possibilities. On the one hand, the collection is a set of unconnected verses – disordered, and fragmentary – left open for readerly appropriation and on the other it functions as a metonymy for the now scattered and destabilized communities which helped these poems into being, holding out the possibility of their re-formation and reconstitution through the promise of its own monumental integrity and authority.[17]

Herrick's move from manuscript into print is certainly not novel, although his self-conscious determination to resist some of its implications may be so. Sixteenth-century poetic anthologies like *Tottel's Miscellany* (1557) represents the first significant translation of occasional poetry and its associated coterie values into the marketplace, a process which, it has been argued, begins early modern poetry's slow transition into a separate discourse that is eventually transformed into 'literature'.[18] Part of this long cultural transition involves converting the reciprocity of the manuscript coterie environment into a more clearly defined hierarchy between writer and reader, and much work has been devoted to unpicking the manner and means of this conversion.[19] According to this argument, the anonymous marketplace of print compels publishers to construct an authorial figure whose biography provides a point of departure for interpreting the poems and as the author-figure becomes a more powerful determinant of meaning, the reader's authority is progressively eroded.

Herrick resists such erosion through the use of textual strategies that act to dissolve distinctions between author and reader. Mary Thomas Crane draws a comparison between *Hesperides* and John Bodenham's collection, *Belvedere, or The Garden of the Muses* (1600) through their shared use of italicized *sententiae*. She argues that Bodenham's work belongs to a tradition of humanist 'gathering' which emphasizes the common ownership of literary texts by taking snippets of existing work and reordering them into new patterns of meaning, creating what she calls an 'editorial model of authorship'.[20] The vestiges of this 'gathering' tradition that Crane notes within *Hesperides* are not simply a throwback to earlier traditions (although it is a useful reminder that Herrick, born in 1591, is a Jacobean poet) but an acknowledgement at the level of the collection itself that his poems are composed from fragments of other poets' works.[21] Other critics have also highlighted aspects of this levelling within *Hesperides*. Randall Ingram's study notes that Herrick 'is an exemplary reader – adapting, translating, redacting other texts and, most importantly, keeping them alive', modelling in his own poetic practice the reciprocal work that he anticipates that his reader will perform on *Hesperides*'s poems.[22] Stephen Dobranski explores one moment of redaction: Herrick's use of the Latin tags 'Desunt nonulla' (some things are missing) and 'Caetera desunt' (the rest is missing) in two poems, the usage of the second supplying a hint to his 'most astute readers' that Herrick has deliberately omitted a fragment of Virgil's verse from his translation, leaving an intertextual lacuna for his reader to interpret.[23] Herrick's construction of the collection as a miscellany further extends the opportunities for this dialogue. Adam Smyth's work on readers' marginalia in printed multi-author miscellanies demonstrates how readers of these texts take possession of the poems within them. They amend, alter and answer the poems they meet, either through marginal annotation, by altering individual words within poems or by transcribing them into their own manuscript books. The early modern reader of poetry, Smyth argues, is one who expects and intends to collaborate in the making – and transformation – of a poem's meaning.[24] I suggest here that Herrick's disordering of his poems and his iteration of their status as reused and reusable pieces of text is intended to drive that collaboration.

However, Herrick is also most interested in a particular kind of reader, a Latinate figure practiced in commonplacing and miscellany-making, who recognizes that the reconstitution of old texts in new forms is the means by which they are perpetuated. He hedges defensively against lowly ranked and uneducated readers, who are typed as destructive and unpleasant in both body and mind.[25] His ideal is the elite reader of the manuscript coterie, who belongs to the environments where Herrick's poems will have perpetual value. It is not print which bestows immortality on this poet but the particular audience who is now reading its poetry in print. The disruption of these readers' former coteries by the Civil War and the subsequent divisions which reach into them (it is noteworthy that Herrick writes and prints verses for both parliamentarian and Royalist friends) supplies a second reason, closely related to the first, for Herrick's choice of the miscellany form. *Hesperides*' paratext presents the collection as a metonymy for its communities of origin, which represents their fractures, their diversity and their communality through its own fragmentations and reconstitutions.[26] The process through which Herrick and his readers might read a volume of poetry as a symbol of community and identity also develops from the practice of writing occasional poetry for circulation in manuscript.

In comparison to its 1402 poems, only sixty-eight of Herrick's poems are preserved by extant miscellanies. The likelihood is that far more circulated but the poems which have been preserved are those that resonate with the groups who compile the majority of surviving miscellanies: university students, Inns of Court men and minor courtiers. Herrick's poetry is popular because of his ability to compose exemplary interpretations of the commonplace poetical themes that appeal to these readers – the inconstant mistress, the farewell to poetry or the supposed wife, the erotic blazon or the drinking poem. Several are written in dialogue with or dedicated to university friends including the 'Oberon' sequence he shared with Sir Simeon Steward and 'His Age', dedicated to his best friend from university, John Weekes. The very popular 'The Farewell to Sack' and 'The Welcome to Sack', and Herrick's short lyrics 'The Admonition', 'The Bubble' and 'The Curse' reflect the constant interest of student miscellanies in drinking and in portraits of cruel mistresses and indifferent lovers. Unsurprisingly then, one of Herrick's most appreciative environments was his university, Cambridge, and in the manuscript version of 'His Age', Herrick names some of the friends that formed his coterie there:

> Hinde, Godderick, Smith,
> and Nansogg, sonnes of Chine,
> and pith Such who know well
> to beare the magick bowe, and spell
> allmighty bloud, that canst doe more
> then Joue and Chaos did before [27]

This poem, a meditation on old age which imitates Horace's *Ode* II, 14:1, values the oral performance of poetry in the company of close friends, who, though now lost, are symbolically recalled to the group by the recitation of their poems. The in-joke is that all the friends were alive at the time of composition and perhaps present at its reading.[28] The whole poem, Herrick's poem, is also their poem. The function of poetry here is to perpetuate the coterie by embedding its ethos within its verses; to construct a world where poetry reflects an origin in many voices and whose full meaning is evident only to those who belong to that world.[29] Perhaps one of the most pointed demonstrations of the difficulties of translating this ethos into print is Herrick's deletion of all these names for the print version, in the process rendering the coterie anonymous and silencing their contribution to the poem's initial creation and meaning, a gesture which may also be driven by actual loss, given the death of Martin Nansogg in 1631.

This ideal of community hinted at by the individual poem foreshadows the manuscript miscellany's capacity to relate its compilers and readers to their socio-literary communities, a capability to which *Hesperides* aspires. One of the most important manuscripts of Herrick's poetry is the Alston manuscript, now catalogued at the Beinecke Library, Yale, as Osborn b 197. Alston is an example of how a fresh generation of Cambridge students read Herrick's work and the volume reframes Herrick's poems for a 1640s audience at around the same time that Herrick is compiling his own miscellany for print. Its history illustrates a typical readership for Herrick's manuscript poetry, how closely patterned the structure, content and intention of *Hesperides* is on this tradition and how the miscellany functions as a metonymy for community.

Alston's texts have a high degree of textual authority, demonstrated both by stemmatic analysis and by evidence that its compiler, Tobias Alston, had indirect connections with the Herrick family and through his siblings and cousins at Cambridge to Herrick himself. Now disbound, the miscellany consists of twenty-one quires of a single paper stock folded in octavo.[30] The leaves are carefully ruled and paginated; catchwords are used throughout. The main hand, a small neat italic, enters the poems contained on the first 243 pages. This hand writes four times on the unpaginated flyleaf of quire one (fol. 1r), 'Tobias Alston his booke' and underneath this is the name 'Henricus Glisson Med. Do[r]' which appears to be written in the same hand. In the top left-hand corner are the names 'Norris' and 'Norton'. On fol. 1v is written 'Henricus Riche' again in what appears to be the same hand as the Tobias Alston inscriptions and on the verso is written in a different hand 'Henricus Glisson' and 'James Tabor'. On fol. 2r is written *Eius Liber* John Whitehead, an eighteenth-century owner who adds some lines at the end of the manuscript. The opening quires contain a sequence of twelve poems, eight of which are attributed either to Herrick or to 'R. H' including several dubia and the complete 'Oberon sequence' by Herrick and Steward. The Alstons were a Suffolk family which included several familial branches, and Tobias was the son of William Alston of Sayham Hall in Sudbury.[31] Herrick's mother Julia, his sister Mercy and her husband John Wingfield lived in the village of Brantham in Suffolk, twenty miles from Sudbury, where Robert is likely to have visited, a probability reinforced by his poem 'To his faithfull friend, Master John Crofts, cup-bearer to the King', addressed to the third son of Sir John Crofts of nearby Little Saxham hall.[32] The source of the poems by Herrick in this miscellany is probably Tobias's half-brother Edward, who matriculated at Queen's College, Cambridge in 1615 but migrated to Trinity Hall, taking his MA in 1619, when Herrick was still resident there.[33] Herrick also had a contemporary, during his time at St John's College, Cambridge named Edward Alston, a cousin of the previous Edward, and either or both of these men could have supplied the poems by Herrick which are copied in this volume. The evenness of the hand and the care taken in transcription means the volume is likely to be a fair copy of a number of smaller collections, of scribal separates and printed songs which had probably been accumulated over several years by several Alstons and their friends. An epitaph on Gustavus Adolphus of Sweden (d. 1632) is copied on page twenty-four and the last datable poem in the hand which copies Herrick's work is on page 241 and is entitled 'Vpon Admiral Trumps Picture Concerning his Overthrowing of the Spanyards 1639', a reference to the naval Battle of the Downs which took place in late October 1639. The date of copying must be after 1632, and is most likely to be *c.* 1640–5. The evidence of additional names on the flyleaves, assuming that they were entered contemporaneously and after the compilation of the volume, demonstrate that its subsequent readers were likely to have been students and fellows at Caius College during the late 1630s and early 1640s, when four Alstons, cousins of Tobias, matriculated there.[34] A James Tabor matriculated at Caius on 9 April 1634 and was a scholar until 1640 and a fellow from 1641 to 1649. Henry Glisson who was admitted to Caius on 1 July 1625 stayed there as a student and fellow until 1640. He became a physician in 1639 so his identification as 'Henricus Glisson Med. Do[r]' is entered after that date.[35] 'Norris' and 'Norton' were probably John Norris who matriculated at Caius in 1640, and John Norton of Naughton in Suffolk, who matriculated there in 1639.[36] The miscellany also contains two apparently unique satirical epitaphs on Dr Peirse of Caius College.[37]

Unsurprisingly, its contents reveal a strong connection between the compiler and both Cambridge and Suffolk: twelve poems deal with events and people at Cambridge between 1615 and 1637 including the exchange of poems on George Ruggle's *Ignoramus* (1615) and epitaphs on the death of Dr Whaley, Vice-Master of Trinity College (1637).[38] Five deal with similar topics in Suffolk including an elegy for the sexton of Hadleigh, John Hills, in 1625, a short masque performed for a visit of James I to Little Saxham and a copy of a pair of libels on Ipswich men, all locations within twenty miles of Tobias Alston's home at Sayham Hall.[39] Not all of these poems directly reflect Tobias Alston's personal experience – there is no evidence for example that he attended Cambridge at all – but they emphasize the scope of a typical seventeenth-century miscellany. The miscellany is an avatar for Alston's communities: familial, local, educational, political and national and draws them together under the emphatic 'Tobias Alston his booke' and as the evidence of the flyleaves indicate it was also a collection which has an interest for those familiar with the socio-literary registers of this particular miscellany, but who may not have been personally acquainted with Alston.

Herrick's use of standardized titles and shared incipits, his addresses to named relatives, patrons and friends, his care at times to offer titles which give some context to the poems' composition and the enormous variety of genres he deploys all have contemporary parallels in manuscript miscellanies.[40] The aspect of *Hesperides* which has been most heavily criticized by modern critics, its ready mixing of elegant lyrics with scatological and bawdy epigrams, is one which is characteristic of most manuscript miscellanies from this period which combine canonical poetry with short, crude epigrams depicting mutual acquaintances and social inferiors as objects of ridicule and revulsion. The very brevity of Herrick's poems points to a poet composing in and thinking about a manuscript environment of reading, since the labour of writing militates against lengthy stints of copying and the manuscript miscellany frequently offers cramped spaces for the transcription of new poems.[41] Alston and other miscellanies like it offer a clear precedent for *Hesperides*'s apparently idiosyncratic combination of autobiographical and familial verse with a wide variety of other forms, themes and tone, but Herrick's boldest gesture is to accede to the miscellany's metonymic role just at the point when the communities which generate its poetry are close to breakdown, and to do so by using print to 'recontextualize' his work. The term describes the practices of compilers who 'put texts in new contexts, changing their frame of reference, and, so, their referential capabilities'.[42] Deftly reversing the strategy of encouraging the reading community to fragment the text, he suggests that through the promise of permanence in print, his gathered texts can act to reconstitute its community of readers. This intention is revealed in *Hesperides*'s paratext, the preliminary matter of title pages, frontispieces and errata lists that make up the book's opening signature.[43] Like the whole volume it is the product of the poet's and publishers' collaboration and whilst it is boldly utilized to give a coherent political and personal identity both to volume and author, it also introduces a variety of strategies to establish the new frame of reference for reading his poetry in 1648.

The volume opens with an engraving of a bust of the author, located in a sylvan glade where cherubim fly, clutching bands of (presumably) laurel and bay leaf, whilst Pegasus and various winged cupids cavort in the background. With only one commendatory poem it is not particularly ostentatious; the simplicity and prettiness of its presentation augmented by the large image of a crown on the title page.[44] This image doubled as an advertisement (the Crown was the shop of Herrick's publisher, John Williams) and a statement of political intent since the illustration is an enlarged emblem of St Edward's Crown, used for Charles I's coronation. Williams uses this very sparingly, in fact only twice between 1650 and 1660, when an even larger version adorned Thomas Fuller's *A Happy Handfull, or Green Hopes in the Blade*, written in anticipation of the return of Charles II.[45] The publishers behind *Hesperides*, John Williams and Francis Eglesfield, continued to serve the Royalist cause following the regicide and the latter participated in the clandestine publication of Charles I's bestselling *Eikon Basilike*. The publishers' affiliation then underscores a likely political motive for their publication of a volume of poetry as large and expensive to undertake as *Hesperides*. Its placement of an ostentatiously large crown is a bold statement of loyalty at a time when Charles I, having escaped from London, was being held in army custody at Carisbrooke Castle in the Isle of Wight.[46] Furthermore, Charles's agreement to an engagement with the Scots, led Parliament to vote in January 1648 to abandon the idea of further negotiations with him shortly before *Hesperides* appeared in the bookshops of Williams, Eglesfield and the Exeter bookseller, Thomas Hunt.[47]

The paratext both presents and then immediately undermines any singular authority over its contents. The bust of the artist and the crown of the monarch indicate a problematic absence in the text of the authorities which guarantee its poetry. When the lyrics of *Hesperides* evoke the poet, they focus on his speaking or singing voice, but the volume's sole visual image of the poet is of an immobilized and truncated (if venerated) artist, whose achievements are celebrated by a graven inscription. The bust (which is never explicitly identified as an image of Herrick) is both memory and monument, and the elegiac note it strikes as well as the opening dedication to the Prince of Wales hints both at memorialization of the recent past and at a proposed transition to a future when the poet's permanent monument in the poetic landscape will be the book in the reader's hand. An address to them is presented in the misquotation from Ovid's elegy for another classical elegist Tibullus on the facing page: 'Effugient avidos Carmina nostra Rogos'.[48] Early modern editions opened with the plaintive subjunctive 'effugient', '*may* escape', whereas modern ones read more firmly 'diffugiunt', '[they] *do* escape'.[49] Herrick did not need to change this mood, but he did make the more significant substitution of 'nostra' ('our') for Ovid's 'sola' ('only') and by so doing he reshaped his borrowed line into an epigraph. The conversion to an epigraph, defined both a summary sentence of a work's idea and an inscription on a building, foregrounds a promise to a knowledgeable Latinate reader of their community's partial survival.[50] Emphasized by the designation of Herrick (probably by his publishers) as 'Esquire', a sign of rank to which he was entitled owing to his education rather than birth, it establishes that the author and his readers, like those of the Alston miscellany, are members of the educated elite who share a mutual responsibility for these poems' existence and survival.[51] The collective pronoun 'our' reiterates the ideal of poetry presented in 'His Age', and hints again at voices evoked and renewed in their absence.

Yet the jocularity of that poem is missing; the environment of manuscript is renewed here but without life.[52] The medium and occasion are married together to register real losses. The epigraph, crown and bust indicate that the book is intended by Herrick and his publishers as a metonymy acting simultaneously as the temporary and inadequate substitute for the poet-singer and for the culture which supports his songs. *Hesperides*'s multiplicity of forms, genres and voices supply the contexts in which his work has the richest meaning, but the fullness of the poet's presence is pitifully limited by the shortcomings of print. The book acts as a means of ensuring that his songs will continue to be sung by an elite and expressly Royalist diaspora as the tense political situation is blended with their dissolution by print and war. A further promise of that renewal is illustrated by Herrick's appointment of the Prince of Wales as the governing deity of the world of the book.

> Well may my Book come forth like Publique Day,
> When such a Light as You are leads the way:
> Who are my Works Creator, and alone
> The Flame of it, and the Expansion.
> And look how all those heavenly Lamps acquire
> Light from the Sun, that inexhausted Fire:
> So all my Morne, and Evening Stars from You
> Have their Existence, and their Influence too.
> Full is my Book of Glories; but all these
> By you become Immortall Substances.[53]

The poem unites the poetic and political worlds by granting the role of creator to the young Charles, making him the essential authorizing figure of both. Herrick's transition from manuscript to print is naturalized as a passage into 'Publique Day', as the volume, named after the daughters of Darkness, is led into the light, and the ethos of the court is revealed to govern the sphere of printed poetry as readily as it does that of manuscript. As the patron of poets, Charles lends his light to its minor stars, made visible only when the Sun rises and sets, a metaphor which transforms Herrick's transitional poetics into a reassuring image of the cyclical order inherent in primogeniture.[54]

The theme of a scattered diaspora reunified by a single authorizing voice inflects the poetic voice in the address to the reader that follows, 'The Argument of his Book'.[55] This poem defines the world of the book in terms of disparate elements united by form and the authorial 'I':

> I sing of Brooks, of Blossomes, Birds, and Bowers:
> Of April, May, of June, and July-Flowers.
> I sing of May-poles, Hock-carts, Wassails, Wakes,
> Of Bride-grooms, Brides, and of their Bridall-cakes.
> I write of Youth, of Love, and have Accesse
> By these, to sing of cleanly-Wantonnesse.
> I sing of Dewes, of Raines, and piece by piece
> Of Balme, of Oyle, of Spice, and Amber-Greece.
> I sing of Times trans-shifting; and I write
> How Roses first came Red, and Lillies White.
> I write of Groves, of Twilights, and I sing
> The Court of Mab, and of the Fairie-King.
> I write of Hell; I sing (and ever shall)
> Of Heaven, and hope to have it after all.

The poem's chronology reflects the Horatian ideal of *de Arte Poetica*, which Ann Moss notes insists that poetry starts 'at the midpoint of narrative and moves both backwards, in the memory of participants in the action, and forwards, in their anticipations, in prophecies, in signs and omens of things to come'.[56] 'The Argument' examines moments of fragmentation and reconstitution, when disparate elements are drawn together and transformed into unities; the poem itself becomes a meditation on the process of constructing the poems, the miscellany and the author himself.

The opening quatrain is a cyclical development of the relationship between time and transformation, beginning in the middle of the year, the third line returning to dwell on social rites of passage which encompass both individuals and communities and which, as with a wedding ceremony, serve to unite them. This note of transition and creation is maintained by references to objects which are both solid and liquid, which are simultaneously created and naturally occurring, without distinction being made between either process: '*Balme ... Oyle ... Spice*, and *Amber-Greece ... Roses ...* and *Lillies White*'. These lines emphasize that it is poetry alone that can refine and fix moments of pleasure so that they can be repeatedly revisited and re-experienced. Material experiences are re-invoked: the sensuousness of touch, taste and smell are moments about which the poet chooses to 'sing' rather than to write, substituting one sense impression, that of listening to music, for another, the feel and scent of oils, dews and waxes, all substances which turn to liquid, as words do when they come in contact with music.[57] So a poem that is visually dominated by the authorial 'I' roots itself both in a material and a literary world which are mutually constitutive, and it situates its own creation within their intersection.

However, Marjorie Swann argues the composition of the 'Argument' as an epic-sonnet in epigrammatic couplets disrupts its claims to wholeness and instead emphasizes its concern with disparity and separateness. This competing structure, she suggests, frames the whole volume for its reader. '*The Argument*' fragments the volume into its constituent parts and the poem becomes an index of the *topoi* available in the book, indicating the heads available to the reader leafing through the book with his commonplace book in hand. What Swann reads as a gesture to the common placing technique of splintering texts is also a signal to the would-be compiler of a new miscellany. The very brevity of the poem in its treatment of its portentous topics makes it a witty joke, one enhanced by the fact that Herrick, complying with Horace's assertion that his advice refers only to epic, promptly begins 'The Argument' with the epic *propositio* 'I sing', and parodies the hierarchy of genres by offering up an epic-sonnet.[58] It converts Herrick's own assertion of his authorial power, the 'argument' of his book into a playful and self-deprecating gesture that wryly reflects his expectation, even at the very beginning, if he succeeds, his 'works' will be returned to their constituent parts, as lines, couplets and whole verses are transcribed into the commonplace books and miscellanies of his readers. 'The Argument', therefore, places the entire book as part of a cycle of fragmentation and re-integration of existing parts into new forms, which must and should be left open to further fracture by the reader, a movement necessary for the perpetuation of the poem and the performance of community. The poem's focuses are on the three elements which underpin this process: chronological time, poetic form and the reader's activity. The authorities within the text, the exiled prince and the exiled poet, are vulnerable figures caught in an uncertain transitional moment, stabilized only within the world that the other can create, now a fiction on both sides. The presentation of the book is marked by poetic singularity and monarchical loyalties but closer inspection of its paratext and opening poems reveal the shifting collaborative, imitative and communal basis on which this appearance of wholeness is built. It is a whole constructed of disparate parts which offers the attractive promise of community, unity, rhythm and balance but which also contains within it the processes of decline, disintegration and fragmentation, a promise and process which are inescapably interdependent.

The volume's summoning of and then refusal of a linear personal or political narrative reflects only too well the situation of both poet and country in 1647, but it also captures its own construction as a volume assembled in a manner which links it not only to the poetic anthologies of the late sixteenth and early seventeenth century but also to the manuscript miscellanies in which Herrick's contemporaries had transcribed his earlier work.[59] *Hesperides* itself becomes an attempt – through paper and typeface – to reify a transient oral culture of voice, music and lyric, whose generative socio-cultural community is now destabilized by war and looks to print to secure its legacy. The sequence of poems which commences the book evokes a sequence of ideal reading environments. 'To his muse' extols the aural environment: 'there you may hear your own lines read' and the reader is instructed that the appropriate response to a poet's work is to compose a new poem in answer to it or to speak those lines anew, substituting his or her voice for that of the poet.[60] Here we finally encounter his ideal readers, who are, in fact, in a conflation of orality and literacy, ideal singers.[61] He describes in the dream poem 'The Apparition' a convivial gathering of friends participating in verse exchange, except that these friends are a roll-call of the great poets of the classical and contemporary periods, re-convening in Elysium. Elysium itself is within the garden of the Hesperides, an elegant conceit which can be broadened to incorporate the idea of the Blessed Isles, the implied former condition of Britain: [62]

> There thou shalt hear Divine Musæus sing
> Of Hero, and Leander; then Ile bring
> Thee to the Stand, where honour'd Homer reades
> His Odisees, and his high Iliads.
> About whose Throne the crowd of Poets throng
> To heare the incantation of his tongue:
> To Linus, then to Pindar; and that done,
> Ile bring thee Herrick to Anacreon,
> Quaffing his full-crown'd bowles of burning Wine,
> And in his Raptures speaking Lines of Thine.[63]

The image creates the kind of dialogic exchange that Herrick values, a mutual knowledge and appreciation by great poets of each other's work, as Anacreon whose works Herrick imitates, re-appropriates those lines and by voicing them, adds his own lustre to Herrick's reputation. Pugh suggests that this is an intertextual gesture intended to demonstrate poetic solidarity between generations of poets who live on through each others' use and re-use of their work: 'an ongoing symposium on the virtual space of poetry'.[64]

What Herrick wishes to recreate in *Hesperides* is an echo of oral exchange and the shared poetic solidarity of a fraternity of poets and friends, locating his poetry within the tradition of the manuscript verse miscellany. Using the forum of print, he emphasizes the shared community of readers and writers and the flexibility and interchangeability of both roles, a gesture which he realizes is complicated by his use of a medium which draws a clear distinction between both. Herrick seeks to create a text which invites and facilitates this reconstitution but which nonetheless will retain its physical and symbolic integrity, to in some way stand in for and sustain the communities which have produced him, his poetry and the book, the only places in which his work will be perpetuated. His characterization of these two aspects as oppositions in play encapsulates *Hesperides*'s complex position as the work of a reader as well as a writer, and of manuscript as well as print.

3 SEARCHING FOR SPECTATORS: FROM *ISTORIA* TO HISTORY PAINTING

Liam Lenihan

In the final decades of the eighteenth century the phrase 'history painting' is common currency in the writings of certain distinguished neoclassical artists. The literary output of artists such as Joshua Reynolds, James Barry and Henry Fuseli captures a significant aspect of the professional aspirations of ambitious London-based painters. A history painting was typically a large work, usually in oil, based on classical or biblical literature. Over the years such pictures also focused on significant historical events or notable moments in modern literature – the works of Shakespeare and Milton were common sources for artists in eighteenth-century Britain. However, despite eloquent treatises, lectures and campaigning pamphlets by celebrated artistic figures it is apparent that history painting was an extremely problematic genre. History paintings were generally not popular with the wider public. Nor were they commercially viable as most wealthy British patrons wanted portraits by contemporary artists such as Reynolds and Gainsborough or cherished works by the Old Masters like Raphael, Titian and Rubens.

A fascinating aspect of the writings of James Barry, one of the most compelling advocates of history painting, is his address to the audience. His writings, in large measure, constitute a search for spectators. In essence, Barry tried to create an audience for the kind of art he aspired to create. Yet this appeal to the public illustrated the extent to which the classical rhetoric of art, refined by Barry's Renaissance predecessors, was displaced by the modern vernacular of aesthetics.

In the context of this shift from rhetoric to aesthetics it is apparent that books shape material things, in this case paintings, and are in turn shaped by such material. Beginning with the Renaissance concept of *istoria* – the painting that tells a story – provides the context for the examination of an idea, or, more accurately, books about an idea, in late eighteenth-century Britain. The idea is that of history painting. At the core, it is intriguing to investigate the extent to which Barry's commentaries on history painting simultaneously draw on and dissect the notion of *istoria* in the search for spectators. Barry's commentaries on his *Progress of Human Culture* (1777–84), a series of six monumental paintings that act as allegories for the evolution of civilized society demonstrate this fragmentation of the idea of what constitutes *istoria*.

The *istoria* was first systematically discussed by Leon Battista Alberti in the 1430s. To execute such a work correctly – a work requiring knowledge of perspective, anatomy, cartography and geometry – Alberti maintained that the painter must be a liberal artist whose endeavour is related to literature and science. In fifteenth-century Italy, this desire to see painting recognized as a liberal art gained considerable support, particularly amongst the early Cinquecento – most prominently Leonardo da Vinci. Da Vinci argued for the pre-eminence of painting over poetry and defended it against the charge that it was a simply mechanical craft against humanist thinkers such as Angelo Decembrio and Mario Equicola:

> You have placed painting amongst the mechanical arts ... Painting does not speak, but is self-evident through its finished product, while poetry ends in words, with which it vigorously praises itself. If you call painting mechanical because it is primarily manual, in that the hands depict what is found in the imagination, you writers draft with your hand what is found in your mind.[1]

Three centuries later James Barry, in his *Lectures on Painting*, informs students in the Royal Academy of Arts in London that they should look to Leonardo as a model of an artist who unifies artistic concerns with intellectual pursuits: '[h]is enthusiasm, though great, is always equalled by the coolness and solidity of his judgement; truth and energy go hand in hand in whatever I have seen that was really his'.[2] Barry's writings continually advocate a medium appropriate to the search for 'truth and energy' in art.

In his first published work, *An Inquiry into the Real and Imaginary Obstructions to the Acquisition of the Arts in England*, Barry put the following to the British public in 1775: '[h]istory painting and sculpture should be the main views of every people desirous of gaining honour by the arts. These are tests by which the national character will be tried in after ages'.[3] Throughout his career, Barry had considerable trouble convincing people of the veracity of such a claim. His writings are, in many ways, a search for spectators, an attempt to create a public for works that were (in his and our lifetime) distinctly unpopular. This is not to say Barry's artistic output was poor; quite the contrary, but his work was never fashionable and consequently never sold well. Barry found it impossible to secure himself a patron for huge history paintings like his late masterpiece, *The Birth of Pandora*, completed shortly before the painter's death in 1806.

The ambition to create monumental allegorical pictures, usually oil paintings, based on classical or biblical literature was not confined to artists who struggled in their endeavours to grasp a large audience's attention. Henry Fuseli, a contemporary of Barry's, was an artist whose name became a byword for sensation and excitement as a result of provoking canvases like *The Nightmare*, which he exhibited in the annual exhibitions of the Royal Academy throughout the 1780s. In 1785 a newspaper critic in London noted that '[g]ypsies, witches, and flying Devils seem to have engrossed the attention of many artists' and Fuseli was the acknowledged leader of this trend.[4] Yet Fuseli, as professor for painting at the Royal Academy, invokes the image of a very different type of picture that the salacious sights of his journalistic counterpart in his 'Fourth Lecture on Painting'. This lecture is the second of two on 'Invention', with a subtitle on the artist's '[c]hoice of subjects; divided into positive, negative, repulsive':

> The first demand of every work of art is that it constitute one whole, that it fully pronounce its own meaning, that it tell itself; it ought to be independent; the essential part of its subject ought to be comprehended and understood without collateral assistance, without borrowing its commentary from the historian or the poet; for as we are soon wearied with a poem whose fable and motives reach us only by the borrowed lights of annexed notes, so we turn our eye discontented from a picture or a statue whose meaning depends on the charity of a Cicerone, or must be fetched from a book.[5]

Here the imagery Fuseli uses to describe a history painting (*c.* 1800) is indebted to the ever-expanding book industry of the mid-to-late eighteenth century. This is unsurprising because Fuseli began his career in London as a writer and translator, working for both Joseph Johnson and Andrew Millar. His reference to 'the borrowed lights of annexed notes' is particularly telling in the context of one of the most successful novels of the age, Laurence Sterne's *The Life and Opinions of Tristram Shandy, Gentleman*. At the beginning of volume five Sterne, speaking through the novel's narrator, Tristram, satirizes the modern artist's dependency on extraneous matter (such as footnotes) by bathically intoning: 'Shall we for ever make new books, as apothecaries make new mixtures, by pouring only out of one vessel and into another?'[6] Barry echoes this critique of plagiarism in *An Account of a Series of Pictures, in the Great Room of the Society of Arts, Manufactures, and Commerce, at the Adelphi*, a 1783 commentary on his six monumental paintings that serve as an allegory for, as the title of the exhibition indicates, *The Progress of Human Culture*:

> Artists of no compass of mind or genius, are notwithstanding necessitated to fall into this beaten track, and will content themselves, as Sterne happily expresses it, with pouring the same water from one vessel to another, and think they do something when they change particulars ... when they alter or add to the mere material, without adding to the subject.[7]

Painting in its highest form, for both Barry and Fuseli, transcends the artist's ability to mimetically replicate natural objects; it displays an understanding of the world beyond mere appearances. Technical skill makes an artist a craftsman, appealing to the senses – the eye – of the viewer. Knowledge makes the artist an intellectual, engaging the mind of the viewer. This idea was not new. It evolved alongside the 'rebirth' of classical learning and science in fifteenth-century Europe, particularly in Italy, where artists began to claim their place among the thinking men of the age.

During the Middle Ages artists were seen as craftsmen, skilled in individual trades, but during and after the Renaissance great artists proclaimed themselves designers, architects, and draughtsmen, as well as painters and sculptors. In their art the many facets of learning were united, not divided. In a poem 'Sol pur col foco il fabbro il ferro stende' ('Only with fire the artisan shapes the iron') from *c.* 1532, Michelangelo draws attention to the poetic inspiration behind the practical craft of an artist: 'The smith when forging iron uses fire/to match the beauty shaped within his mind'.[8] The implication is that the smith does not just copy nature as it is seen; he shapes beauty in its essence, as it is perceived by the mind. After the Renaissance, the highest forms of art came to be seen as those that fused manual dexterity, with brush or chisel, with intellectual grandeur. For painters like Barry, working in an age where neoclassicism was the dominant style, history painting was regarded as the highest of forms.

The idealization of a form, in this case history painting, within the writings of artists raises the inevitable question of who people such as Barry wrote for? What was the intended audience? Our understanding of this question is complicated by the knowledge of the fact that Joshua Reynolds, Barry's eminent contemporary and first president of the Royal Academy of Arts in London, wrote about the need for great works of arts, like history paintings, but rarely attempted such work himself. Barry served as professor of painting at the Royal Academy (1782–99). Yet it has been estimated that in the years 1781–5, those immediately after the Academy's move to its grand new home in Somerset House, the proportions of history paintings in the prestigious, annual exhibitions never rose to more than 20 per cent of the total work displayed. Portraiture and landscape, supposedly lesser genres, accounted for roughly 70 per cent.[9]

Such knowledge complicates our understanding of the Royal Academy, a prestigious body patronized by the king, comprised of learned men (though generally not gentlemen; most were self-made men from relatively humble backgrounds). Therefore any discussion of the relationship between the material and nominal existence of the republic of taste, a term for cultural centres like the Royal Academy of Art, alerts us to the difficulty of defining this realm:

> Wherein lies the authority to legislate, and who possesses the social credit to represent the social and cultural totality? ... Is its materiality – the physical paint, canvas, and so forth – capable of being extracted from the culture in which it was made, first seen, preserved, collected, or from the multiple meanings which accrue to it over time.[10]

Such questions about the materiality of the supposedly enlightened, cultural domains throughout the late eighteenth and early nineteenth century – be it in terms of who represents it and what works define it – help us to refine the context in which we read James Barry on history painting. But first, we must begin with *istoria*.

I

Leon Battista Alberti's *Della pittura* (*On Painting*), the first modern treatise on the theory of painting, appears in 1435–6. Artistic practices in the Florence into which Alberti's work arrives are at a crossroads. The old and new order stand side by side. Cennino Cennini's *Libro dell'arte*,[11] almost contemporary with respect to time and place to *Della pittura*, encapsulates the medieval approach to painting that precedes Alberti's thought. While Cennino's work is preoccupied with all aspects of the trade in conjunction with a speculative assessment of its status as an intellectual pursuit, it does not prepare the reader for the originality of Alberti.

Although Alberti is ostensibly writing about painting for painters, his methodology is quite distinct from that of a craftsman, like Cennino. To an extent, this difference can be explained by looking at Alberti's relatively affluent background, one very much at odds from that available to the working-class Cennino. Alberti was the illegitimate son of a wealthy Florentine banker and received what was then a pioneering type of education, known as humanism. As a young man he probably entered the school of the humanist Gasparino Barzizza at Padua. In 1421 he was enrolled in canon and civil law at the University of Bologna, and by 1424–5 new interests seem to have led him to philosophy and the natural sciences, notably mathematics. By 1434, around the time he began *On Painting*, Alberti's assimilation of recently discovered writings by Greek and Roman authors of antiquity appeared as comprehensive as any young humanist.

A brief overview of *On Painting* illustrates its importance and the profound impact it had on the history of European art. The first part of the treatise explains the optical and geometrical principles behind perspectival projections. Perspective transforms the nature of painting and an understanding of it provides Alberti with compelling evidence for the dignity and elevated intellectual status of the artist. Thus mathematics facilitates our understanding of the plane, in itself the essential means by which an artist of true quality surveys nature and organizes his representation of it: 'I hope the reader will agree that the best artist can only be one who has learned to understand the outline of the plane and all its qualities'.[12] Yet the best artists, using mathematics, can achieve something greater than the mere organization of space; they can move towards what Alberti calls *istoria*.

Istoria dominates the second and third part of *On Painting*. *Istoria*, roughly translated as 'story', is the highest challenge a painter can tackle: it is a composition with human figures that, ideally, conveys a narrative. If successfully executed, such a picture can display a painter's grasp of all facets of the art, be it a command of the skills necessary to represent nature or an understanding of qualities like form and unity. For example, in book two Alberti offers a succinct summary of *istoria* that demonstrates the extent to which practical skill is intertwined with intellectual understanding:

> Composition is that rule of painting by which the parts of things seen fit together in the painting. The greatest work of the painter is not a colossus, but an *istoria*. *Istoria* gives greater renown to the intellect than any colossus. Bodies are part of the *istoria*, members are part of the bodies, planes are part of the members. The primary parts of painting, therefore, are the planes. That grace in bodies which we call beauty is born from the composition of the planes.[13]

So defined, *istoria* offers the painter access to the idea of a fascinating fusion: the practical skills – drawing, painting, mathematical, generally technical – are also intellectual and thus allied to another ability of the liberal, educated humanist: literary interpretation. To represent a scene from classical or biblical literature the artist must comprehend the story rather than merely illustrate it.

Debate surrounds the intention of Alberti regarding the status of painters and patrons. David Rosand has argued that *On Painting* contributed to the social elevation of artists 'by defining theirs as a liberal rather than a mechanical art', yet Michael Baxandall has described the treatise as 'a handbook in the active appreciation of painting for an unusual kind of informed humanist spectator'.[14] However, while the exact nature of his intended audience may be unclear, what is apparent is Alberti's desire for a new kind of art – one distinct from the idea propagated in Cennino's guide to the workshop. Alberti's conception of the forms worthy of an *istoria* departs from conventional medieval representations of the human body and so ushers in a new era in art.

Leonardo da Vinci ambitiously developed the idea that painting was a discipline superior to the liberal arts, notably poetry. Leonardo conceived of painting as a science grounded in empirical observation and a rational understanding of the natural phenomena represented in art. Consequently, Leonardo argued for painting as an art that achieved a mathematically proportional harmony that embraced the diverse aspects of the natural world:

> If the painter wishes to see beauties that would enrapture him, he is master of their production ... In fact, therefore, whenever there is in the universe through essence, presence or imagination, he has it first in his mind and then in his hands, and these are of such excellence that they can generate a proportional harmony in the time equivalent to a single glance, just as real things do.[15]

Leonardo's ideas were taken up in Florence and Venice around 1550. However, painting came to be seen as a liberal art, not a science. The establishment of the Accademia del Disegno in Florence in 1563 under the patronage of Duke

Cosimo di Medici substantiated the art's new liberal status. Yet it must be acknowledged that the foundation of the academy was part of a larger transformation in Florence as it moved from a republic to absolutist rule. The Accademia was an attempt to weaken the artistic guilds as political entities and so create a sizeable body of well-trained but docile artists who worked under Giorgio Vasari's supervision on the huge fresco cycles in the Palazzo Vecchio as well as the refurbishment of the main churches in Florence.

What we thus find are a small number of outstanding artists, exemplified by Michelangelo (representative of the Florentine school) and Titian (representative of the Venetian school), who enjoyed relative autonomy on certain projects. Michelangelo and Titian are only some of the very few artists who rose to attain the social status Alberti mapped out for them in the earlier part of the previous century.

During the mid-to-late sixteenth century, when the aforementioned artists emerged, theories on the art of painting develop in an interesting manner. Against the condemnation of the imitative arts in general in Plato's *Republic*, one of the two philosophical works that dominate discussions of painting in sixteenth-century Italy, we see artists turning to Aristotle's *Poetics*. While there is not sufficient space here to discuss these developments in detail it will serve our purpose to examine Giorgio Vasari's *Lives of the Artists* and responses to it as an example of the influence of the *Poetics* on theories of painting. This will tender the final piece of information, since it relates to *istoria*, regarding the context necessary to understand what happens to theories about history painting in late eighteenth-century Britain.

In the second edition of Vasari's *Lives*, 1568, he contrasts Raphael with Michelangelo. Vasari wrote his *Lives* to illustrate the cultural and intellectual importance of the visual arts in general and in Florence in particular. He placed Michelangelo at the summit of the whole history of art but he was aware of 'limitations [that] made him an awkward choice as the model artist'.[16] In his 'Life of Raphael', Vasari considers the younger artist's reaction to Michelangelo on his arrival to Florence from Urbino in 1504. Vasari suggests that 'Michelangelo's focus on the male nude is due to the fact that he was by training and temperament a sculptor' and 'as in antiquity, regarded the creation of large-scale, freestanding figures as the pinnacle of achievement'.[17] Conversely, 'painters have a different and more wide-ranging job to do – something which Raphael understood instantly'.[18] In Vasari's much-quoted and influential distinction he maintains that Raphael knew that 'he could never attain the perfection of Michelangelo' and 'like a man of supreme judgement, [surmised] that painting does not consist only in representing the nude human form, but has a wider field'.[19] In Vasari's *Lives* Raphael has become a painter whose work is equivalent in many ways to that of a poet. Raphael is the painter of variety, not simply the ideal nude; the painter of life, who, like the poet, can affect a union between the ideal nudes and the manifold particularities of nature.

Two centuries later, Fuseli echoes Vasari's praise of Raphael when he contrasts him with Michelangelo. While Fuseli's Michelangelo is the sublime creator of singular beauty, his Raphael is viewed as a dramatist:

> To give the appearance of perfect ease to the most perplexing difficulty, was the exclusive power of Michael Angelo. He is the inventor of epic painting, in that sublime circle of the Sistine chapel which exhibits the origin, the progress, and the final dispensations of theocracy. He has personified motion in the groups of the cartoon of Pisa ... as sculptor, he expressed the character of flesh more perfectly than all who went before or came after him ... The inspiration of Michael Angelo was followed by the milder genius of Raphael Sanzio, the father of dramatic painting; the painter of humanity; less elevated, less vigorous, but more insinuating, more pressing on our hearts, the warm master of our sympathies.[20]

Vasari set the tone for Fuseli's depiction of Raphael by treating the 'wealth and variety' of his 'pictorial invention as basically poetic'.[21] Between the first edition of *Lives* in 1550 and the second in 1568, Vasari recognized that Michelangelo's successors – such as Pontormo and Daniele da Volterra – could not fruitfully learn from their master. Thomas Puttfarken has assiduously linked Vasari's poetic treatment of Raphael to the emergence of Aristotle's *Poetics* after 1550, particularly in relation to the idea that the way the imitative arts could be defined as arts of knowledge like poetry.[22] Consequently, like poetry, painting began to acquire a hierarchy of genres. The conception of *istoria* was again refined. Rather than express interest in the scientific imitation of nature as a whole, Italian thinkers placed greater emphasis on the significance of human actions. Puttfarken points out that in Domenichi's 1547 translation of Alberti's *On Painting* the definition of *istoria* is relayed in Aristotelian terms, preoccupied with action or plot. A painting was now looked at as 'a whole [that] must involve and absorb the spectator's mind, hold his attention and arouse his feelings and passions', not 'through particular instances of sympathy or empathy, but through necessary, causal even logical structure and development of the whole plot'.[23]

II

In 1783 James Barry published a commentary in excess of 200 pages to accompany the exhibition of his series of six oil paintings, *The Progress of Human Culture*, at the Society of Arts.[24] Barry's *Account of a Series of Pictures in the Great Room of the Society of Arts, Manufactures, and Commerce, at the Adelphi* concludes with a bold declaration of his ambition: 'I set out in this work with a firm persuasion, that a more intimate union might be effected between the ideal and the mechanic of the art [of painting], than has been generally imagined.'[25] This dramatic statement of intent draws on the Aristotelian idea of unity, notably unity of action. Barry's second commentary, published exactly ten years later in 1793, makes this clear. In *A Letter to the Society of Arts* the seriousness of Barry's artistic intent is linked to its moral purpose – a unified representation of a civilized society is itself a measure of civility:

> We are now at the close of the eighteenth century, the whole of the art [of painting] is called for, the animating soul is necessary, and if mind or intellect be wanting, care, expense, and curious decoration or mere trifles can avail nothing[26]

But a few lines below this ambitious statement Barry wrote that he completed the prints based on the paintings in *The Progress of Human Culture* 'in the midst of the satisfaction I had received from the impression this work made on the public mind'.[27] The aesthetic imperative, which is to draw upon every resource available to painting ('the whole of the art') on an epic scale, is clearly linked to the civic function of the paintings. No mere decoration could make the impression Barry wished to make on the public mind. He sought to unite every separate element of the series, to make of the disparate parts 'one subject or totality'.[28]

Each monumental painting in the series is an allegory for the progress of human civilization. The first painting, *Orpheus*, focuses on the mythic Grecian musician as he leads people from the darkness of barbarism to the light of civilized society. *A Grecian Harvest-Home*, the second picture, attempts to capture Arcadian Greek life. In the foreground young men and women dance around the double figure of Sylvanus and Pan; a farmhouse lies in the idyllic rural background and is surrounded by ritualistic male and female enjoyments and employments – courtship, marriage, child-rearing and sports such as wrestling. The third work, *Crowning the Victors at Olympia*, celebrates ancient Greek civilization at its classical peak by representing a parade of victors receiving their laurels at the Olympics. The fourth painting, *Commerce* or *The Triumph of the Thames*, turns to contemporary Britain, here attempting an allegory that honours the civilizing effects of trade. *The Distribution of the Premiums in the Society of Arts* is the fifth composition and it depicts a prize giving ceremony at the Society of Arts, a modern example of the promotion of civic values. The final work, *Elysium and Tartarus* or *The State of Final Retribution*, is a dynamic imagining of a classicized heaven in which great legislators, scientists and philosophers, theologians, writers and artists consult. For example, in a group to the left of the picture, Roger Bacon converses with Archimedes, Descartes and Thales opposite a group composed of Sir Francis Bacon, Nicholas Copernicus, Galileo and Sir Isaac Newton. This space of virtuous luminaries, the majority of the picture, is protected from the civil wrongs of Tartarus (hell) by gigantic guardian angels.

Figure 3.1: J. Barry, *Elysium and Tartarus*, first published 1792, etching and engraving (black ink), 41 x 92.4 cm. Reproduced by permission of the Crawford Art Gallery, Cork.

Barry's 1783 *Account* references Raphael's Stanza della Segnatura as the exemplar he is following with reference to *The Progress of Human Culture*. Yet he is keen to point out that 'Raffael enjoyed all the advantages the heart of man could wish for':

> [he] had a fair opportunity of putting forth all his strength, in a country which afforded a continual occasion for the exercise of his abilities; his profession was considered as not less necessary than ornamental, and his great work of the *Camera della Senatura* was carried under the auspices of those two great and distinguished encouragers of the art, Julius the Second, and Leo the Tenth; he was assisted in his work by the counsels (such as they were) of the great luminaries of that age, Bembo, Castiglione, Bibbiena, &c.[29]

Barry's interpretation of the assistance Raphael received in the planning and execution of his work in the Vatican, especially the 'four great pictures' in Pope Julius II's private library, demonstrates the extent to which *istoria* reveals itself as a fragmented entity in the form of a commentary on a series of history paintings.[30] Essentially, the context in which the artist paints for the spectator has fragmented and this in turn is reflected in the book the artist produces for his readers/viewers. Read in this way, Barry's commentaries about his paintings expose the tension underlining the necessity of their production in the first place – the search for spectators.

To illustrate this point let us compare Raphael's Stanza della Segnatura with Barry's *Progress of Human Culture* in terms of the purposes they served for their respective patrons. Raphael's Stanza was designed to be the private library of Pope Julius II. The frescos on the ceiling and walls were painted between 1508 and 1511. Recently Christiane Joost-Gaugier has persuasively argued that the learned humanist Tommaso Inghirami, *Preposito* of the Vatican Library (Papal Librarian from 1505–16), was the 'author' of Raphael's Stanza scheme. A colleague of distinguished humanist scholars such as Pietro Bembo, Baldassare Castiglione and Egidio da Viterbo, Inghirami was immensely learned, a gifted orator, an ally of Julius II and ideally positioned to aid Raphael in his undertaking. Raphael would indeed have benefited from Inghirami's assistance considering the 'single-theme easel pictures he had painted previously in Florence' up to 1507 were utterly different in 'form and content' to the 'complex humanistic themes' he executed on a large scale shortly after his arrival in Rome in 1508.[31] With the guidance of Inghirami, a learned Papal Librarian and humanist scholar familiar with Greek and Latin literature, and the support of a powerful and difficult but adventurous patron, Julius II, Raphael possessed many advantages over artistic successors such as James Barry.

The programme that underpinned Raphael's Stanza della Segnatura operated successfully on a number of levels without fundamentally disrupting its overall unity. The Aristotelian necessity for a causal, or certainly logical, structure and the sense of the pictures as the development of a (wholly integrated) plot in line with the Albertian notion of *istoria* work in harmony with the demands of the patron, Julius II, and his chief advisor on the project, Tommaso Inghirami. The breadth of Inghirami's knowledge and his range of skills used in service of the Vatican – he was a famous orator influenced by Cicero, an actor who favoured the plays of Seneca in his youth, an antiquarian, diplomat and poet, a humanist scholar keen to reconcile classical pagan and Christian learning, Secretary of the Conclave and Librarian of the Vatican – is reflected in the Stanza della Segnatura. All this stood in service of Julius II. Literally, Inghirami's immense knowledge of books (classical and Christian) shaped Raphael's paintings:

> In planning the new library, Fedra [Inghirami] created a triumph, glorifying his patron and the world that absorbed his papal interest with the most articulated display of unity built on the wealth of diversity from the past ever achieved in the decoration of any known library ... In its display of scenes inspired by classical antiquity, as in joining heaven and earth in the cosmology of the universe, the chamber is not only a symbolic triumph, incorporating a mission to defend Julius's temporal and spiritual authority, but also an aesthetic triumph. Exultantly grandiose in its arrangement of form, content, and space, the unifying concept of the room embodies the role of Julius as successor to Justinian, whose biography Inghirami knew well.[32]

Barry's *Progress of Human Culture* inadvertently inverts this unity of programme and purpose in the context of the relationship between the artistic and social function of the painted image. *Istoria*, now the history painting, comes between the artist and the patron, as does the writing that seems to clarify it.

In 1772 the Society for the Encouragement of Arts, Manufactures and Commerce, founded in 1754, invited nine distinguished artists (including Barry) to decorate their Great Room at the Adelphi, a space designed by Robert and James Adam. The artists declined the offer. Yet in March 1777 Barry proposed to the Society that he undertake the entire decoration of the Great Room without a fee provided the Society supply canvases, paints and models. The Society agreed and he began work in April. In 1783 and 1784 two exhibitions were held from which Barry hoped to receive critical and financial reward. He achieved the former (with many qualifications) but not the latter and felt his ambition neglected by the general public.

A most significant feature of Barry's commentaries on *The Progress of Human Culture* is the way its constituent parts undermine the unifying concept of the series. The resulting tension can be described as a tension between metaphor and metonymy. The uses of the terms metaphor and metonymy to describe Barry's delineation of the public sphere in his commentaries draws on a distinction made by Paul De Man in *Allegories of Reading*: '[t]he inference of identity and totality that is constitutive of metaphor is lacking in the purely relational metonymic contact'.[33] For De Man, the use of metaphor infers a totalizing identity that absorbs every part of the writer's subject matter. For Barry, the totality that is *The Progress of Human Culture* infers a series of paintings that, according to his explanation, make of their disparate parts 'one subject or totality'.[34] Metonymy, the relational association of part to part, undermines this inference of totality. The incorporation of each part of Barry's subject into his series reveals the contingent nature of his seemingly universal conceptualization of the public sphere in these modern *istoria*.

The Progress of Human Culture seems to prove the point De Man made about what he calls the principle of generalization in literature, which he states 'does *not* operate between the part and the whole but is determined by the relationship that the different parts, as parts, establish between each other'.[35] This overall structure of a text – the 'rhetorical structure' as De Man calls it – is constituted by metaphor, which infers totality, but it can be undone by the play of metonymy.[36] De Man states that '[t]o name the world is to make the representation of the world coincide with the world itself' and that 'metaphor is precisely the figure that depends on a certain degree of correspondence between "inside" and "outside" properties'.[37] Barry's *Progress of Human Culture* attempts to imagine a correspondence between the artist's imagined republic of taste, conceived in universal terms, and the reality of late eighteenth-century Britain. Yet his commentaries on the series serve, at times, to illustrate not the link, but the distance, that stands between what is within and without each work of art.

Ultimately Barry's commentaries, both the *Account* of 1783 and *Letter to the Society of Arts* of 1793, demonstrate the extent to which the idea of *istoria* had become fragmented. In the Stanza della Segnatura Raphael's visual lexicon is held together by Tommaso Inghirami's immense learning, a learning that seamlessly unifies the contemporary politics of Julius II's papacy with classical and Christian learning. By contrast, in Barry's monumental canvases modern artistic values, such as a 'commitment to accurate historical portraiture', clash with the generalizing tendency implied by the necessity to create a whole, in Aristotelian terms, that occupies the spectator's mind.[38] For example, in *Elysium and Tartarus* Barry 'assiduously turned up pictorial records of those virtuous men whom he wished to include' but, as William L. Pressly points out, so ambitious a programme 'placed severe strains on his artistic resources'.[39] In what is a pragmatic art historical evaluation, Pressly makes a point that strangely mirrors De Man's theoretical observation about the relationship between metaphor and metonymy: '[t]he numerous elect form a sea of heads which threatens to overwhelm the painting by turning it into a catalogue of the famous, and the sources at times are so familiar that they prove impossible to incorporate into the main body'.[40] In essence, the parts undo the whole, and throughout Barry's commentaries the reader observes an artist expending huge intellectual energy in a valiant but unsuccessful search for spectators. Unlike Raphael's patron, Julius II, Barry's intended audience were members of a diffuse public who could not be appealed to on the ground that a certain visual code was being utilized in accordance with treatises such as Alberti's *On Painting*. In the end Barry looked for virtue in the indecipherability of his visual symbols, turning to the commentary of the historian and the poet or finding in the borrowed lights of annexed notes (against his contemporary Henry Fuseli's censure), in descriptions of his art – all the time shaping readers as viewers for his difficult but ambitious art:

> It is an absurdity to suppose, as some mechanical artists do, that the art ought to be so trite, so brought down to the understanding of the vulgar, that they who run may read: when the art is solely levelled to the immediate comprehension of the ignorant, the intelligent can find nothing in it, and there will be nothing to improve or reward the attention even of the ignorant themselves, upon a second or third view; so much for what was wanting in historical art.[41]

4 RETURNING TO THE TEXT OF
FRANKENSTEIN

Graham Allen

One could be forgiven for thinking that there was little left to say about Mary Shelley's *Frankenstein*. Over the past thirty years or so the novel has been at the centre of various disciplinary reforms and revolutions, from the rise of feminist literary criticism to the canon-changing re-evaluation of Romantic literature in Britain, the United States of America and elsewhere. It has become one of the most talked about, one of the most taught, and one of the most written about texts of the Romantic period. One perhaps could be forgiven, also, for being a little tired of *Frankenstein*. Scholars of Mary Shelley have themselves shown signs of such a weariness in the past ten years or so, as one can see from such book titles as *The Other Mary Shelley: Beyond Frankenstein*, or *Iconoclastic Departures: Mary Shelley after Frankenstein*.[1] The desire of critics and scholars dedicated to Mary Shelley's work to get 'beyond *Frankenstein*' is understandable. We need to remember, however, that in order to 'go beyond' something, we should have a good idea of what that something is. It turns out that, despite a certain collective weariness with *Frankenstein*, and despite a perceived over-concentration on this one, famous novel, we did not know that novel sufficiently, and in many cases were in fact talking about a novel 'we', rather than 'the Author of *Frankenstein*', had invented. Despite calls for a move 'beyond *Frankenstein*', some of the most important recent developments in Mary Shelley scholarship can be said to be *returns to* the novel. I want in this essay to at least begin to demonstrate two things: first, that going *beyond Frankenstein* involves returning to *Frankenstein*; and, secondly, that returning to *Frankenstein* involves recognizing that returning to *Frankenstein* is impossible. I have elsewhere discussed the importance of the idea of *the return*.[2]

There are two main trends in this *return* to *Frankenstein*. The first concerns the subject of book history and has been thoroughly explored by William St Clair. It turns out that despite what one might imagine, despite what many in fact have imagined, *Frankenstein* was not widely published as a novel until the final two decades of the nineteenth century. The huge impact *Frankenstein* clearly had on the nineteenth-century British and European imagination was not caused by a wide readership for the novel. St Clair, in his magisterial *The Reading Nation in the Romantic Period*, presents the story of *Frankenstein's* limited readership through the nineteenth century in a manner which severely challenges some of the assumptions we have had about the novel's history as a literary text.[3]

The other trend concerns textual criticism, and in particular it concerns Charles E. Robinson's seminal, facsimile edition of what he calls 'The *Frankenstein* Notebooks'.[4] The novel was first published in 1818 by Lackington, Hughes, Harding, Mavor & Jones, published again (under Godwin's supervision) in 1823 by G. & W. B. Whittaker, and then re-published in 1831 by Colburn & Bentley, as part of *Bentley's Standard Novels*. Those who have studied the novel in some detail may be aware of the 1818 *Thomas* copy, which Mary Shelley corrected and annotated and left, with Mrs Thomas, in Genoa, when she left Italy in 1823.[5] What Robinson's scholarship has given us, as an addition to this already sizeable series of variants, is an immaculately edited facsimile of the two-volume manuscript draft copy of the novel produced in 'two hard-cover notebooks ([August or September)] 1816 [to] 17 April 1817' and a part (Notebooks C1 and C2) of the three-volume fair copy produced from '[? eleven] soft-cover notebooks (18 April – 13 May 1817)'.[6] If that were not enough, his scholarship, building on but also correcting the work of previous scholars, has also given us a much more solid idea of the lost, original story, what he calls the 'Ur-Text', that Mary Shelley wrote, immediately after the famous decision to hold a ghost-story writing competition in the Via Diodati, between '([? 17] June – [August or September] 1816)'.[7] Both the proofs for 1818 and the revises have been lost.

This scholarship and availability of the facsimile draft and part-fair copy complicates what was already a highly contentious area of study. As Robinson states, describing the critical debates which have revolved around the 1818 and 1831 versions:

> the substantive changes that MWS made in her revised edition are so extreme that many teachers and students of *Frankenstein* consider 1818 and 1831 as two different novels. Among the significant 'alterations' made in 1831 are the following: a transformation of Elizabeth from a cousin to a foundling having no blood relation to Victor; a new chapter to accommodate a much longer exposition about Victor's childhood; and a more explicit and earlier introduction of the doppelganger theme when Victor alludes to Aristophanes's myth of the circular and then divided primal human beings in Plato's *Symposium*.[8]

What has been characteristic of some of the best *Frankenstein* criticism of the past thirty years has been a debate about the politics of the changes made in 1831 to the 1818 version, with until recently a growing consensus that 1818 was a more politically radical text than 1831.[9] For my part, for example, I have attempted to build a reading of both 1818 and 1831 versions which demonstrates a greater level of importance, on the subject of education and its relation to reason, in the passage Robinson refers to when Victor apparently alludes to Aristophanes. In fact, I have argued that the allusion is more directly to the work of Godwin, Mary Shelley's father.[10]

The draft copy and remaining parts of the fair copy unsettle a good deal of this debate as it has been conducted over the past thirty or so years. One cannot any longer simply take scholarly editions of 1818 and 1831 and play them off against each other. This is true for a number of reasons. Robinson's facsimile edition poses a number of what are quite simply foundational questions and challenges to traditional *Frankenstein* criticism. The issue I have in my mind in this essay, however, concerns the collaborative nature of the draft and fair copy, and ultimately the authorship of Mary Shelley's and Romanticism's most famous novel. 'Establishing a final and exact count for the PBS words in 1818', Robinson writes, 'is impossible, although ... I have hazarded a number in excess of 4000'.[11] The exact estimate is impossible because of, amongst other things, the unavailability of the proofs and revises. However, Robinson's work has given us a huge amount of assistance in what has always been, for ideological and for interpretive reasons, a highly controversial subject; that is, P. B. Shelley's part in the authoring of *Frankenstein*. Donald H. Reiman, in his 'Foreword' to *The Frankenstein Notebooks*, compares the relationship between P. B. Shelley and Mary Shelley in this instance to that between Ezra Pound and T. S. Eliot over the authoring of *The Waste Land*.[12] That could be seen, of course, as a less than neutral analogy. Robinson attempts a more moderate stance, although some would of course view his borrowed figuration as equally problematic:

> If ... MWS is the creative genius by which this novel was conceived and developed, we can call PBS an able midwife who helped his wife to bring her monster to life. His 'hand' is in evidence in each of the extent *Frankenstein* Notebooks ... [and he was also involved, of course] in the printing, publishing, and reviewing of the novel.[13]

The issue of collaboration in authorship is one which appears to be growing in importance in Shelley studies and Romantic studies generally, and it is one which almost invariably brings with it gender-based issues regarding the politics and psychology of authorship. Zachary Leader, for example, in a fine examination of the issue in his *Revision and Romantic Authorship*, contrasts Byron's perceived abandonment of his work after composition to Mary Shelley's maternal understanding of authorship as parenting: 'The good parent', he writes, attempting to paraphrase Mary Shelley's attitude towards authorship, 'like the good author, neither abandons its offspring nor seeks wholly to control or shape them'.[14] It is this paternal-maternal understanding of authorship, which perhaps allows

Robinson's midwife figuration to stand as an accurate enough trope. Leader goes on: 'Though Percy Shelley may not have intended his alterations to make the novel's characters take on his voice – formal, cultural, "Ciceronian" – they did, and Mary Shelley doubtless knew or sensed as much, approving'.[15]

There have been some who have argued that P. B. Shelley should be considered a co-author of *Frankenstein*, most significantly of them perhaps, since his argument was presented within a scholarly edition of the text, James Reiger.[16] This approach is misguided in many ways, and I will say why below. However, it is also clear that serious implications for the tradition of interpretation which has grown around Mary Shelley's novel present themselves to us when we return to *Frankenstein* in its collaborative draft and fair-copy texts. At a very simple level, some of the canonical readings of the novel have to be revised or even discarded when we actually look at the textual evidence.[17] I cannot claim to have yet attempted any sustained and rigorous survey of these changes and challenges to canonical readings of the novel. A revision of *Frankenstein*-criticism on this basis would be a huge undertaking, one which in itself would be best embarked upon in a collaborative spirit. I have been more concerned, so far, in making sure that my own reading of the novel is written in full knowledge of who wrote what. Robinson's 'Frankenstein Notebooks' have, quite simply, taught me that I have to relearn how to reread Mary Shelley's most famous novel. We are dealing here, often, with individual words or small phrases or solitary images. But then patterns of words and their figurative dimensions are what we invariably build our interpretations of such a text upon. A good example would be the series of names by which the creature is nominated. To take some draft examples: a change from 'creature' to 'being' to 'an animal' occurs on the first page of chapter 6 (vol. 1, ch. 3 of the 1818 novel), and this change is in Mary's hand.[18] On the next page, however, Victor's 'A new creation would bless me as its maker and source; many happy and excellent creatures would owe their existence in to me' is altered in a number of places: 'creation' to 'existence', 'maker' to 'creator', 'creatures' to 'beings' and then 'natures', 'existence' to 'being', and these changes are, chronologically, Percy's, Mary's, and then two more from Percy.[19] On draft vol. 1, ch. 10, p. 114, Percy prefers 'being' to Mary's 'wretch' and then later to her 'creature'.[20] In the scene on Montanvert, as the creature comes towards him with super-human speed and agility, vol. 2, ch. 2 of the 1818, Victor states: 'I perceived, as the shape came nearer, (sight tremendous and abhorred!) that it was the wretch whom I had created'. The word 'shape' is P. B. Shelley's alteration to the neutral 'he', although the word 'abhorred' (I will come back to the significance of that word later) is Mary Shelley's original.[21] In draft vol. 1, ch. 6, p. 69, Mary Shelley changes 'life' to 'animation' ('Pursuing these reflections, I thought, that if I could bestow animation upon lifeless matter').[22] However, a few pages later, as Victor reflects with horror on his achievement of this process, it is P. B.

Shelley who substitutes 'animation' for 'life' ('A mummy again endued with animation could not be so hideous as that wretch').[23] We cannot tell whether Mary,
or Percy or someone else substituted 'wretch' for the underlined and capitalized
'He'.[24]

There is evidence of a fascinating interplay between Mary and P. B. Shelley
in terms of word choice in the draft and fair-copy, and these have a potentially
vital role in any future reading of the novel. There are more extensive additions
made by P. B. Shelley. These include the extended comparison between serv-
ants in Geneva and in England in vol. 1, ch. 5, 1818,[25] and, quite significantly
for readings which would simply take the novel as a critique of Shelleyan, male
Romanticism, much of M. Waldman's Enlightenment statement about the
labours of scientific ('philosophical') men, including: 'The labours of men of
genius however erroneously directed scarcely ever fail in ultimately turning to
the solid advantage of mankind.'[26] For those who would read Mary Shelley's
novel as a critique of male Romantic modes of quest and politico-aesthetic ide-
alisms, the fact that it was P. B. Shelley who inserted this disastrous piece of
encouragement to the budding Victor must be somewhat disturbing. If we are
determined to read *Frankenstein* as a critique of P. B. Shelley, how far are we prepared to allow, in the face of indisputable textual evidence, that he contributed
significantly himself to that critique?

Such a question brings us back to the gender issues which asserted themselves as soon as we began to think about the issue of collaborative authorship.
Much has been made of the gender politics surrounding the characters who
figure as the story's first readers within the novel. I am referring of course to
Walton and to Margaret Walton Saville, his sister, and bearer, as we know, of the
same initials as Mary Wollstonecraft Shelley. Does Walton learn from Victor's
and the creature's tragic story that a rejection of the female domestic sphere and
the values of that sphere are ultimately harmful to oneself and to everyone else
with whom one comes in contact? Is Mary Shelley's famous novel an example
of what Anne K. Mellor calls 'female Romanticism', and does it direct its critique of 'male Romanticism' towards its readers via the mediation of Walton's
writerly relation to his alienated, readerly sister? These are, in reductive form,
some of the issues that critics have been debating for a good thirty years now. Yet
who is actually the novel's first reader? The answer has to be that the first reader
of *Frankenstein* is that significant male other who is not just given anonymous
responsibility for penning the novel's rather anxious 1818 'Preface', but who is,
far more radically, encrypted within the novel as an interpretive force, a force of
interpretation. We are familiar now with arguments, from Robinson and Anne
K. Mellor, that the novel encrypts within its own time frame the author's own
gestation within her writerly mother's womb.[27] We need to supplement that
textual-historical possibility by recognizing that P.B. Shelley, as a collaborative

interpreter, is also encrypted within the novel's pages. *Frankenstein* as a novel includes within itself it own first, interpretive reception, so that the novel we return to has always already been read, subject to interpretation. Another way of stating this is that some of the novel's symbolically significant figurative and lexical patterns and networks are interpretations (through additions) made to the novel by P. B. Shelley, and, in fact, are also interpretations (through additions) by Mary Shelley of P. B. Shelley's interpretive interpolations. My one example in this essay emerges if we return to the word 'abhorred'.

In the draft of what would become vol. 3, ch. 7, the creature, addressing Walton over the dead body of his creator, states:

> Why do you not hate Felix who drove his friend from his door or the man who would
> have destroyed the saviour of his child? Nay they are virtuous and immaculate beings
> – While I the miserable & ... trampled on, am the devil to be spurned & kicked &
> hated!

P. B. Shelley cancels 'the devil', however, and adds what we now have in both 1818 and 1831, 'an abortion'.[28] So we have, in 1818, 'I, the miserable and the abandoned, am an abortion, to be spurned at, and kicked, and trampled on'.[29] The further changes evidenced there I presume were made at the proof stage. The alteration from 'devil' to 'abortion' is, I would argue, a hugely significant and a brilliantly accurate interpretation of the lexical and semantic network Mary Shelley has built up around the story of creature and creator and which pivots on the at least partly homophonous relationship between the word 'abortion' and the word 'abhorred'. To prove such a statement one would have to enter into a long discussion of Enlightenment theories of pedagogy, Godwin's and Wollstonecraft's politico-philosophical and novelistic writings and their influence on P. B. and Mary Shelley, and the on-going negotiation (political, philosophical, psychological and aesthetic) between those last, forever related authors on the meaning and the consequence of the writings of those parental influences. A whole reading of *Frankenstein* can be built upon the notion, the uncanny, rationally disturbing notion of an 'abortive man' and that figure's generation in others (for which read 'us') of 'abhorrence'. But it is no ordinary reading, since it already exists, before a critic such as myself can construct it, and it exists as subject and object of a reading, within the still uncanny, protean, unstable series of texts we call *Frankenstein*.

The formative, dialogic force of reading makes the novel we call (in the singular) *Frankenstein*, so that any reading of the novel is in fact a *return* to reading, a return to a reading which already exists within the text as object and subject. Reading is not something we simply bring to *Frankenstein*, it is something that has already happened, something that created the text in the first place. Our reading of the novel is, even the first time we read it, a re-reading. This is true for any book which has been proofed, edited, annotated, modernized, amended, materially re-presented. So, true for every book, then. But in *Frankenstein* we find this rule writ large. This novel novel undermines any notion we might entertain concerning the novelty of our reading. It reminds us, instead, that all reading is dialogic, collaborative and has always already begun. I have spent a lot of my career writing critically about a critic who argues, persuasively at times, that all reading worth our attention is *mis-reading*.[30] My answer to that claim is increasingly that all reading worth our attention is self-consciously *re-reading*.

All serious reading knows that what it reads is the product of generative reading. All reading is re-reading. The 'Frankenstein Notebooks' reminds us of this fact, and of the uncanny tropes and reversals such an insight and practice offers up. Where some critics have been mistaken on the issue of P. B. Shelley's contribution to Mary Shelley's novel is in re-staging the issue in terms of a conflict over authorship; as if writing, being an author, were detachable from the sometimes agonistic, often collaborative, but always collective act of re-reading. I want to end this brief look at *Frankenstein*'s readerly origins by giving an example of the manner in which that insight and practice gives us fresh perspectives on readings of the novel which occurred in Mary Shelley's own time. My example concerns Walter Scott and his important review published in *Blackwood's Edinburgh Magazine* in 1818. Scott ends that fascinating review by stating the following: '[S]o concludes this extraordinary tale, in which the author seems to us to disclose uncommon powers of poetic imagination'.[31]

Scott, like many of the novel's first reviewers, thought that P. B. Shelley was the author of *Frankenstein*. P. B. Shelley had, after all, sent him the novel personally and had couched his letter in terms that had clearly left room for the possibility, at least in Scott's mind, that P. B. Shelley wished, like many others in the period, to publish his novel anonymously. 'The Author', P. B. Shelley writes,

> has requested me to send you, as a slight tribute of high admiration & respect, the accompanying volumes. / My own share in them consists simply in having superintended them through the press during the Author's absence. Perhaps it is the partial regard of friendship that persuades me that they are worthy of the attention of the celebrated person whom I have at present the honour to address.[32]

So it is no wonder then that Scott foregrounds the novel's 'powers of poetic imagination'. He carries this on, by praising the literary and linguistic style, even say 'voice', with which the novel is written:

> It is no slight merit in our eyes, that the tale, though wild in incident, is written in plain and forcible English, without exhibiting that mixture of hyperbolical Germanisms with which tales of wonder are usually told, as if it were necessary that the language should be as extravagant as the fiction.[33]

Scott thinks he is commenting on an author's narrative and literary style here. He is, in fact, as we know, unknowingly praising the product of a collaborative project of reading and writing, and re-reading and re-writing. He ends by, as he thinks, paying P. B. Shelley the compliment of stating that the author of *Frankenstein* displays: 'the same facility in expressing himself in verse as in prose', before, by way of an illustration and confirmation of this judgement, quoting the last eight lines of P. B. Shelley's 'Mutability', first published in *Alastor and Other Poems* in 1816:

> We rest. – A dream has power to poison sleep;
> We rise. – One wandering thought pollutes the day;
> We feel, conceive or reason, laugh or weep;
> Embrace fond woe, or cast our cares away:
> It is the same! – For, be it joy or sorrow,
> The path of its departure still is free:
> Man's yesterday may ne'er be like his morrow;
> Nought may endure but Mutability.[34]

As Scott explains to his readers, these lines from 'Mutability' are quoted in the novel by Victor Frankenstein (vol. 2, ch. 11), just prior to the sublime face-off between creator and creature on the *mer de glace* facing Montanvert and, beyond it, Mont Blanc, a mountain P. B. Shelley had so powerfully represented and responded to in *History of a Six Weeks' Tour* co-written by P. B. and Mary Shelley and published anonymously in 1817.

Scott quotes the lines from 'Mutability' as quoted in *Frankenstein* as proof that the poet is also a significant novelist, not knowing that the significant novelist was in her (not his) novel quoting his (not her) significant poetry. My point is that although he does not know it Scott is absolutely right to quote these lines and highlight their thematic importance for the novel as a whole. He is right because the quotation of the quotation highlights the fact that Mary Shelley welcomes P. B. Shelley into her novel in a wholly positive and meaningful (meaning-making) fashion. Arguments, such as those made by Anne K. Mellor, that P. B. Shelley marred Mary Shelley's text by introducing into it his 'Ciceronian', overly ornate and Latinized, sentences, cannot cope with the fact that even before the process of collaboratively revising the draft notebooks began, Mary had invited P. B. Shelley into her novel through her own use of quotation, along with covert and overt allusion. Scott is also completely right in his use of quotation, since these lines echo throughout Mary Shelley's post-*Frankenstein* works, always reinforcing her realist response to the more extreme forms of perfectibilist idealism in her husband's and her father's writing. For Mary Shelley, human life is not so much perfectible as ambivalent, strung out between hope and despair, Enlightenment and the inconsolable fact of tragedy, and if we read her work closely, we frequently find Shelley's 'Mutability' directly or implicitly incorporated into her texts in order to reinforce that world vision.

Scott is not misreading *Frankenstein* in his review. He is responding, rather brilliantly, if blindfolded as it were, to the originary process of reading and re-reading, out of which the novel was created. *Frankenstein*, like all literature, is created out of quotation, citation, echo, allusion, the iterability of all language. It is intertextual, and so the product of re-reading. But far more interestingly, perhaps, it is the product of a specific intellectual exchange and collaborative partnership that we are only now, after two centuries of literary criticism, beginning to take seriously.

There is a nice touch with which we can end. As Mary transcribes the words of her husband into her famous first novel, she makes one mistake and leaves out an 'h' in the penultimate line. P. B. Shelley appears to have restored this missing 'h', transforming 'is' into his original 'his'.[35] In other words: P. B. Shelley corrects Mary Shelley's quotation of P. B. Shelley's 'Mutability' in a novel published anonymously and ascribed by many to P. B. Shelley but actually authored by Mary Shelley in collaboration with P. B. Shelley. There is much more still to learn about *Frankenstein* and what is often called, appropriately, as I have been suggesting, 'The Shelley Circle'.

5 'CASUALTY', MRS SHELLEY AND SEDITIOUS LIBEL: CLEANSING BRITAIN'S MOST CORRUPT POET OF ERROR

Nora Crook

> Let us remark that hardly any great poet, certainly no modern one, has been so *inaccurately printed* as Shelley. Helps to the very necessary revision are in existence, and ought quickly to be used.[1]

William Allingham's observation in his anthology *Nightingale Valley* (1860), quickly took on a life of its own: 'I know no works of any great modern poet which need to be more carefully revised for the press than those of Percy Bysshe Shelley' ('O. T. D.', 1867).[2] 'Certain passages begin to be famous as crucial subjects for emendation; and the master-singer of our modern poets shares with his own masters and models the least enviable proof of fame, – that given by corrupt readings and diverse commentaries' (Swinburne, 1869).[3] 'The texts of Shelley's poems are in many cases as defective or corrupt as if he were a classic instead of a modern writer' (H. S. Salt, 1887).[4] Surprisingly, this last is still *just* true, if by 'texts' one understands 'edited reading texts' and 'many' is whittled down to 'quite a few'. It will be less true by the time this is published. But only when the two major collective editions in progress, the Longman and the Johns Hopkins, are complete (as is expected within the next few years) will Salt's pronouncement finally be put to rest.[5]

The 'helps' no doubt included Richard Garnett, whom Allingham knew to have access to Sir Percy and Lady Shelley, owners of most of the manuscripts from which Mary Shelley (1797–1851), Shelley's first editor, had drawn her editions.[6] Friends of Shelley, with information about his working methods, were still alive; manuscripts, such as one purportedly found on Shelley's corpse, were being rediscovered. But Allingham's chief 'help' when he came to correct, as he thought, 'Lines to an Indian Air' was his own insight into Shelley's characteristics. The second stanza of the Indian girl's plea to her lover to descend from his chamber runs thus in Mary Shelley's editions of 1839–47:

> The wandering airs they faint
> On the dark, the silent stream –
> The champak odours fail
> Like sweet thoughts in a dream;
> The nightingale's complaint
> It dies upon her heart,
> As I must die on thine,
> O beloved as thou art!

Allingham noticed that the third line broke the *abcbadcd* rhyme scheme of the other two stanzas, and emended 'fail' to 'pine', suspecting some tampering with the text:

> We believe that the 'fail,' in the third verse, caused the same word to be slipt into the second, under the notion of making the iteration more exact; but such merely verbal and mechanical iteration is not in place here, and destroys the rhymic structure of the lyric in a very un-Shelleyan manner.[7]

His privileging of the 'rhymic' structure (which shows the attention that Victorian readers brought to these matters) was misplaced. Shelley is a great experimenter with rhyme, but he is just as likely to prefer verbal structure. Here he needed 'fail' in order to be able to gather the words *faint, fail* and *die* for the final stanza, which begins, 'O lift me from the grass / I die, I faint, I fail'. A great admirer of Calderón, Shelley adopts a typical Calderónic device, whereby three elements are elaborated separately and then finally reassembled.[8] Allingham was not aware of this, nor was he in a position to know that Shelley's manuscripts do not have 'pine'. Yet, as I shall later suggest, even the immeasurably better informed modern editor is sometimes thrown back on an armoury little different from his.

Those were the days, the 1860s, before editing Shelley's poetry became the professionalized and solemn activity that it is today. Allingham's note ushered in a glorious free-wheeling decade of Shelley emendation, when *literati* could denounce a particular reading, and propose what Shelley had really written, certain of attention, at least. Between 1867 and 1869 the pages of *Notes and Queries*, their forum, hummed with readers adducing passages that had puzzled them for years and discussing the corruption of Shelley's texts. Authenticated misinformation was eagerly shared. J. W. Dixon, proposing to emend a case of Shelley's 'delight' with 'the light,' wrote that 'an intimate friend' of Shelley

> assured me that Shelley in his MS. often used the small Greek theta for th. Let any one write the words 'the light' after such a fashion, and it will be seen how easy an

unlearned printer might mistake a small theta ... for a d. ... By-the-bye, 'P. B. Shelley,' in large capitals, is inscribed or rather cut on the walls of the dungeon of the Castle of Chillon; it is on the righthand wall. The genuineness is unquestionable.[9]

Some went further. Completing an imperfect line in 'The Triumph of Life' ('And near him walk the [   ] twain'), in which 'him' is Plato and the 'twain' are Aristotle and Alexander, 'A Cobbler' supplied what Shelley *ought* to have written: 'I suggest "Macedonian" as the word Shelley would have employed, had it occurred to him, being sonorous, simple, adequate, and poetical'.[10] From the forum there emerges a sense of a loose group, great admirers rather than idolators, with a sound knowledge of prosody, who read their Shelley carefully, and assume that he meant something even where he seems to write nonsense. The Shelley of the Chartists, who had taken *Queen Mab* as their Bible, is not theirs (though one of the forum, William Michael Rossetti, republican and radical-leaning, thought that the best, most original portions of *Queen Mab*, as poetry, were the angry declamatory passages). They are confident that blemishes, including grammatical irregularities, may be eliminated, obscurities clarified, and Shelley shine forth as one of the greatest poets of modern times. This is the readership at which the landmark Shelley editions of 1870–92 were originally aimed, at least by their editors.

Explanations for Shelley's flawed texts were advanced: 'More than half of Shelley's poems were written during what I may call his *imprisonment* in Italy, from 1819 to 1822; during which time ... he was unable to correct the proofs' wrote Thomas L'Estrange.[11] 'O. T. D.' blamed Shelley's method of composition,

> which was to omit a line or an epithet here or there when it did not readily present itself in the heat of composition, and pass on with the remainder of his work till the muse was in a more indulgent humour, when the omission would be happily filled up.[12]

Rossetti attached more blame to the printers 'or here and there a hasty slip of [Shelley's] own pen'.[13] The ungallant L'Estrange blamed Mary Shelley, who

> though anything but a beauty, was a girl endowed with powerful force of character. In England she found herself and Shelley *deconsidered* in the social world; and when he went – Wednesday, March 11, 1818 – to reside in Italy, *she* resolved and determined never to return.[14]

Mary Shelley's editing as such was not censured. This, however, was to change. Rossetti, whose long instalments of suggested emendations to *Notes and Queries* secured him a contract to re-edit Shelley's poetry for Moxon,[15] later explained the sorry state of Shelley's texts as due to: 'Shelley himself, Casualty, and Mrs. Shelley'.

Mrs Shelley brought 'deep affection and unmeasured enthusiasm' to the task. 'But ill health and the pain of reminiscence curtailed her editorial labours', and, he added, trying to sound tactful and not succeeding, 'to judge from the result, you would say that Mrs. Shelley was not one of the persons to whom the gift of consistent accuracy has been imparted'.[16] Rossetti (who, with a few exceptions, still did not have direct access to Shelley's manuscripts) was high-handed in his emendation of the faults due to 'Shelley himself' – mostly grammatical sole-cisms. Modern editors reject his policy, winsome though he could be in going about it, as when banishing the spurious word 'tookedst' from Shelley's transla-tion from *Faust*: 'Editors are a hard-hearted race. None had hitherto sufficient pity to alter "tookedst" into "tookest"'.[17] But there remains 'Casualty' – the fortuitous and piecemeal manner in which Shelley's manuscripts have become available – [18] and 'Mrs Shelley', whose reputation as Shelley's editor has fluctu-ated greatly over nearly 200 years.

It sank when in 1958 Charles H. Taylor, Jr demonstrated that she had cut corners in editing the *Poetical Works* (1839), and used hand-corrected pages of two imperfect 'pirate' editions of Shelley's poems as press-copy.[19] Two 1960s articles by Joseph Raben accused her of editorial malfeasance.[20] But in 1969 both Irving Massey and Jean de Palacio praised her work.[21] Palacio, possibly her most even-handed critic, details in his lengthy chapter the many respects in which her procedure is censurable, but concludes by judging her work overall to be of 'remarkable probity ... she almost always respects the text and her inexactitudes are only rarely disastrous'.[22] At present, following important critical articles in the 1990s, her reputation oscillates between the perspectives of critics like Susan Wolfson and Neil Fraistat,[23] who acknowledge the constraints under which she worked, but tend to emphasize her negative legacy, and of those who, like Michael O'Neill and the late Betty Bennett, salute her achievement, Bennett maintaining that 'her editorial standards, stated or implied, stand up well even by modern standards'.[24] Yet although the story of her editing has now been often told, there remain aspects worth underlining or reinterpreting that bear on the choices facing an editor today, and that I will now illustrate (with a caveat that what follows is not a comprehensive view of this complicated subject).

It is indeed when Shelley went to Italy and began to leave proof-correction to others that trouble began, and this continued after he drowned in 1822. In the winter of 1822–3, living in Genoa with Leigh Hunt and his family, Mary Shel-ley sat down to extract from Shelley's legacy of loose papers and notebooks what was to become a substantial part of *Posthumous Poems of Percy Bysshe Shelley* (1824). She wrote to Claire Clairmont on 19 December 1822:

> There is but one fireplace in the house ... So I am obliged to pass the greater part of my time in Hunt's sitting room ... I rise at nine, breakfast work read and if I can at all indure [*sic*] the cold, copy my Shelleys Mss. in my own room & if possible walk before dinner – after that I work – read Greek etc till ten when Hunt & Marianne go to bed. Then I am alone ... I am alone.[25]

As she went through Shelley's twenty-five or so working notebooks, some soaked in the sea-water that had drowned him, she would have encountered a record of his minutest actions – where he dipped his pen, or turned the feather of his quill into a paintbrush, or doodled, or swatted a fly, or blotted his page with fine sand (all preserved to this day). Even today the transcriber may experience a strange, sad feeling of Shelley's absence and his simultaneous presence, in spite of the faded ink, the repair glue, the Bodleian library stamps. 'I am torn to pieces by memory', she wrote in 1839 in the throes of editing the *Poetical Works*.[26] But she also remembered the sheer hard slog. Although she returned to some of Shelley's manuscripts for checking in 1839, she never attempted a root-and-branch revision of her 1822–3 work:

> Did any one see the papers from which I drew [*Posthumous Poems*] the wonder would be how any eyes or patience were capable of extracting it from so confused a mass, interlined and broken into fragments, so that the sense could only be deciphered and joined by guesses which might seem rather intuitive than founded on reasoning. Yet I believe no mistake was made.[27]

She has attracted condescension and reproach for that last sentence, but she was making a limited claim, as the context helps to clarify: to have assembled the fragments in the right order and not created hybrid monsters. She was not setting up to be word-perfect (she continued to give small tweaks to the poems up until 1847). Even so, that 'I believe' concedes that she may have made mistakes, though she herself cannot see them. Often her confidence was justified; her arrangement of 'The Triumph of Life', for instance, has been endorsed by G. M. Matthews (1960) and all subsequent editors. But in some cases, unaware that Shelley had made a fair copy of a poem of which she possessed a rough draft only, she was wrong.[28]

Rossetti's complaint of inconsistency was also justified. Mary Shelley disliked proofreading. It shows in the printing errors that affect all her own novels and in this remark:

> 'The disagreeable and, to [Alfieri's] sensitive temperament, irritating task of correcting the press, seems to have exercised an injurious influence over his temper and genius. According to his own account, it dried up his brain, quenched the fire of youthful enthusiasm, and prevented his ever again writing with equal vigour and felicity.'[29]

We detect a slight irony at the expense of Alfieri's super-sensitivity, but 'disagreeable' evidently expresses her view. She would lose concentration at points, and substitute a synonym, such as 'turned' for Shelley's 'changed'.[30] Her riot of sigla befuddled Shelley's later editors, who could only guess at their significance. She has two ways of showing indecipherable text (square brackets and long dashes). But square brackets double as indicators of the lacunae in Shelley's original manuscripts, along with suspension points, triple em-rules, and unbracketed blank space. Sometimes she omits to indicate a lacuna altogether. Her closing up Shelley's blank in the line 'Fresh spring, and summer and winter hoar' in the lyric 'O World, O Life, O Time', gave rise to a notorious squabble. Rossetti inserted 'autumn' after 'summer' to correct the metre. Swinburne exploded:

> the melodious effect of its exquisite inequality – I should have thought was a thing to thrill the veins and draw tears to the eyes of all men whose ears were not closed against all harmony by some denser and less removable obstruction than shut out the song of the Sirens from the hearing of the crew of Ulysses.[31]

Rossetti was abashed into withdrawing 'autumn', but access to Shelley's drafts has vindicated, not his insertion, but his perception that there *was* a metrical deficiency (which Shelley would presumably have remedied had he published the stanzas).[32]

Yet cases of her minute fidelity to Shelley's preferences have been overlooked, as in her omission of apostrophes in past tense verb-forms to indicate elisions (distinguishing between 'vein'd' and 'veined', for instance). Shelley's manuscripts omit them, nor does he seem to have desired printers, traditionally trained to improve authorial punctuation,[33] to put them in. The odd ones in his printed texts seem to be there through force of habit on the part of compositors of the old school, and the same may be said of those in Mary Shelley's editions. (Byron's printers, by contrast, regularly put them in.) Rossetti, editing in 1870, when the typographical convention was as outdated as the full-bottomed wig, felt it necessary to do the reverse, to indicate sounded final *-ed* with a grave accent, and many editors have followed. However, Shelley apparently expected anyone with an ear to be able to tell whether a final *-ed* was sounded or not, or wanted to factor in a certain freedom of interpretation as to how a line might be read.

Later editors have confirmed many of Mary Shelley's suspected transcription errors, and succeeded in reading words that defeated her. Yet it is no exaggeration to say that she taught all subsequent editors how to read Shelley's rough draft hand. It is comparatively easy to crack one difficult word when the rest have already been deciphered.[34] Indeed, she is today more likely to be criticized not for her slips, but, rather, for promoting a depoliticized, inoffensive Shelley for middle-class consumption, a 'pure poet of the lyric moment',[35] later to degenerate into Arnold's infamous ineffectual angel. Her first intention, expressed within three months of Shelley's death, was to look into the best way of 'republishing S's works *as well as* the writings he has left behind' (20 September 1822; my italics), and was still thinking of doing this as late as 5 October 1823. But a long letter, begun 20 October 1823, to Leigh Hunt, then still in Italy, suggests that no best way had been found:

I am yet undecided whether to print a Vol. of unpublished ones [or] of the whole together – I encline [*sic*] to the former – as it w^d be a specimen of how he could write without shocking anyone – and afterwards an edition of the whole might be got up inserting any thing too shocking for this Vol. but I sh^d be very glad of your opinion.

By 3 November 1823 the idea of a collected edition (which would have included Shelley's most controversial poems) had been postponed without Hunt having had a say: 'My S's poems are ready – I publish now the unpublished only'.[36] Neil Fraistat comments: 'Perhaps the most crucial decision Mary Shelley made about the volume was to defer trying to publish Shelley's complete works, which would have prompted all of the by-now-familiar complaints and resistances'.[37] Fraistat recognizes her tactical reasons, but it is worth probing further: was this effectively her decision? What did she mean by 'without shocking anyone'?

Arguably, Mary Shelley's really crucial decision had been to publish with John Hunt, Leigh Hunt's brother, and publisher of the recently failed *Liberal*, the periodical that Leigh Hunt, Byron and Shelley had started up just before Shelley's death. It was her first direct negotiation with a publisher, and John Hunt was direct and cordial towards her. In any case her options were limited. A bridge between 'respectable' publishers and 'unrespectable' radical ones such as Cannon, Carlile, Clark, Hone and Benbow, Hunt was one of the few in the mainstream who would have willingly risked publishing Shelley at this time.[38] He was a fighter, praised by Jeremy Bentham for his energy and courage, and likened by Byron and Horace Smith to the seventeenth-century parliamentarians Prynne and Pym and the republicans of ancient Rome.[39] She initially approached him on 11 September 1823, shortly after her return to England. Already the idea of a complete edition hung in the balance. She proposed that he publish 'such MSS as I have of our S— and he agreed to it ... The present volume would consist of unpublished pieces' though this was 'not yet settled'.[40] This suggests that John Hunt had neither ruled out a complete edition nor agreed to one.

Mary Shelley had told Hunt that two Shelley admirers had offered to part-sponsor the collection of unpublished work, but there is no record of them offering sponsor a collected *Poetical Works*, and they do not appear to have had the means.[41] There was a glut of unsold Shelley in 1823–4, and until that had shifted, a republication had few attractions to a publisher. Charles Ollier, who had published all of Shelley's volumes after 1817 except *Swellfoot the Tyrant*, had lost by his investment. Bankrupted in the spring of 1823, he sold off most of his stock, the greater part of the Shelley items at a knockdown price to Simpkin & Marshall, who made up a remainder edition called *Poetical Pieces*, first of four works, and later, when copies of *Hellas* ran out, of three works (1823). *Poetical Pieces* did not fly off the shelves.[42] On 28 October 1823 Mary Shelley asked Charles Ollier to deliver his remaining stock (nine titles) of Shelley's printed poems to John Hunt. Hunt later attempted to sell these off separately, and was advertising them all in July 1824, though he had received as few as twelve copies of certain titles.[43]

The exclusion from *Posthumous Poems* of Shelley's hard-hitting unpublished political poems and popular songs of 1819–20 is also frequently adduced as an indication of Mary Shelley's wish to elevate Shelley above politics. This group includes *The Mask of Anarchy*, 'To the Lord Chancellor', 'England in 1819', 'Corpses are Cold in the Tomb', 'Song: To the Men of England', 'To S[idmouth] and C[astlereagh]', 'A New National Anthem' and 'A Ballad', all except the last collected or published for the first time in 1839–40.[44] That she transcribed most of them into the fair copy that she used in 1823 to assemble work for *Posthumous Poems* suggests that there was a period during which she had intended to publish these.[45] As Michael O'Neill has pointed out, *Posthumous Poems* did not exclude political poems *per se*.[46] Four items are overtly political: 'Ode to Naples', 'Liberty' ('The Fiery Mountains'), 'Political Greatness' and fragments of 'Charles the First'. But unlike the 'popular' group, none is obviously about contemporary British politics. The nearest are some powerful lines about social inequality in 'Charles the First', displaced onto the 1630s, which may be why Mary Shelley tucked them tactfully away at the back of the volume. She explained laconically in 1839 why the public had had to wait so long for the others: '[I]n those days of prosecution for libel they could not be printed'.

Among London publishers in 1823 John Hunt was one of the most vulnerable to such prosecution. In 1821–2 he had been jailed in Coldbath Fields Prison for seditious libel. In late 1822, after his release, he was indicted for blasphemous libel as 'a person of wicked and malicious disposition' by the Constitutional Association (a vigilante group) for publishing Byron's *Vision of Judgment*. In late 1823, nearly a year later, he was still awaiting trial.[47] Things then got worse for him. On 15 January 1824, during the crucial period when Mary Shelley was preparing *Posthumous Poems* for the press, he was convicted, and the sentence was deferred. During the next six months the threat of another term of imprisonment hung over him. Just how little he could afford to step out of line during this period is vividly brought home by his recently discovered letter to Edwin Atherstone of 24 February 1824. Atherstone had submitted some work that John Hunt reluctantly rejected, advising him to 'find some less *prosecutable* publisher' or to make alterations. 'What I fear is ... that some Individual or Gang should insist that it is libellous or blasphemous, and (out of spite to the Publisher rather than to the Work itself) prosecute forthwith'.[48] It appears that it was not so much that Mary Shelley wanted the public to embrace the ethereal poet and dampen the angry radical (she still intended to publish an edition containing Shelley's 'shocking' poems), as that she would bring harassment and ruin on her publisher unless material was excluded that might serve as a pretext for a malicious prosecution.[49]

A collected edition would have been financially risky for John Hunt while a selective one that included the popular political songs (which contained *ad hominem* attacks on living named individuals) would have been foolhardy, especially in the wake of his conviction of 15 January for publishing 'a mere piece of burlesque poetry', as he complained with bitter incredulity in the same letter to Atherstone.[50] The final decision as to what to include in *Posthumous Poems* may have been taken only after this verdict. Whether the 1824 exclusions were the result of Hunt's veto or of Mary Shelley's second-guessing is of course unascertainable. Probably she always expected to negotiate with Hunt over particular items. It is worth noting that had Hunt been acquitted, it would have been less easy for the Constitutional Association to have then brought an action against *The Mask of Anarchy*.

The equation of 'writing without shocking anyone' with 'depoliticization' is also worth further scrutiny. I would suggest that behind Mary Shelley's concern lies Hazlitt's accusation in *Table Talk* (1821) that Shelley wrote less 'to convince or inform' than 'to shock the public' with irresponsible and volatile thought-experiments, and (elaborating on the metaphor of *shocking*) Hazlitt's wish that Shelley would stop 'the incessant, alarming whirl of his Voltaic battery', because he brought 'disgrace and discredit' upon the cause of 'science and virtue'. By this Hazlitt particularly meant *The Revolt of Islam* and *The Cenci*. It was the first public attack on Shelley from a prominent radical. Leigh Hunt privately remonstrated angrily with Hazlitt, and told Shelley that he had done so.[51] Significantly, Mary Shelley's letters to Leigh Hunt of 1823 frequently include news of Hazlitt, and her remark appears pointed towards this loose cannon. Shelley's unpublished and uncollected work contained no denunciations of Christianity (apart from the doctrine of hell in *Peter Bell the Third*) or Jesus, no praise of 'lawless love', no topics so revolting as be fit only to entertain the devils in hell. A volume of such work (as distinct from a collection of his published works) would be a sufficient answer to Hazlitt, and any whom he claimed to speak for. In the event the tactic was partly successful. Hazlitt's review of *Posthumous Poems* disappointed her, but he acknowledged that Shelley could write political poems that were, in his terms, situated and responsible. He singled out 'Ode to Naples' for high, if back-handed praise: 'immediate and strong local feelings have at once raised and pointed Mr. Shelley's style, and made of light-winged "toys of feathered cupid," the flaming ministers of Wrath and Justice'.[52]

Commentators who have pointed to the language of martyrology in Mary Shelley's writings about Shelley are describing something palpably there, but such language cannot be separated from her political intentions. Motives that emerge from her preface to *Posthumous Poems* are the reparative and the punitive: making the reading public feel what it had lost by Shelley's death and shaming Shelley's enemies in the midst of their triumph.[53] It is the widow's cry, not to Heaven, but to the public, for justice. They lie behind her inclusion of *Alastor* (anomalous, given that this was a collection of posthumous and fugitive poems), in which the death of the unnamed poet is mourned as 'a grief too deep for tears', and continues into her notes for her later editions. She had in front of her (perhaps literally; Shelley had owned a copy and was using it during the last year of his life) one of the most outstanding examples of a book that had virtually overnight turned the tide in favour of one who had been branded a public criminal, – the *Eikon Basilike*, a compendium, purportedly of Charles I's own apologia, meditations and prayers, which, published ten days after his execution in 1649, produced an immediate reflux of feeling towards the dead king. Charles's Christian virtues (including those of forgiveness of enemies, piety, and sobriety) were foregrounded, and he began immediately to acquire the status of a martyr who had died for his religious beliefs, and his judges the opprobrium of murderers. William Godwin, whom Mary Shelley found on her return to England immersed in writing his four-volume *History of the Commonwealth*, was to explain the eventual loss of the Commonwealth as due in part to the immediate publication of *Eikon Basilike*, 'an event that could not have been foreseen'.[54] *Posthumous Poems* was Mary Shelley's attempt to produce just such an unforeseen event, on behalf not of a Christian king but of a far worthier object, his antithesis, an atheist and republican poet. Certainly she knew the tactical importance of seizing the day. When Hunt advised her to delay publication for a year she answered (9 February 1824): 'Alas, my dear friend, "there is a tide in the affairs of man" – Shelley has celebrity even popularity now – a winter ago greater interest would perhaps have been excited than now by this volume – but who knows what may happen before the next'.[55] One great difference between the two books is that whereas *Eikon Basilike* went into thirty-five editions in a short time, *Posthumous Poems* was promptly withdrawn because of pressure applied by Shelley's father, who wished his son's name to be forgotten; John Hunt was forced to destroy the unsold copies. It was mostly left to unauthorized publishers (with one of whom Mary Shelley clandestinely cooperated) to disseminate Shelley's work between 1824 and 1839.

Wolfson and Fraistat see (in different ways) Mary Shelley as shaping a Shelley for a discriminating readership, one prepared to pay a handsome price for his refined and difficult poetry, signalled as such by mottoes in Italian and Latin. Wolfson, additionally, sees Mary Shelley's notes to the editions of 1839–47 as installing herself as Shelley's ideal, sympathetic reader. However, her seven editions of his poetry and prose, not counting re-impressions, suggest a greater plurality of readerships than that judgement encompasses. There was: 1) a collected *Poetical Works* in a four-volume pocket edition (1839), with an expurgated *Queen Mab*; 2) an enlarged one-volume edition (1840, new impression 1844), with the expurgated portions restored; 3) a two-volume collection of

Shelley's prose, *Essays, Letters from Abroad, Translations and Fragments* (1840); 4) the same (with some additions and light revision) in one volume (1845); 5) a one-volume selection, *Minor Poems of Shelley* (1846); 6) a three-volume revised pocket edition of the *Poetical Works*, replacing the four-volume one, with *Queen Mab* expurgated again (1847); 7) a one-volume collection of Shelley's *Works* containing both the *Poetical Works* (incorporating the three-volume revisions, but with an unexpurgated *Queen Mab*) and the 1845 *Essays, Letters*.

Both editions of the *Poetical Works* were at first priced the same (12*s.* in 1844).[56] Neither the reader seeking protection from Shelley's irreligion nor the reader seeking exposure to its full force enjoyed a financial advantage over the other. However, in 1846 Moxon started lowering prices, making the unexpurgated one-volume Shelley the cheaper, at 10*s.* 6*d.*[57] Then came the now largely overlooked *Minor Poems* edition of 1846. This was Moxon's reaching out to a popular readership, and cost only 2*s.* 6*d.* in paper. It undoubtedly had more than Mary Shelley's *imprimatur* (she may even have suggested it), and there is no reason to suppose that the selection was other than hers. Many small corrections hitherto thought to originate in her 1847 editions start with this unassuming 24mo-size volume,[58] the print small but not cramped – no Book Beautiful, though some owners bound their copies in tooled leather. It excluded dramas, translations, very short fragments and Mary Shelley's prefaces and notes. 'Minor' did not mean 'shorter lyrics' or 'poetic gems' but, in effect, any original complete poem by Shelley of under 1,000 lines. All of Shelley's published shorter political poems are there, except for 'To the Lord Chancellor', *Peter Bell the Third*, a poem Mary Shelley disliked because of its attack on Wordsworth, and the inferior 'A New National Anthem'. *The Masque* [*sic*] *of Anarchy* is upgraded to a principal poem, alongside 'Julian and Maddalo', 'Lines Written among the Euganaean Hills', and *Epipsychidion*.[59] The first two cantos of *Queen Mab*, now called 'Ianthe', are in an 'Early Poems' section. These editions collectively suggest a spectrum of possible purchasers shading all the way from the refined and fastidious to members of groups such as working men's associations, shop assistants and lower-paid clerks. The multi-volume pocket editions of the poetry, elegant, expurgated, and portable, seem aimed to catch the boudoir, the circulating library, the pious and the traveller abroad. The one-volume editions, which contain Mary Shelley's own translation of the shocking original Cenci story, are more utilitarian, with cramped print and double columns; some survive in plain cloth, others are leather-bound in gentleman's library style. The *Minor Poems*, though *Queen Mab* is expurgated, refuses to fit into a narrative of a Shelley mediated through Mary Shelley's self-promoting notes and packaged and priced to choke off the masses. The compendium *Works* of 1847 was a bargain (and still is for the book-collector).

Today Shelley's poetry shocks nobody, though it still has the power to incense (the *ODNB* biographer of Castlereagh characterizes his lines on the politician as 'some of the most vicious in the history of British political satire'). Shelley's current editors, the teams contributing to the Longman and the Johns Hopkins editions, have now spent more hours of their lives in trying to restore as nearly as possible 'what Shelley wrote' than Mary Shelley did in placing his writings in the public domain. Modern editors now have access to so much information that, to adapt Shelley's words, the poetry is in more danger of being 'concealed by the accumulation of facts' than by intuitive speculation.[60] Yet at some points it is still necessary to give up a particular crux as irresolvable or decide that the error, if it is that, lies within the bounds of the tolerable, or fall back on Shelley's inferred intentions. For example, in the 1816 *Alastor* (ll. 530–2), 'knarled roots' clench the soil with 'grasping roots' – almost certainly a mistake. Emendations to the first 'roots' have been proposed ('knots', 'trunks', 'stumps'), but no manuscript evidence has survived to suggest what Shelley originally wrote, and modern editors have let the printed text stand. Again, the 'tookedst' that bothered Rossetti might be regarded as indicating Shelley's intended deliberately crabbed pronunciation, or even a joke (Mephistopheles, the speaker, has just announced that he does not speak in a noble style), and also let stand. A third instance, the posthumously published *Julian and Maddalo*, presents more problems, as in this extract from Shelley's press-copy (the latest and most authoritative copy-text), where the protagonists debate free will and determinism:

'Aye, if we were not weak – & we aspire
How vainly to be strong!' said Maddalo
'You talk Utopia.' 'It remains to see'
I then rejoined, '& those who try may find
How strong the chains are which our spirit bind;
Brittle perchance as straw ... We are assured
Much may be conquered, much may be endured
Of what degrades & crushes us. We know
That we have power over ourselves to do
And suffer – what, we know not till we try (ll. 177–86)[61]

In the draft copy, for line 179 Shelley has 'know' for 'see', which made a perfect rhyme,[62] and *Posthumous Poems* also reads 'know'. Mary Shelley's source for her *Posthumous Poems* text is lost, but it was presumably an earlier fair copy with 'know'; 'see' was therefore, inferentially, Shelley's miswriting at the very final stage, and all editors have emended accordingly. However, the more one looks into the matter, the less open-and-shut the case for emendation appears. A few lines later Shelley repeats 'know' as a rhyme-word, this time with 'do' (this particular 'know' is rhymeless in the draft, where the couplet has not yet evolved). Shelley tended not to repeat rhymes in such close proximity, but this might be a case where he did intend to do so, 'know' being a key-term in 'Julian and Maddalo'. It occurs, tellingly, twice in the above extract. Julian, the speaker, distinguishes two kinds of 'knowing': general assurance of our capabilities, and particular knowledge of these capabilities derived from doing and suffering. But there is also a distinction between 'see' and 'try', the first distinguishing *spectators*, who look on the struggles of others, as Maddalo and Julian will shortly do when spying on the Maniac's agony, from *actors*, who put themselves to the trial, as, ironically, Julian does not – a distinction effaced by emending 'see'. Granted, the rhyming defect seems conclusive against retaining 'see'. Except that this is 'Julian and Maddalo', and Shelley was experimenting with an informal, conversational style, where a little studied laxity in rhyming was in keeping. A few lines on he drafted a couplet rhyming 'yoke' with 'spoke', and then for his press copy omitted some lines, making the line ending in 'spoke', now rhymeless (and incidentally avoiding repeating a 'yoke / spoke' rhyme fifty lines back). In short, Shelley might for more than one reason have made a last-minute change from 'know' to 'see' at press-copy stage. A modern editor debating whether to stick by the press copy or emend from Shelley's draft has much information, but still not enough. In the end, the decision depends on whether or not the editor considers that 'see' destroys 'the rhymic structure … in a very un-Shelleyan manner'.

The entire question of 'latest' intentions is a famously vexed one, especially for a writer like Shelley, who compared the creative mind to a 'fading coal' and who left so many of his works as rough or roughish draft. One way out of the crux described above would be to regard Shelley's draft, his press copy, and Mary Shelley's *Posthumous Poems* edition as each having its own validity. A marked development in some recent critical essays is to quote from minimally cleaned up transcriptions of draft, often illustrated by reproductions of notebook pages.[63] Sometimes the draft, with its doodles, jottings and ink-spills, is treated as co-extensive with the printed text. Nancy M. Goslee would recommend a wise multi-perspectivism. Each stage of the draft should be considered as 'in effect an independent work which we are free to interpret and then relate, as one among many versions, to the final text'.[64] Nevertheless, she holds on to the idea of Shelley's final intention, of which his printed text (where it exists) is its manifestation. Such a multi-perspectivism, if it is not to be confined to a small and privileged coterie of specialists, implies ready access to a 'library' of differently presented Shelley's texts. It is not hard to imagine what such a library might comprise: 'definitive' edited print editions; unedited texts – digitized versions of Shelley's early editions, such as are already available on books.google.com and Internet Archive; electronic reproductions of Shelley manuscripts, in high-resolution facsimile. The first are in progress; the last do not yet exist, but there is no technical reason why they might not, given money and willingness of the owners to make them available in this form.[65]

Which leads to the question of the relationship between readership and economics. The Longmans and the Johns Hopkins, aimed at the postgraduate school and the research library, are priced beyond the means of the average private buyer.[66] They are the modern successors to Forman's beautiful and scholarly Library edition of 1876–7, and their readership heirs of the *Notes and Queries* readers. The editors' aim is definitiveness, but all recognize that in editing poems from Shelley's rough draft no reading text can be strictly definitive, and that no two editors are likely to come out with a text that is exactly the same. One can imagine these editions being supplemented by the facsimiles envisaged above (free or by subscription), which, aided by faithful diplomatic transcriptions, might even in some cases become the citation source of choice in scholarly articles. But such transcriptions, particularly of rough drafts, are not pleasurable to read, particularly aloud. The eye is interrupted by different levels and sizes and by the deletions throughout. If it is true that elegant presentation signalled to the working classes that Shelley was out of their league, facsimiles say to the common reader 'Scholars only'. There is no substitute for the reading text.

Yet reading texts of Shelley have never been more available – at the click of a button, on websites purveying inspirational quotes, in selections, such as Bartleby.com, or 'complete' in Project Gutenberg or at the University of Adelaide. Shelley figures in global poetry discussion groups undreamed of by the 1860s contributors to *Notes and Queries*. 'Does anyone know the poem "A DIRGE" by Shelley?' someone asks of the web, and Yahoo answers, 'Though I do not like all Romantic poetry I find in this poem by Shelley a force and greatness I could not disregard'. Such sites almost invariably reproduce the out-of copyright Hutchinson text of 1904. As the canon of minor eighteenth-century authors was perpetuated well into the nineteenth century until the Romantics went out of copyright in the 1850s and 1860s,[67] so copyright laws ensure that an edition published over 100 years ago, famously unreliable and incomplete, will continue to transmit Shelley's poetry, or at least the canon as it was in 1904, to the greatest number of people for the foreseeable future, enabled by 'Casualty', the invention of the internet. If more accurate and complete versions are to prevail, and the gap narrowed between high Shelley textual scholarship and Shelley on meaningfulnicesayings.com, key intermediaries will be affordable Shelley selected editions, transmitting up-to-date texts, but with reduced annotation, carrying on the function at present performed by current editions of Dent's *Percy Bysshe Shelley: Poems and Prose* (1995); Norton's *Shelley's Poetry and Prose* (2002) and Oxford's *Percy Bysshe Shelley: The Major Works* (2003). One might even envisage an e-book incorporating a modern text of Shelley's complete poetry, together with one of Shelley's prose.[68] Which would be something not seen these 150 years: a counterpart for the twenty-first century of Moxon's 1847 one-volume edition of the *Works*, edited by Mrs Shelley.

6 WRITING TEXTUAL MATERIALITY: CHARLES CLARK, HIS BOOKS AND HIS BOOKPLATE POEM

Carrie Griffin & Mary O'Connell

Charles Clark

In 1828 the 22 November edition of the *Mechanics' Magazine* reported on the invention of a new portable printing press. The inventor, Mr Charles Clark of Great Totham in Essex, wrote to describe his machine and the motivation behind its construction. Confessing that after his first 'peep into a printing office' he felt surprise at the relative simplicity of the press, he set about producing a smaller version which would be made of cheaper materials.[1] The illustration Clark sent to accompany his letter shows a machine of about 6 ft in length. The platten, measuring fifteen by ten inches, and the table holding the type, were both made from highly polished stone; the rest of the press was made from elm wood. The editor of the magazine includes a note supporting Clark's assertions that the impressions produced by his machine were 'fully' equal to the Colombian or Stanhope Press. Clark describes the two chief recommendations of his portable press as the ease of use, even for someone unacquainted with printing, and the affordability: thirty shillings in comparison to £25 for a press of similar size. The letter concludes with Clark's hope that his invention would be of interest to people who would take pleasure in 'printing little trifles for their own convenience or amusement'; he cites the example of William Cowper who owned a bellows press and was described by his biographer as a 'printer as well as a writer of poetry'.

Clark himself was a printer as well as a poet, although he enjoyed considerably more success in the former venture. A minor figure in the nineteenth-century book trade, where Clark receives scholarly attention it is as a footnote in literary history. He is remembered for the invention of his press that he operated from Great Totham Hall, mainly producing pamphlets and poetry before acquiring a larger press in 1846. He also wrote satirical verse, often in the local Essex dialect, and more frequently as shameless imitations of Thomas Hood. Hood's volume of comic verse *Whims and Oddities* (1826–7), which displayed the poet's talent for punning word play, was obviously an influence on Clark who was known for his love of perpetrating the 'double entendre occasionally'.[2] Clark was also a self-styled 'bibliographic farmer' and a noted antiquarian who delighted 'in nothing half so much as in collecting'.[3]

The entry on Clark in the *Dictionary of National Biography* describes a man 'possessed of some small literary impulse' who 'occupied his leisure' composing and printing poems which are 'for the most part exceedingly silly and indecent'.[4] In fact, Clark seems to have been possessed of quite a strong literary impulse; he was, as he described it, a 'Bibliomaniac'.[5] In addition to his activities as a printer and satirist, over 300 letters preserved in the Essex Public Records Office testify to the fact that Clark was an avid collector of rare volumes who acted as a supplier to the London bookseller and publisher John Russell Smith. He also had close links with the bookseller P. H. Youngman and corresponded with John Clare.[6]

Born in 1806 to Robert Clark and Mary Ann Pond, Clark was raised in Heybridge, Essex. An only child, he attended the Rev. J. S. Dunn's school in Witham. The family seem to have been quite well off, living in a house built by Clark's grandfather and farming 100 acres. In 1823, they moved to nearby Great Totham, becoming tenants of Great Totham Hall. Aside from his attendance at school in Witham, information about the early period of Clark's life is scant. We do know that he began to write poetry in 1825 and, although he continued to farm, began printing on his private press in 1828. His first production of any significance was a work entitled *A History, Antiquarian and Statistical, of the Parish of Great Totham in the County of Essex* (1831) written by Clark's friend and neighbour George W. Johnson. The book was seventy-two octavo pages and was financed entirely by Clark. Despite some later unenthusiastic assessments of the quality of Clark's typography, contemporary opinion is almost universally positive. Johnson, in his preface, writes that no one 'would believe that the typography of the work was the unassisted labour of a private individual'.[7] While continuing to print pamphlets and broadsides, Clark turned his attention to poetry and produced an imitation of Hood's *Epping Hunt* entitled *Tiptree Races*, which was printed in nearby Maldon by Youngman in 1833.

Clark's next project united his interests in printing and farming as he published Thomas Tusser's *Hundreth Good Points of Husbandrie* (1834). In a prefatory note to this work, Clark surmised that his dual occupation of farming and printing, 'the very same pursuits that form the subject of [the] work', would make the edition 'somewhat of a curiosity'. In the same year Clark collaborated with John Russell Smith for the first time. Smith was a London bookseller and bibliographer who had recently opened his own shop at 4 Old Compton Street in Soho following an apprenticeship at nearby John Bryant's. Smith was particularly interested in topography and local dialects and was known for his promotion of dialect study. Having published a ballad by John White Masters in Kentish dialect, Smith suggested to Clark that he might profitably write a similar colloquial work in the Essex vernacular. The result was Clark's long poem *John Noakes and Mary Styles* (1834). Clark and Smith became friends as well as literary associates, and the pair often frequented the races at Tiptree, at least until Smith's marriage in 1844. The friendship had added benefits for Clark, as Smith often allowed him to borrow books from his shop.[8]

In 1830 Thomas Hood announced an intended sequel to *The Epping Hunt* which would concern Epsom Races. With no sign of publication by 1838, Clark altered his own *Tiptree Races* sufficiently to reissue it as *Epsom Races*; he writes, 'I'll let Hood sing of Epsom – but is seems / That he will not' (ll. 4–5). Clark was a fervent admirer of Hood, and his letters are full of references to *Whims and Oddities* and the *Comic Annual*. It is clear that Clark sees himself as a potential rival to 'the celebrated punster'.[9] In the appendix to *Tiptree Races* he praises Hood's 'Nocturnal Sketch', advertised in 1832 as the only example of 'blank verse in rhyme'.[10] Hood's technique was to rhyme the last three words of each line. Clark ends his appendix with a poem in similar style, except his lines end with four rhymes, intended 'to surpass Mr. Hood's specimen'. Clark also prints an extract from a review in the *Literary Gazette* which reinforces the comparison: 'C.C is the man who has thus challenged his [Hood's] laurels; and if he does not look sharp, "C.C" will carry them off'. Early on in the poem he confesses that it is 'plain' he is '*Robbing Hood!*' although the fact that he signed the poem 'Thomas Hood Esq, The Younger' would seem to make such an admission unnecessary. In 1839 Clark wrote a short satire entitled 'A Doctor's Doings, or The Entrapped Heiress of Witham' seemingly in protest at Dr Henry Dixon's marriage to a young woman, Georgiana, in January 1839. The following lines display the general tenor of the piece, as well as Clark's ability to stretch a simple pun to the limit:

> Though se-*duc*-tion's a most foul offence,
> There's a thought makes our case seem less black;
> Those who *pond*-er it o'er should reflect
> The offender is only a *quack!* (ll. 48–52).

Smith advertised and sold the poem despite the threat of legal action from Dr Dixon. Although the first edition was removed from circulation, Clark printed a second edition, which was again advertised by Smith. Dixon reiterated his threats and Clark was forced to issue a lengthy apology in the *Chelmsford Chronicle*.[11] Of more immediate consequence was the delivery of a solicitor's bill of over £51 to Totham Hall, which was paid by Clark's father. Despite the financial cost to his family, Clark wrote to Smith speculating that they might usefully capitalize on the notoriety surrounding the poem and make money by selling new copies. This episode seems to have cost Clark his father's goodwill towards his printing ventures. Smith was no longer welcome at Totham Hall, and Clark's increasing debts to the bookseller makes it clear that Robert Clark decided to withdraw a certain degree of financial support. Such speculation is reinforced by the fact that the next few years saw Clark attempt various new ways to make money, including notifying the owners of uncollected dividends and hoping for a reward.

While Clark's printing activities were curtailed for a few years, he turned to writing, and composed a bookplate poem in February 1843 entitled 'A Pleader to the Reader not a Heeder' which was eventually published in *Notes and Queries* in 1852 as 'A Pleader to the Needer when a Reader', and which is the subject of this paper. In 1846 he obtained a larger press, enabling him to move from printing pamphlets and short works to books. He exchanged his old press at Sharwood's Foundry for three sizes of black letter type. The first production on the new press was Sir Egerton Brydges's *Human Fate*.[12] 1849 and 1850 saw the respective deaths of Clark's parents. Clark had written to Smith in March 1850 of his intention to leave Totham, and his father's death a few months later hastened his move back to Heybridge. The tenancy of Great Totham Hall was taken over by John Pond and Clark announced his intention of establishing himself as a printer in Heybridge. Clark's last surviving letter was to John Russell Smith and is dated 1853. Although he was mentioned in *Notes and Queries* as 'well known and esteemed as a zealous antiquary', and his bookplate poem was often praised in the publication, Clark sank into obscurity and died on 21 March 1880 and was buried on 27 March in Heybridge. He left no will and his grave is unmarked.[13] He was mentioned in Henry Plomer's history of nineteenth-century private presses as having received more notice than he deserved and his works were described as poorly printed 'scraps of doggerel' that would only be 'creditable to an amateur'.[14]

His Books

Charles Clark's antiquarian interests centred not just on printing; as already mentioned he appears to have been a voracious collector of arcane and unique items, cuttings and ephemera. Books – rare and scarce volumes in particular – were his preference, and at the time of his death, his personal library is thought to have been substantial. Brignull notes that, following his death in March, 'his estate, including his press, type, and 2500 books was sold by auction over two days at the end of June'.[15] Clark's estate, fittingly, consisted mostly of the tools of his trade – books, type and press – all three elements of his work imaginatively linked after his death as they certainly were during his lifetime. However, they most likely found new owners, and were certainly fragmented, at his death, and his carefully-amassed book collection – effectively the material for his printing activities – ceased to be a library once the auction began. There is evidence to suggest, however, that the fragmentation of Clark's collection had begun during his lifetime. Clark was, as we have seen, a prodigious borrower and lender of books, but his permanent collection – large by any standards, and especially those of a Victorian gentleman farmer – required that Clark was also a regular purchaser. Since there is evidence of his literary dealings with Youngman, the bookseller and printer at Maldon, it is reasonable to assume that he was a customer of the shop both as a young man and after he moved with his family to Great Totham in 1823 and began to write in 1825. Maldon is the closest large town to Heybridge, which is unlikely to have had a bookseller (although Heybridge flourished as a busy port town served by a canal in the early part of the century, until the arrival of the railway). After the move to Great Totham (which is further north than Heybridge) in 1823 it is likely that Youngman's shop in Maldon was too distant for the young Clark to visit regularly. He evidently, however, still maintained contact with Youngman, using his address as a delivery-point, as evidenced in his letter to Thomas Frognall Dibdin (10 June 1837) in which he asks Dibdin to dispatch a manuscript by 'either of the Maldon coaches, which start from the Bull, Aldgate, and the Green-Dragon, Gracechurch Street, addressed to me, to the care of Mr. P. H. Youngman'.[16] But his new and profitable relationship with John Russell Smith, the London bookseller, meant that Clark had an important central contact not just for the sale of his own productions, but also for the acquisition of new books and items for his own library.

Clark and Smith were active and regular correspondents, as evidenced by the large collection of surviving epistles that passed between them, now preserved at the Essex Public Records Office, Chelmsford.[17] As noted above, Smith and Clark cooperated in literary and economic enterprises, but it is clear that Clark was a customer of Smith's too. Smith, with ready access to the varied and interesting London book-market, must have supplied Clark with items that were not always available locally. Indeed Clark was in debt to Smith, certainly by 1841, for various books,[18] yet his last dated item of correspondence held at Essex Public Records Office is a book order to Smith, dated 1853. Clark seems to have been financially unstable around the time of the death of his father in 1850; he wrote to Smith that same year announcing that he would move back to Heybridge (where he presumably paid no rent), apparently with a view to earning a living by printing alone. His brush with libel, resulting in a bill of '£51 and some odd shillings'[19] owed to Dr Dixon's solicitor, his bizarre money-making schemes (one, as mentioned above, involved the notification of owners of uncollected dividends, in hope of reward; another attempted to import *The Book of Mormon*, then unavailable in England),[20] and the death of his father, presumably the financier of his printing activities, meant that Clark most likely had to find alternative ways of earning. He had swapped his portable press for a common wooden press and some black-letter type, but issued booklets and broadsides only from Heybridge after 1851.

Clark apparently – most probably owing to his lack of commercial success, and his debts – began to sell off parts of his book collection in the decades after his father's death in 1850. Despite being in debt, Clark also continued to purchase books, and it is reasonable to assume that he culled parts of his library in order to finance the acquisition of new volumes. One of the books in his collection was the manuscript that is now Egerton 2433, held at the British Library, London, a volume that was bound between boards sometime in the nineteenth century. We know that it belonged to Clark because he pasted his printed bookplate poem, this one dated by hand to 1859, on the inside cover (see Figure 6.1). This is only one volume in a library that must have varied between 2,500–3,000 volumes throughout Clark's collecting life, but it is a signifier of Clark's collecting activities, his zeal for antiquarian materials, and more broadly, Victorian interest in retrospection.

The history of Egerton 2433 is complicated when we come to examine its provenance post-1500. There is a vacuum into which the book disappears for 300 years, remerging, as if from a time machine, in the 1900s and in the hands of Clark. One of the manuscript's flyleaves bears the coat of arms of the Egerton family. In 1829 Francis Henry Egerton, eighth Earl of Bridgewater, bequeathed to the British Museum sixty-seven manuscripts and £12,000, monies which became known as the Bridgewater Fund. This sum was augmented in 1838 by £3,000 by Egerton's cousin Charles Long, Baron Farnborough; both bequests were to be used by the Museum to contribute to and enlarge the Egerton series of manuscripts. On another of the volume's flyleaves is inscribed the note: 'Purchased of J. Harvey, 1878'; the note was written by a cataloguer at the British Museum, and the manuscript was purchased using funds donated by Long and Egerton;[21] it seems likely, then, that the manuscript belonged to J. Harvey after it belonged to Clark. The most likely scenario is that Clark sold the manuscript at some point between its acquisition in 1859 and the 1870s, probably as part of his programme to raise funds by offloading part of his personal book collection.

A PLEADER TO THE NEEDER WHEN A READER.

AS all, my friend, through wily knaves, full often suffer wrongs,
Forget not, pray, when it you've read, to whom this book belongs.
Than one Charles Clark, of Totham Hall, none to't a right hath better,
A *wight*, that same, more *read* than some in the lore of old *black*-letter.
And as C. C. in *Essex* dwells,—a shire at which all laugh—
His books must, sure, less fit seem drest, if they're not bound in *calf*!
Care take, my friend, this *book* you ne'er with grease or dirt besmear it;
And o'er my books when book-*worms* *puppies* will continue to "*dog's-ear*" it!
While none but awkward *puppies* will continue to "*dog's-ear*" it!
No marks the margins must de-*face* from any busy "*hand*?"
Marks, as re-marks, in books of Clark's, when e're some critic spy leaves,
It always him so *wasp*-ish makes, though they're but on the *fly*-leaves!
Yes, if so they're used, he'd not de-*fer* to *deal* a fate most meet—
He'd have the soiler of his *quires* do penance in a *sheet*!
The Ettrick *Hogg*—ne'er deemed a *bore*—his candid mind revealing,
Declares, to beg "a *copy*" now's a mere pre-*text* for stealing!
So, as some knave to grant the loan of this my book may wish me,
I thus my book-*plate* here dis-play, lest some such "*fry*" should *dish* me!
—But hold,—though I again declare WITH-holding I'll not *brook*,
And "a *sea* of trouble" still shall take to bring book-worms "to book!"

Figure 6.1: Clark's Bookplate © The British Library Board, British Library, MS Egerton 2433.

His Bookplate Poem

The only evidence of Clark's engagement with the Egerton 2433 MS is his pasting of his bookplate poem onto the inside cover-board. This is significant in itself, and we return to this material act of appropriation and ownership below. For now, it is clear from Clark's impulse to collect, repackage and retransmit 'trifles' from the medieval and Renaissance periods led to his accumulation of 'literary rarities', items like, for example, Thomas Tusser's will.[22] Clark himself, in the same letter to Dibdin, acknowledges both his interest in the acquisition of older materials and texts and the evident expense of his interests, describing himself as 'one who delights in nothing half so much as in collecting, as far as his humble means warrant, some musty specimens of the venerable black-letter lore of the olden times'. That the manuscript lacks the visual appeal that, say, the high-grade codices of the Middle Ages have for Clark's contemporaries is therefore unsurprising. It does not materially evoke the highly-wrought, artistic book-production of the Middle Ages in its decoration, *mise-en-page*, historiated initials, fronds, miniatures and formal book-hand; on the contrary, the manuscript that Clark was so keen to have back unblemished from lenders is a poor exemplum and both visual appeal and space are clearly sacrificed for text. Indeed Egerton 2433 is almost certainly the product of an unpractised hand, the later-medieval book scribe-owner who compiled a collection of medical and folkloric texts. The manuscript, as we might expect, is written in one hand throughout, and is a small quarto paper volume, which has been heavily trimmed, at the expense, in places, of text, to ensure that it fits the neat nineteenth-century binding. It has fifty-four folios, measures 190 x 157 mm, and is dated to the late fifteenth century. The texts are copied in a large and undisciplined hand, which has an untidy appearance; there is some rubrication, and some spaces have been allowed for decorated initials. The contents – all of which circulated widely and, thus, were readily available for copying – are perhaps typical of the personally compiled handbooks owned by medical professionals in the later Middle Ages: a Galenic surgical treatise, some bloodletting tracts, medical receipts and charms, and two Middle English astrological/astronomical treatises (The *Wise Book of Philosophy and Astronomy* and *The Book of Destinary*).[23]

Clark's bookplate poem aside, the manuscript displays some signs of provenance and investment. In the first instance, the physical evidence bears witness to the decision of the scribe to impose his own authority on the texts he copies, figuring himself as author by inscribing his name – habitually at section breaks or at quire ends – in the manuscript. At fol. 15r, for example, he writes 'quod Brunfylld' at the end of the page, and again at fol. 18r; this is varied to 'par' Brunfylld at various points throughout the manuscript. Whoever Brunfylld was, he was certainly keen to ensure that other readers would be in no doubt as to the identity of the puported author of the text and the compiler of the book; of course that Brunfylld *is* the author is an impossibility, since the codex is a compilation of texts that have been in circulation since at least the early fourteenth century. By inscribing his name in the book, Brunfylld ensures his place in the history of that book, forcing editors of texts to acknowledge his role in the chain of textual transmission and taking his place, alongside Clark and J. Harvey, in the list of owners.

Clark firmly ensured, however, with his composition, production and dissemination of his bookplate poem, that his name would be the one that remains materially linked to the volume now preserved in the British Library. At the time of writing three versions of Clark's bookplate poem have been discovered. The first is an early draft manuscript version, in fair copy and in Clark's own hand, preserved in Essex Public Records Office; we designate this 'E'.[24] This, an early draft of the bookplate poem, runs to twenty-two lines, and is entitled 'A Pleader to the Reader not a Heeder!' We reproduce it in full here; transcription is ours:

A Pleader to the Reader not a Heeder! [E-Version]
[10 February 1843]

As all, my friend, through wily knaves full often suffer wrongs,
Forget not, pray, when it you've read, to whom this Book belongs.
Than one Charles Clark, of Totham, none to it a right hath better, –
A wight, that same, more read than some in the lore of old black-letter!
And as C.C. in Essex dwells – a shire at which all laugh –
This Book must, sure, less fit seem drest if 'tis not bound in calf!
Though of this sightly volcano's worth the owner would not "croak,"
Where's he who can with truth assert it seems but one of smoke!
Oh! if so 'twere deem'd, I'd not de-fer to deal a fate most meet,
I'd have the carper of these quires do penance in a sheet!
This Book, too, friend, take care you ne'er with grease or dirt besmear it;
While only awkward puppies will continue to "dogs-ear" it!
And o'er my books when book-worms "grub," I'd have them understand,
No marks the margins must de-face from any busy "hand!"
Marks, as re-marks, in books of Clark's, where'er some critics spý-leaves,
It always me so wasp-ish makes, though they're but on the fly-leaves!
– The Ettrick Hogg – ne'er deemed a bore, – his candid mind revealing,
Declares to beg a "copy" now's but a pre-text for stealing;
So as some day some knave to grant the loan of this may wish me,
I thus my book-plate here display lest some such "fry" should "dish" me!
But hold – though I must just delcare with-holding I'll ne'er brook
And "a sea of troubles" still shall take to bring bookworms to "book"!!

E was most likely part of one of Clark's regular correspondences with John Russell Smith (he habitually sent him manuscript versions of poems of his own composition), and is signed 'C.C.' and dated in an authorial hand. A later version of the poem is recorded in an 1852 volume of *Notes & Queries*, most likely submitted by Clark under one of his many aliases, 'Bookworm'.[25] This version is designated 'N', and was obviously revised by Clark with a view to publication; this version is twenty lines, omitting some of the more awkward syntax. The authors have taken this version from *Notes & Queries*:

A Pleader to the Needer when a Reader [N-Version] [10 July 1852]

As all, my friend, through wily knaves, full often suffer wrongs,
Forget not, pray, when it you've read, to whom this book belongs.
Than one CHARLES CLARK of TOTHAM HALL, none to't a right hath better,
A *wight*, that same, more *read* than some in the lore of old *black*-letter!
And as C.C. in *Essex* dwells – a shire at which all laugh -
His books must, sure, less fit seem drest, if they're not bound in *calf*!
Care take, my friend, this book you ne'er with grease or dirt besmear it;
While none but awkward *puppies* will continue to 'dog's-ear' it!
And o'er my books when book-*worms* 'grub', I'd have them understand,
No marks the margins must de-*face* from any busy 'hand!'
Marks, as re-marks, in books of CLARK's, whene'er some critic spý leaves,
It always him so *wasp*-ish makes, though they're but on the *fly*-leaves!
Yes, if so they're used, he'd not de-*fer* to *deal* a fate most meet-
He'd have the soiler of his *quires* do penance in a *sheet!*
The Ettrick *Hogg* – ne'er deemed a *bore* – his candid mind revealing,
Declares, to beg a 'copy' now's a mere pre-*text* for stealing!
So as some knave to grant the loan of this my Book may wish me,
I thus my book-*plate* here display, lest some such 'fry' should 'dish' me! –
But hold – though I again declare WITH-holding I'll not *brook*,
And 'a sea of trouble' still shall take to bring book-worms 'to book!'

The third version is pasted, as mentioned above, into at least one of Clark's numerous manuscripts – Egerton 2433 [B]; this does not vary from the N-version and it is reproduced from the MS in Figure 6.1. The poem found in Egerton 2433 is dated by hand to 1859, and we take this date to relate, as explained, to the acquisition of the book. Clark apparently returned to his 'whimsical' poem as his book collection increased in the late 1840s, and because he revised it for publication – and for the printing of his own bookplate – we take the N and B versions as the base texts for the discussion here.

That Clark reserved use of the bookplate poems for rare volumes in his collection only is both implicit in his verse and explicit in the note that he submits to *Notes & Queries*. Clark records that the verse is '[A]ttached as a book-plate to each of the volumes and MSS forming a *portion* of the extensive and curious library at Great Totham Hall' (emphasis ours). His habit, then, seems to be to attach the plate to what he sees as rare books only, significant in view of

Clark's penchant for the accumulation of 'literary rarities'.[26] This impulse is echoed in the poem itself, which is apparently composed with the express purpose of indicating ownership, in the first instance, of the rarer, more arcane volumes in Clark's collection and, also, to draw attention not just to his collecting habits, but his preferred collectibles. Moreover, Clark is careful to identify himself not just as a collector but as an avid reader of the antique materials he acquires, describing himself as a '*wight*, that same, more *read* than some, in the lore of old *black*-letter!' (l. 4). We must assume too that Clark, who was certainly an unashamed borrower (from, as we have seen, Dibdin, Youngman, and Smith), was also a *lender*, and was particularly keen to ensure that borrowers do not forget who owns the book (l. 2). Thus our bookplate poem author sees himself as a full participant in the literary landscape of early Victorian Britain, and he succinctly demonstrates his various literary activities in the short verse that he, very deliberately, pastes into the most valuable, most unique – and surely the most desirable – items in his library. He intends it to be accessible to the most discerning readers: borrowers of his antiquarian volumes, and subscribers to *Notes & Queries*.

The poem, thus, can be read as a humorous yet carefully composed personal statement on the way in which Clark wishes to be viewed by his peers. Inscribed, arguably, is a certain awareness on the part of the author himself that he is a figure on the purlieu of the literary mainstream of the 1840s and 1850s. This can be read as a certain defensiveness: Clark has a 'right' (l. 3), as a gentleman farmer and amateur scholar, to be a philanthropic bibliophile; he is aware that, living in Essex ('a shire at which all laugh'; l. 5) some distance from London and quite a way from Edinburgh, that he might be considered regional, and therefore, less worthy or serious, than some of his correspondents and associates. Although the centres of literary culture were London and Edinburgh, he attempts to address this perceived imbalance both textually and materially: his reference to his calf-bound books (l. 6) must surely have had more impact when physically attached to one such volume; and readers of *Notes & Queries* are invited to imagine a handsome library at Totham Hall consisting of valuable, rare volumes bound in the best leather of the day, as impressive as the collections which must have so often been admired and extolled in that publication. The knaves (l. 17) of whom he is so suspicious are surely, too, asked to consider Clark a serious book-collector who takes pride in what he wishes to be seen as a valuable and desirable library.

The highly visual and provocative rendering of his book collection in the poem is just one aspect of what emerges as a salient concern of Clark's: the material condition of his books and that materiality as a signifier of his status and interests. It can be read as a succinct, witty and effective statement of Clark's general concerns, evidently with the material condition of books and texts, and with related issues such as printing and recovery, copyright law, borrowing and exchange, the demarcation of books, and with very current debates on cultures of medievalism and older, antiquarian volumes.

The antiquarianism and arcane interests of Clark are undoubtedly manifest in the poem in various ways, not least in the form and style of 'A Pleader to the Needer when a Reader'. The bookplate verse (N and B versions) consists of twenty lines varying between fourteen and fifteen syllables in rising duple (iambic) metre. Having some lines as 'fourteeners' is strongly reminiscent of ballad metre and the words such as 'knaves' and 'wight' used throughout clearly suggest Clark's wish to associate his bookplate poem with the manuscripts on which he pasted it. However, the overwhelming sense of the purpose of the poem arises from a consideration of its textual appeal married to its visual impact: attaching a bookplate to a book is a material act of appropriation, and Clark reinforces the idea of appropriation in his poem by repeated stress on his opening warning: 'Forget not, pray, when it you've read, to whom this book belongs' (l. 2). He ensures that the reader or borrower does not forget: his name occurs three times in the poem alongside expressions of possession such as 'my books' (l. 9); 'books of Clark's' (l. 11); and 'my book-*plate*' (l. 18). Moreover, the texts contained in the books are also owned by Clark, and he expresses a concern to guard against the dishonest borrowing of his volumes for illicit copying (l. 16). Although the singular, overarching purpose of the poem appears to be a statement of ownership and a warning to potential readers to take care of his books, Clark, however, also uses his bookplate to advertise himself as a producer, consumer, and lender of books. By publicizing his bookplate poem he publicizes himself as a collector of note; he ensures too that the bookplate poem is circulated more widely than it might do pasted into a rare book by offering it to *Notes & Queries*. Clark conflates his various identities – poet, printer and book collector – in one clever material statement.

Nonetheless, Clark was a self-confessed amateur who, based on the evidence of his surviving correspondence, struggled to maintain his passion for books and printing. Despite obvious desires to impact on the national literary scene, much of his printing and collecting has a distinctly regional flavour (impulses shared with his correspondent and friend, John Russell Smith), and he inscribes his sense of locality and place in his verse, mentioning 'Totham Hall' (l. 3), the location of his press and his home for some thirty years, and figuring himself as a local champion of taste and culture, clearly working against a central literary nexus that would 'laugh' at him and his kind. This sense of the marginal, however, is nowhere more keenly felt than in the sense of importance in the material text. Clark demonstrates not only his position as a discerning collector of manuscripts and scarce books but as someone who worked to ensure the integrity of those books. He issues a conventional warning against physically damaging his books with 'grease or dirt' (l. 7); and he is particularly keen to ensure that no prospective reader writes on them: 'No marks the margins must de-*face* from any busy *"hand!"* / Marks, as re-marks, in books of Clark's, when e're some critic spy leaves' (ll. 10–11). Clark, dependent as a regional, liminal figure on the cusp of a thriving, vibrant and somewhat exclusive book-business on the goodwill of borrowers to return his books, is also reliant on their respect for the physical object. But the irony of this statement, expressed in a bookplate poem printed by the author is clearly lost on Clark; he 're-marks' (l. 11) volumes as his own, using the '*fly*-leaves' (l. 12) to insist upon ownership in a bold and authoritative manner, thereby affecting the material book almost indelibly.

Yet it is surely Clark's related activities as a printer that make him acutely aware of the materiality of the text. His book-collecting informs his choice of material for printing and, in turn, dictates the appearance and style of what he prints. Clark's obvious preferment was to replicate the look of documents and books printed by the early printers (who sought to imitate the manuscript book); his reference to '*black*-letter' (l. 4), thus, is not merely a device to allow the reader to imagine Clark's choice of reading material, but directly corresponds to his *modus* in his chosen hobby; as he writes to Thomas Frognall Dibdin about his printing of some work that he sends him:

> [P]robably you will deem my humble Reprints, &c., somewhat the more interesting, when you are informed, that their typography, such as it is, is the production of a person who never put a single letter into a composing-stick in any regular printing-office in his life! – they were produced by quite an amateur in the 'Divine Art' of the immortal William Caxton. They are the work, too ... of one who delights in nothing half so much as in collecting, as far as his humble means warrant, some musty specimens of the venerable black-letter lore of the 'olden times'.[27]

For Clark, the printing of the work, and therefore the labour, skill and art that contribute to the appearance of the text, would outweigh the subject matter and, arguably, the literary qualities, of his outputs. Collecting, and the material, visual manifestation of that antiquarianism, is the primary concern here expressed, but allied to that is printing: the material, physical rendering of a text. The linking of the two reveals a complex, theoretical perspective that pervaded Clark's literary activities: that the physical text is important, and can signify, and that in itself is articulated, as if to strengthen its impact, in his own book-related compositions – in his writing textual materiality – and his rendering of these concerns in the real, material form of a bookplate. Clark, like many of his Victorian contemporaries, undoubtedly realized the significance of the form of a text. Not only are his letters sprinkled with the ontology of materiality but he took care to advertise his concerns with the same in his self-penned poem. The poem, when encountered in its natural context – on the inside cover of one of Clark's collectables – has an immediate effect on the reader; however that effect is at first material.

Designed as a visual alert to the reader, and as a signifier regarding the value of a particular volume, the poem itself reinforces Clark's insistence on the material quality, state and appearance of his precious books. Thus Clark's complexity as a collector and a publicist is revealed, as is his own unique participation in the whirlwind of Victorian book culture.

At first glance, Clark appears an obscure, eccentric, amateur printer from Totham. His pseudonym 'Bookworm' probably best describes him; a man obsessed with punning, printing and purchasing books. Beyond the scope of this paper, and the subject of a forthcoming study, one of the most fascinating aspects of Clark's career is his relationship with John Russell Smith, and their exchange of books. Friends and regular frequenters of the races, Clark and Smith also seem to have operated a formal trade of rare books. Clark's letters to Smith are typically concluded with lengthy book orders, sometimes for as many as sixty volumes. Clark also acted as a supplier for Smith, a bookseller who specialized in antiquarian texts. As noted above, a study of this singular figure sheds light on the manner in which London booksellers operated with regional centres of trade, and more particularly how a self-confessed 'amateur' printer, living in 'a shire in which all laugh' contrived to amass a library of 2,500 volumes and print over 100 broadsides and thirty-eight pamphlets from his portable press at Totham.

7 CHARLES DICKENS'S READERS AND THE MATERIAL CIRCULATION OF THE TEXT

Robert McParland

Reading the fiction of Charles Dickens has helped some travellers far from home to pass the time and to stay connected with the human community. Among these readers of Dickens, one could hardly be farther away from civilization than Isaac Israel Hayes, a sailor at sea in the Arctic. For Hayes, a volume of Dickens was among his most precious possessions:

> Upon leaving the brig I had selected from the narrow shelf which held the little library that I learned to love so well during the last long winter, three small books, which I thrust into my already crowded clothes bag. They were the before mentioned volume of Dickens, the 'In Memoriam', and a small pocket Bible; all parting gifts from kind friends to me when leaving home; and all doubly precious, for themselves, and for the memories which they recalled.[1]

These books, embodying memories of loved ones at home, were soaked and torn and their backs were loose. Yet, they served both a practical and an emotional purpose, and so he held onto them as one would hold to a tether something precious and secure: 'I kept them under my head as helps for a pillow and for their companionship'.[2] For Americans like Hayes, Dickens's fiction, whilst mostly set in Britain, provided a memory of home and a resource for self-construction. His writing entertained them and served as a model for their own self-expression in letters and diaries.[3] In Hayes's account we see the book was regarded both as an object and as a companion; perhaps a talisman of sorts. When a Dickens story was read aloud on a ship, in camp, or at home, it was a common amusement, a space where the wide world came in and sentiment and theatricality was shared. His popular texts were sites of connection.

While Charles Dickens's critical reception has been frequently assessed, his popular audience, the one that most counted in market and social terms, has not. An attempt may begin to reclaim the forgotten voices of this significant public: the diverse audience of one of the most popular novelists of the nineteenth century. This essay asserts that the wide consumption and reproduction of Dickens's work by American audiences contributed to shaping the development of American literature and culture by launching imitations, circulating socially shared themes and caricatures, promoting business, and fostering shared sentiment. In the process of recovering the response of Dickens's audience, it is important for us to account for the transpositions of the material text. Dickens was abundantly printed, in many formats.[4] The process of making books through the appropriation of Dickens's serialized texts had an important impact upon readers' reception of his works. The material form in which Dickens's stories appeared and the movement of each Dickens story through various cultural frames had an impact upon how it was read. Dickens's novels were reprinted in differently priced editions to meet the needs of different audiences. In the passage from publisher to printer through shipper to bookseller and on to the reader, signs, symbols and discourses underwent transformations as they passed from Dickens's pen through the communications circuit. Publishers had to consider printing and production costs, physical transportation, including geographical distance, and the need for middlemen such as agents and booksellers, in their efforts to match supply with demand. This affected the appearance, availability and pricing of print products and how they were received. The serialization of Dickens's stories contributed to the distribution of his novels.[5] Meanwhile, commercial competition over Dickens's works intertwined with the development of American culture. From his first appearance in America with *The Pickwick Papers*, Dickens was both a popular celebrity and a hotly contested commercial property. Reprinting Dickens for profit, publishers engaged in a reprint culture that Meredith McGill has suggested 'offered a model of national identity'.[6] The appearance of Dickens's fiction, or other authors' serialized stories, essays, and news in American newspapers and periodicals, created what McGill calls 'a sense of near-simultaneity that was crucial to the imagination of the federal form of the nation'.[7]

The wide circulation of Charles Dickens's novels performed the role of creating unified fields of exchange and information. They contributed to written and spoken language and empowered people through the expression of sentiment in both their autobiographical and letter writing, in their oral reading, or personal theatricality. In serial publications, in cheap and expensive editions, in theatre productions and adaptations, the writings of Charles Dickens entered the unique situations of American readers. While each reader approached Dickens's fiction in his or her own way, the shared experiences of reading or hearing references to Dickens's characters acted as a reference point for them all. Dickens's novels created a field of discourse, a common ground for communication. They were a source of shared symbols, images and phrases, and a meeting ground for social sentiment.[8] Charles Dickens's immense popularity in America springs, in part, from his ability to communicate effectively with his readers by suggesting a direct personal contact while writing for a mass audience. Their responses suggest that during Dickens's time it was possible for Dickens to forge bonds of connection with his audience. Dickens's ability to do this may be attributed, partly, to his storytelling gifts. His lively caricatures, winding plots and resolutions, and his narrative voices offered an abundant panoramic world and suggested the immediate face-to-face encounters he later actualized in his public readings.

Dickens's readers had regular contact with the author and his works. Texts intersected with their lives, arriving in instalments, unfolding alongside their own personal life stories and activities. As Dickens's characters became familiar to his readers, they came to think of these characters as living people and wrote letters to the author expressing their concerns about what future instalments might bring. As Martyn Lyons notes,

> A new relationship was created between the writer and his or her public. American readers, it was reported, crowded the docksides to greet the ship bringing the next installment of Dickens's *The Old Curiosity Shop*, so eager were they to learn the fate of the heroine, Little Nell.[9]

This popular response to the serialization of his fiction answered for Dickens what Reinhard Wittmann has called the need for an author to connect with a reading public. This need led to 'intensive contact' with these readers, 'leading to a spiritual community created by the book'.[10]

The reading of Dickens's novels, in serial publication, was a social ritual practised in many homes and discussed in public arenas. His stories promoted a bond of connection with his readers, as Kathleen Tillotson and John Butt point out, and, as Hughes and Lund note, the serial promoted a vital 'intimacy between reader and story'.[11] Arriving in a particular material and visual context, the serial created a sense of shared experience and generated a collective anticipation of a story's outcome. Dickens's novels unfolded in this climate, month by month, encouraging an active imaginative relationship between reader, text, and writer. For example, when the ladies of the Wednesday Club of Syracuse, New York met to discuss Dickens, Mrs H. R. Hare noted: 'Charles Dickens, whose tales are household words in every home where the English tongue is heard, was a novelist of the highest rank and the greatest humorist of this century'.[12] While this mention of Dickens's stories as 'household words' plays upon the title of Dickens's own publication, it also appears to be quite consistent with the interests of these common readers who listened to Mrs Hare's lecture. For the group's secretary adds: 'Dickens domestic life was discussed by Mrs. Curtis and several members of the club'. The domestic concern of these women is emphasized by the presence among them of a Household and Economic Club, members of which wrote a 'Help Booklet'.[13]

Dickens's readers who gathered in groups like this shared common texts, stories they read together, often as these stories unfolded in serial instalments in the pages of a periodical. These readers were involved in what Hughes and Lund have referred to as 'creating a home' and 'living in history'.[14] For Americans at this time not only faced the question of what it meant to be an American, they also were facing changes in their experience of community, time and work. Between 1820 and 1860, America's population increased, with residence in cities growing 226 per cent.[15] In both the United States of America and Great Britain, it became more necessary to 'create a home' and to forge community. One way in which the affective bonds of home could be realized was through expressive communal reading and spirited discussion. Dickens, as a source of sentiment that could be shared, provided a vision of connection amid fragmentation, a way to 'live in history' and to imagine one's place within the vast social framework of modern life.

Charles Dickens's writings influenced how people saw the world and sometimes how they expressed themselves in it. As part of the thought and conversation of Americans of all classes, regions, races and sexes, Dickens provided them with a common language, a cast of characters, clichés and images that entered the public mind. At a time when Americans were setting forth a set of values and a vision of life amid their domestic and commercial activities, Dickens's widely read stories and characters provided them with ways of coding strangers, ways to cast their fleeting impressions of people, their appearances and mannerisms. Dickens's cast of British characters enabled Americans to consider their own difference from these British models. He gave his American readers ways of seeing the world and themselves, and models for how they might tell their own life stories.

One American reader of Dickens, Frances E. Willard, an educator and temperance crusader, wrote in 1860:

> Dickens writes strange, startling histories, and your pulse beats faster as you follow the fearful destinies that he reveals; but I suppose you never thought that our own Bridget, in the kitchen, and John, at the stable, have histories scarcely less full of right and wrong forever warring, of passion, and of pain. And we ourselves, if but our strange life out of sight were known, are hardly what the world calls prosaic.[16]

The visceral impact of Dickens's fiction, those moments when the 'pulse beats faster', is recognized here. Willard's response suggests that common readers – Bridget and John – have discovered their secret lives and passions in Dickens's characters. They too have dramatic histories. In Willard's view, some of Dickens's common readers are much like David Copperfield. They realize that they are the heroes of the stories of their own lives – and Dickens has affected them profoundly. Such lives have destinies; they are filled with ethical and emotional conflicts and crises. Willard's perspective encompasses the common reader of Dickens and suggests that readers may see their lives in his fiction.

Dickens appealed to America's common readers, as autobiographies, journals and letters amply demonstrate. Even so, we are faced with questions about how readers like Mrs Willard understood Dickens's novels. Were American readers different from British readers of Dickens? What were the effects of empathy upon the reading process of a common reader, or upon this particular reader's memory and self-concept? How did Dickens name for Mrs Willard that 'strange life out of sight' that she believes is vibrantly at work in the lives of common folks like Bridget and John?

We may meet the interesting 'unknown public' of Charles Dickens's audience in out of the way places: in autobiographies, personal correspondence, publishers' archives, marginalia in first editions of Dickens novels, extant records of nineteenth-century reading circles, library circulation records, or newspaper accounts of audience response at Dickens's public readings. The data is often sketchy – the briefest mention by a reader of having read or heard a Dickens story, often with little further elaboration. But even these brief jottings by Dickens readers begin to tell a story. For example, we may meet readers of Dickens in interviews with common readers. When Richard E. Broome, a farmer in South Carolina who became a lawyer and state assemblyman, was interviewed by the Federal Writer's Project in the early 1930s, he recalled his late nineteenth-century childhood: 'One day mother came by as I was intensely reading a copy of *The Tale of Two Cities* by Charles Dickens. She smiled and said she was happy because I loved to read books.'[17] The intensity of Broome's reading reflects his deep engagement with Dickens's story. He recalls the supportive recognition of his reading by his mother. His interest in Dickens's novel and the praise of his mother merge to create a memory that remains vivid for him many years later. As Jonathan Rose has asked, 'how do texts change the minds and lives of common readers?'[18] Is not Broome's comment about his experience the beginning of an answer to this provocative question?

Dickens is mentioned by the forgotten, like Austin Ward, a Mormon, who could find Dickens's novels in a Mormon library in Utah in 1857: '[T]here was little poetry, and less light literature, though a few standard novels were there, among which I particularly noticed the works of Dickens and Marryat.'[19] Ward's testimony affirms that, by 1857, Dickens's novels had made their way west, across the American countryside. It also reminds us that Dickens's work was read by common readers: ones who were not professional authors, editors, or critics. While there was not much poetry or fiction for Austin Ward to read in the Utah library, there were novels by Marryat and novels by Dickens. The distribution of these novels, inland and far west of the Mississippi River, is significant. Dickens's novels had been brought by water routes as far west as California and they had also been brought by the Mormon community to Salt Lake City. His novels were available for Mormon readers, even though poetry and 'light' reading were virtually absent from the Mormon library. It seems likely that Dickens's stories were important to travellers and settlers because these stories often start from the experience of displacement and lead to the discovery by characters of their home, or their bonds with others. For example, Oliver Twist is orphaned, tossed into a workhouse, and journeys through Fagin's den and the London streets toward the recovery of his inheritance. Little Nell is cast out upon the road and her journey results in her sad passing. Perhaps, some critics say, this theme of displacement arises because Dickens himself felt displaced when he was sent to work at a blacking factory as a child. However, displacement was also the collective experience of many people in the early to mid-nineteenth century. In the nineteenth century, thousands crossed the Atlantic to America, where the growth of the city drew people interested in new economic opportunities from their homes in the countryside. Dickens's readers could regain some sense of home and imaginative connection through their shared experiences of reading his stories.

Readers often repeated the memorable line from *Oliver Twist*, 'Please sir, I want some more'.[20] It is by no means certain that everyone who used Oliver Twist's 'Please sir, I want some more' and Mr Micawber's assertion that 'something will turn up' had read Dickens's works.[21] However, these phrases became familiar slogans among Americans. From Union Army Headquarters, Ulysses S. Grant, thinking of politics, refers to Mr Micawber in a letter of 16 August 1864 to E. B. Washburne:

> I have no doubt but the enemy are exceedingly anxious to hold out until after the presidential election. They have many hopes from its effects. They hope a counter-revolution: they hope to elect a peace candidate; in fact, like Micawber, they hope for something to turn up.[22]

Mr Micawber's phrase was used to describe the growth and hopes of American towns and cities. Mr Josiah Gardner Abbott (1814–91) of Boston, in the Massachusetts State convention debates of 4 May 1853, uses the phrase, claiming that his opponents do not have good reasons for their report. 'What is the reason they give? It is the old argument that was ever potent with Wilkens Micawber – waiting for something to turn up'.[23] The next year, Harriet Beecher Stowe uses the phrase '[Y]et still I find myself easy to be entreated, in hopes, as Mr Micawber says, that something may 'turn up,' though I fear the difficulty is radical in the subject'.[24] By the time of the Civil War, Mr Micawber's phrase was particularly pervasive and perhaps resonant for a society hoping that something would soon turn up. For America, Dickens's phrase echoed a kind of cultural expectancy, a sense of the promise of the vast continent. Panhandlers and miners of the West hoped that the something that would turn up would be gold. James Fowler

Rusling, a New Jersey lawyer and brigadier general, in 1877, writes: 'Individual miners and the lighter companies seemed mostly to have suspended or like Mr Micawber to be waiting for something to turn up'.[25] Orestes Brownson, the transcendentalist philosopher, used Dickens's phrase in support of a more ethereal view: 'But under them all I saw the same spirit, the spirit of the age ... Something, as Micawber was to say, "might turn up" and out of the seeming darkness, light might at length shine'.[26]

Oliver is the subject of many peculiarly negative associations for people who know the popular phrase, or who had an idiosyncratic reading of the story. For example, we might consider what acquaintance the following people had with Dickens's novel: in Catherine Ann (Ware) Warfield's fiction we hear: '"Yet all alike", I repeated. In vain alike, I mean flatter their vanity ever so little and they are at your very feet asking "for more" like Oliver Twist; more bread for amour propre, the insatiable!'[27]

Oliver appears to have gained a bad reputation here. Now he has an 'insatiable' appetite. Poor Oliver does not fare any better in postal employee James Holbrook's diary. There Oliver becomes feline. In New England, January–February 1854, Holbrook tells us, there were lots of money-letters in the post office. It was like getting through a maelstrom, he says. 'And the lion, whoever he was, had an insatiable and indiscriminating appetite, for he consumed supplies coming from three or four neighbouring counties in the State, and like a feline Oliver Twist, continually "asked for more".'[28]

For Robert Barnwell Roosevelt, a one term Congressman and uncle to Theodore Roosevelt, Oliver becomes an unfortunate mink who got into the eggs on a farm: 'We killed that mink. Like Oliver Twist, he returned for more, and met his fate. I had him stuffed.'[29] Indeed, it is natural to wonder if these people read Dickens's story, or derived their knowledge of Oliver from public conversation or hearsay. Oliver is given little sympathy by these writers and is used as a metaphor for vain people, voracious consumption, and hungry minks. Clearly, the process of reading 'involves reader's constructions, such as mental representations, changes in attitude and belief, or affective reactions', as David S. Miall observes.[30] Readers are interpreters, paraphrasers, constructors of meaning who, as Roger Chartier has asserted, 'read between the lines' and 'subvert the lessons imposed upon them'.[31] This is certainly true of Dickens's American audience, who interpreted Oliver in various ways.

There are, of course, archival records from many readers who clearly did read Dickens. Hinton Rowan Helper (1829–1909) certainly knows Dickens's story when he compares convicts with Bill Sykes: 'Low brows, heavy features, and cold steel-gray eyes, gave them the expression with which Cruishank has pictured Sykes in his illustrations of *Oliver Twist*. They were Australian convicts, brutal wretches, whose hands were red with blood.'[32]

Oliver Twist was put to a wide variety of uses by Dickens's contemporaries. Mrs Elizabeth Sweet, a spiritualist, identified with Oliver, as she recalled a Quaker (Society of Friends) school in Poughkeepsie on Church Street, where she was sent by her father when she was a child: 'Obediently, I went, reported myself at the desk, and, like Oliver Twist, wanted to know what was coming next.'[33] Identifying with Dickens's character, Mrs Sweet recalls herself as a young girl looking forward, with anticipation, wondering what the future would bring. Perhaps, in her own experience of reading Dickens's *Oliver Twist*, she was both identifying with Oliver and anticipating how the story would unfold. As David S. Miall points out, studies indicate that 'Readers of literary texts often appear to draw more explicitly and frequently on their active personal feelings: a literary text may speak to an individual through its resonances with that individual's experience.'[34]

Recalling *Oliver Twist* led to different associations for other readers. For instance, Dickens's Oliver and the Artful Dodger were matched with real life scenes of New York City's poor children. Junius Henri Browne, a popular magazine writer, looking at poor children in the city in the 1870s writes:

> Not a few are pale and haggard, and sad-eyed, reminding you of Smike, Oliver Twist, Little Nell, with the promise of better things in them. With education and training, they would be intelligent and worthy men and women. Their eyes look appealingly at you ... Each one was furnished with a little bowl and spoon, and it was interesting to see how quickly the bowl emptied in most cases, and like Oliver Twist, they called aloud for more.[35]

The connection between Dickens and the urban poor is clear. This American journalist associates the children of New York with Dickens's fictional children of London. In this way, he puts out a call for public response that can ensure the potential that these deprived children may have. The image Browne presents is that of the injured Smike, the outcast Nell, and Oliver, holding out his bowl for food. 'Oliver was born in the workhouse, and his mother died the same night', begins Dickens's novel.[36] The workhouse system looms large: 'All relief was inseparable from the workhouse, and the thin gruel issued three times a day to its inmates'.[37] Recalling the novel, Margaret Cabell, in 1858, compares a local workhouse-like building to *Oliver Twist*; it too has been abandoned and orphaned:

> The workhouse has long since been destroyed – the spacious dwelling house alone remaining to attest the folly of the builder. Mrs. Williams occupied but a short time, and then the building, like Oliver Twist was let out to anyone whom they could get to take it.[38]

In Cabell's account, Oliver is the abandoned, cast-off building and she associates the workhouse with *Oliver Twist*. One might expect Ignatz Leo Nascher, a New York social worker and pioneer of geriatric medicine writing in 1909, to also point to *Oliver Twist* in this way. Instead, he uses Dickens's novel to address the issue of crime in the city: 'The term Fagin, after Dickens' notorious character in Oliver Twist is now generally applied to one who induces of children to become pickpockets and shoplifters.'[39] These public references to *Oliver Twist*, or the popular use of Micawber's phrases, suggest the pervasive impact of Dickens in America across gender, class and region. Perhaps they suggest colloquial usage more than reading practices. However, the circulation of these phrases probably began with the reading of Dickens's texts.

This wide availability of Dickens's texts aided American readers in the work of self-definition. The popular texts of this period – advice manuals, tales of the self-made man –suggest that people, during this time of upheaval were trying to understand their places in society. Texts, like those of Dickens, marked out social types, ways to describe how a good businessman could best function, or how a domestic housewife could best fulfil her role. Dickens provided his readers with models, or caricatures, that enabled them to identify features of the world in which they were living. In a sense, perhaps Dickens was still putting labels on the bottles of the blacking factory, or creating signs as did Nicholas Nickleby. Dickens never stopped naming things and he helped his readers to name them. For now the factory was a turbulent, lively society.

'Dickens's delineations are eminently historical and present a better notion of the period than the general history itself', observed Henry Coppee, an educator, in 1873.[40] The serial form in which Dickens's stories appeared reflected this historical consciousness and often suggested a sense of passage and personal development. As Hughes and Lund have pointed out, a serial, with its 'space between numbers', forced readers to pause in their encounter with the narrative and promoted an anticipation of the future.[41] In reference to Dickens's *A Tale of Two Cities*, they write:

> Being within each number was for installment readers living in history, a fictionalized past in which one was not completely sure where all events lead; being between numbers or at the end of the entire text was inhabiting one of those moments at which one glimpses or creates larger patterns, fixing oneself more securely within a scheme of history.[42]

Dickens's readers, living in a transitional period, were dealing with a shift in their awareness of space and time. An increasing pace of life, compression of time, and rate of transition changed perceptions of the individual in relation to the wider society. The change from a nation of predominantly stable agricultural units to an increasingly industrial society caused some dislocation and disorientation, or a need for adjustment and adaptation. Family time proceeded at a different pace than the business clock and railroad schedules. Print served as a means of connection as commercial enterprise urged movement to new territories, scattering family and friends throughout a region, and the roads and rails moved people on new journeys. One way in which people countered the separation caused by these changes was by gathering in associations such as reading circles.

Some circles of readers made Dickens a central part of their small communities, reading him aloud and discussing his stories across several months. For example, at the Wednesday Club in the growing city of Syracuse, New York, on a snowy Thursday, 4 February 1892, the mostly female reading circle heard one of their members read from *Dombey and Son*. The secretary reports:

> The afternoon of Thursday, February fourth found the ladies of the Wednesday Afternoon Reading Circle quite ready for their sleigh-ride into the country to the pleasant house of Mrs. Barrett where, after a nice ride they were received with graceful hospitality and a steaming cup of chocolate. There were ... twenty members and four guests. As it was Dickens' day, the ladies ... all suspended to roll call with quotations from that author.[43]

We see here the graceful hospitality of the parlour theatrical in which warmth and cultivated conversation contrasts with the cold winter outside. It is not noted which quotations were put forward to the group; however, it appears that they made Dickens their topic of discussion at least three times during the 1890s. With a strong interest in Dickens's biography, the women connected Dickens's life with their own concerns. Dickens was portrayed as a self-made man. The secretary writes that 'Mrs. Barrett gave a very interesting history of Charles Dickens, following him from a boy through all the trials and hardships of poverty and toil on to a great and distinguished success of wealth'.[44]

Along with this theme of self-made success and wealth, the Wednesday Club secretary adds that Dickens was married in 1838 and he and his wife were separated in 1858. 'He had five sons and two daughters', she says.[45] Her selectivity here suggests that marriage and family were among these women's central concerns. The secretary notes:

> Mrs Klock read from *Dombey and Son*, the birth and death of Paul Dombey, which selections were fine examples of the pathetic description of those scenes which are constantly occurring in the houses of men, 'The old-old fashion, Death!'[46] Mrs. D. H. Gorving, taking the notes of this meeting, writes that the speaker noted Dickens's childhood writings and his early love of books, 'Being a very delicate child he sought companionship of books, his father had a small collection, out of which Dickens said, came a glorious host to keep him company'.[47]

The reading circle focused on Dickens's *A Tale of Two Cities* and on the French Revolution on 18 November 1896. The secretary writes: 'Especially thrilling was the storming of the Bastile, The flight, imprisonment and death by the guillotine of the helpless King'.[48] She adds that 'Mr. Trowbridge pleasantly filled an intermission' with piano playing 'which was followed by Mrs. Barrett reading selections from Dickens's *Tale of Two Cities*'.[49] History here becomes a 'thrilling' spectacle: a melodrama of flight, imprisonment, and death, 'pleasantly' filled out by parlour piano playing.

In Cortland, New York, the Truxton Club, formed in the winter of 1886, included several individuals who had read Dickens when they were children. The minute book indicates that on 2 February 1886: 'Subject for the evening Cardinal Woolsey [*sic*]. Miss Emma Jones read the Chapter on the Great Cardinal in Dickens *Child's History of England*.'[50] The Cortland group consisted of husbands and wives who, along with their interest in history, had a theatrical taste for Shakespeare as well as for Dickens. On 23 November 1891, eight members met at Mrs Kenney's to read the fourth act of *Romeo and Juliet*. According to the minutes:

> The committee had decided that reading should be the main feature of the meetings. Each one present voted by ballot for three authors whose works they preferred. 'Dickens' received the most votes, eight. They then balloted for a choice of his works and *Pickwick Papers* was chosen. Each member to read ten minutes at a time.

The presence of reading circles like these demonstrates that reading Dickens aloud served as a communal reading experience both in Dickens's lifetime and afterward, reaching readers of all backgrounds, across thousands of miles. Year after year brought an expansion of Dickens sales in America. His work was published, reprinted, and given away. The novels of Charles Dickens, under different covers and formats, through a variety of publishers, became mass-market items. They put identifiable characters, images and phrases into circulation throughout the United States of America. People at a distance from each other shared the same laugh or dwelled upon the same sorrow, as they encountered the same Dickens story.

Another site of this common encounter with Dickens's fiction was the public library. Christine Pawley writes:

> An important aspect of the inseparable development of the middle class and of institutions was the establishment of certain dominant values, often expressed through myths-stories that express key values. Myth construction was one process by which middle and upper middle classes defined themselves as separate from the working class. It was also a means, *mutatis muntandis*, by which the working class defined itself and was defined, as well as part of the process of establishing institutions such as schools and libraries.[51]

The reports of librarians at mid-century, indicate that the novels of Charles Dickens, Walter Scott and James Fenimore Cooper were among their most circulated works. In 1837, Edward Johnston introduced the New York Mercantile Library's *Systematic Catalogue* (1837), which soon included both *Pickwick* and *Oliver Twist*. Records in 1850 show that there were three copies of Dickens's *The Memoirs of Joseph Grimaldi* (1838) along with at least two copies of all of Dickens's novels at the library. Before mid-century, the New York Society Library had 35,000 volumes (compared with 30,000 at the Library of Congress).[52] This increased to 52,000 volumes by 1876. Books borrowed increased from 19,109 in 1861–2 to 32,642 in 1876. The library's ledgers show that from the 1840s onwards, *Oliver Twist* was one of the library's popular charges. It was charged at least four times or more by patrons consistently from 1847–56. From 1854–6, New York Society Library patrons borrowed Walter Scott's *Waverley* novels thirty-eight times (including repeating borrowers). Cooper's *The Pilot, Deerslayer, Pathfinder* and *The Last of the Mohicans* were also popular. Dickens's novels were borrowed less, averaging about a half a dozen times for *Oliver Twist, Old Curiosity Shop, Pickwick Papers* and *Dombey and Son* (New York Society Library Collection).

The Mercantile Library of Philadelphia reported in 1867 that 'the Library is now furnished with twenty to forty of each of Dickens'.[53] The librarian, when asked which books were the most read, said 'the bound volumes of *Harpers*'.[54] (Or so it was reported in *Harper*'s itself). 'We have Scott's novels, but they are much less read than Dickens is'.[55] 'We needed two sets. This was not strange, since the volumes contain half the works of Dickens, Thackeray, Reade and others, to say nothing of the original papers'.[56] At the Boston Public Library, we know that by 1869 about 9 per cent of issues were for American history and literature but that Boston readers read more foreign history than American. We also know that in 1870, the Boston Public Library Lower Hall held many drama texts, including American stage adaptations of Dickens's novels. Dramatic works were a speciality of the library and records show copies of dramatic adaptations of Dickens's *Cricket on the Hearth* by A. Smith and *Dombey and Son* by J. Brougham and a copy of the Wilkie Collins/Charles Dickens dramatic collaboration *No Thoroughfare*. According to the Public Libraries report of 1876: 'In the Boston Public Library the reader will find Dickens's works in 53 volumes'.[57] Harvard University librarian Charles Ammi Cutter, in January 1868, noted 'the marks of incessant use exhibited by the cards' of Dickens, Thackeray, Macauley and Shakespeare. 'The titles of Dickens's works were so often taken out and misplaced, that the experiment of extending a wire over the cards from front to back was tried and proved successful. Being easily unfastened, it does not interfere with the insertion of a new card'.[58] With Cutter's assistance, the Boston Atheneum developed a dictionary catalogue by 1874. This pioneering catalogue, with entries for author, title, and subject, clearly indicated that Dickens was well-stocked at the library. What is notable here is the high percentage of German volumes purchased regularly from Leipzig, from Tauchnitz, and that a Philadelphia publisher, rather than a Boston or New York publisher, was the primary provider of Dickens books to the Boston Atheneum. The Index-Catalogue recorded parts of books and articles in periodicals. Some 105,000 books are recorded, with an annual estimated circulation of 33,000. The library stocked periodical copies of Dickens novels serialized in *Bentley's Miscellany* (*Oliver Twist*) and *Harper's Magazine* (*Little Dorrit, Our Mutual Friend*) and in Dickens's own *All the Year Round* (*Great Expectations, A Tale of Two Cities, Uncommercial Traveller*). Dickens's periodical *Household Words* was also available.

Public library collections of Dickens were responding to a major publishing phenomenon. Harper & Brothers's first effort with Dickens's works was *American Notes for General Circulation*, which, despite the depression lingering over America, the company brought out in November 1842 in plain brown wrappers at twelve and a half cents. The Harpers' volume, a reprint from British sheets, ran in two columns across ninety-two pages. Volumes of *American Notes* were used by American publishers with nationalistic aims to provide an image of the United States of America, even though Dickens was sometimes critical of American habits and mores.

Harpers' edition of *Martin Chuzzlewit* in July 1843 put it in direct competition with Lea and Blanchard's supposed 'rights' to Dickens and with other publishers who were producing and distributing Dickens. The novel sold about 20,000 parts per month. According to Robert Patten, 'The sales figures do not entirely support a conclusion that the *Notes* were a failure ... But there is much truth to the argument that the hostile, or, - even worse, condescending – critical reception of the book affected the public's feeling about Dickens.'[59] Patten points to a lull in publishing production and sales because of 'financial uncertainties, political unrest, and the sort of general depression that feeds upon itself to intensify its effects'.[60] The maximum monthly circulation of *Martin Chuzzlewit* in New York was about 23,000 copies.[61]

Dickens's British publishers countered the overseas competition with their own 'cheap editions'. Dickens could be found in triple-decker novels, 'library' editions, 'people's' editions, 'Charles Dickens' editions and in newspaper and magazine reprints. Along with the Dickens book trade, there was continued reprinting of Dickens's stories in parts in periodicals. As Dickens began his own periodical *Household Words* in Britain in 1850, several American companies, including Harpers, rushed to reprint his stories or his articles from it. Everyone wanted a piece of Charles Dickens. In 1850, the British author remained at the centre of intense disputes between American publishers seeking rights to his work. Some publishers paid Dickens for his stories, while, as in the past, others grabbed and reprinted them. Dickens volumes from his British publishers were distributed by Ticknor & Fields & Little, Brown of Boston and he was 'published' (reprinted) by T. B. Peterson & Lippincott of Philadelphia. In New York, his work was issued by Harper & Brothers, G. P. Putnam, D. Appleton, and a dozen other companies. The 'Editor at Large' in *Putnam's*, September 1854 edition, wrote:

> Here we sell Dickens, in a hundred editions, at every railway station. In brown covers, in yellow covers, in every possible species of cover. We gloat over his *Bleak House*; we devour his *Hard Times*.[62]

A direct comparison of American prospects and British print and literacy appeared in the next issue, with 'A Letter to John Bull'. The writer said, 'I do not think there is an American family in the land which does not take in some newspaper or magazine'.[63] The writer attests to the 'almost universal circulation' of newspapers and magazines in America and criticizes London papers, which 'all are too costly to be taken by the poorer classes'.[64] He says that he has no book trade statistics at hand but that he believes that 'the circulation of books is on a level with that of periodicals'.[65] For, he says:

> No really valuable work is published in England which is not reprinted here: the works of our own authors are widely read; the trade of bookmaking is lucrative, and that of book publishing more so. One publishing house, the Harpers, issue on the average a book a day, the sales of which vary from five to fifty thousand copies.[66]

Bleak House (1852–3) first appeared in the United States of America in *Harper's New Monthly Magazine*, which sold for twenty-five cents a copy. According to Harper & Brothers records, in 1852 Rufus Griswold attempted to obtain the first proofs of *Bleak House*. He authorized one of his associates at the *International Monthly Magazine* who was going abroad to give Dickens a $2,000 advance for the sheets to his next novel. News of this was printed in the New York *Evening Post*.[67] The Harper *Priority List* indicates that *Harper's* paid £360 ($1,728 by Exman's estimate) for proofs of *Bleak House*. Serialization in *Harper's* began in April 1852. The story was published in book form, in two volumes on 21 September 1853. In a letter Charles Dickens wrote of *Bleak House* developments:

> The story has taken extraordinarily, especially during the last five or six months, when its purpose has been gradually working itself out. It has retained its immense circulation from the first, beating dear old Copperfield by a round ten thousand or more. I have never had so many readers.[68]

A serial in 34,000 copies suggests 'striking popularity', Patten states. He points out that 'In 1852 an edition of 1,000 copies was probably still standard for many works'. Drawing upon the work of Michael Sadlier, Patten adds that 'First printings of yellowbacks ranged between 1,000 and 5,000 copies'.[69] The Dickens trade was not seriously affected by the economic trends that affected the American publishing business in the mid-1850s. The *Ladies Repository* reported the wide circulation of *Bleak House* in 1852–3, noting that it generated advertising income:

> *Bleak House*, which appeared in monthly numbers, had so wide a circulation in that form that it became a valuable medium for advertising, so that before its close the pages of the tale were completely lost in sheets of advertisements which were stitched to them.[70]

As Harper & Brothers became one of the most visible of the magazine publishers of reprints of Dickens, the firm of T. B. Peterson at 306 Chestnut Street in Philadelphia became one of the most visible book publishers of Dickens. T. B. Peterson had assumed the rights to publish Dickens and were known as Dickens's publishers, making use of the stereotype plates from Carey (Lea and Blanchard). The company had made a deal with Harper & Brothers for the plates of Dickens's recent novels. Following Carey's practice, they claimed to provide trade courtesy to Dickens, although they had no contractual agreement with him. By 1867, T. B. Peterson had issued twenty-three editions of the novels; this increased to twenty-five within the next two years.[71] In *Philadelphia and Its Manufactures* (1858), Edwin T. Freedley wrote:

> T. B. Peterson's have in their possession the stereotype plates of about six hundred different books, small and great, principally novels. They have invested about $50,000 in Dickens's works alone, of which they print twenty-nine different editions: the only complete series in the United States. The sales annually average 50,000 volumes.[72]

Harper's agreement with T. B. Peterson was generally respected. However, other firms sought to print Dickens's fiction. In one case, T. L. McElrath, in 1854, put out an American edition of *Hard Times*. Harpers responded by issuing the book at one-half McElrath's price. McElrath complained in the *Empire City*, an ephemeral newspaper, that Fletcher Harper had caused his business to fail.[73]

Dickens's entire catalogue continued to be published in Britain and shipped to the United States of America. In January 1856, Chapman & Hall sent 1,898 volumes of *Oliver Twist* to New Orleans and 468 volumes to New York.[74] The *Pickwick Papers* were then sent to New York in 1855–7 to Bangs, an American distributor that carried 1,638 volumes of the novel in 1856 and 507 volumes of it in early 1857. Chapman & Hall issued 1,275 numbers of *Christmas Books Cheap Edition*, in one volume, that were sold in New York. By December 1856, some 975 numbers of the *Christmas Books* were sent to the United States of America. Of these, '75 dozen' were sold to Bangs, New York.[75] 'By 1864, the Dickens competition in America was intense', notes John Tebbel. 'Twelve publishers, at least, were printing him, ignoring courtesy of the trade, but Dickens himself was getting as much as $5,000 for advance sheets of a single novel'.[76] In the months following the war, Appleton received 250 sets of Dickens before December 1865. Another 480 volumes, or twenty sets, were sent to Little Brown and 600 volumes in cloth, or twenty-five sets, went to the Philadelphia publisher Lippincott, which issued a standard edition of Dickens.[77] In December 1865, Scribners was sent 277 volumes.[78] The year 1866 saw four American publishing firms distributing Chapman & Hall produced copies of Dickens. These firms sent their books out through agents and distributors to booksellers throughout the country. In Tebbel's view, Dickens 'sold better in America than they did at home'. Dickens reissues appeared 'to have no end'.[79] The Dickens productions of Harper & Brothers, G. P. Putnam, and T. B. Peterson made their way from New York and Philadelphia across the United States of America through a variety of distributors and book agents, notably including James Cephas Derby, one of the leading distributors of Dickens and other print material from East Coast publishers. Dickens's novels were distributed out of Boston by Ticknor and Fields, a highly respected publisher of *belles lettres*.

As their trade expanded, publishers were locked in a dispute over priority to Charles Dickens. A 'triangular contest' was described by the *New York Times*, 18 May 1867. Harpers, T. B. Peterson and Ticknor & Fields all were claiming Dickens. Harpers claimed a prior arrangement with Dickens, one that Dickens consented to abide by. T. B. Peterson claimed an arrangement with Harpers for reprinting from advance sheets of the Dickens novels. Ticknor & Fields asserted that Dickens had signed a contract with them. A compromise was struck in which Ticknor & Fields would print Dickens stories in book form and the Harpers would serialize his stories in their magazine. However, this arrangement did not please T. B. Peterson, who also claimed priority 'rights' to Dickens, based on its purchase of Lea & Blanchard's plates and catalogue. As Ticknor & Fields put out its 'Diamond Edition', T. B. Peterson's publicly expressed upset with what they believed was Ticknor & Fields's intrusion on their claim to Dickens. Before 1850, they had begun to pay for advance sheets run as serials in *Harper's Weekly* and *Harper's Monthly*. On 16 March 1867, in an advertisement in the *Boston Transcript* they asserted:

> T. B. Peterson and Brothers, Philadelphia, in connection with Harper and Brothers, are the only Publishers in America of the works of Charles Dickens, that have ever paid anything for the manuscripts advanced proof sheets of his various works, so as to enable Harper and Brothers to publish them in America.[80]

The company also placed ads in the *New York Tribune* on 6 April 1867: '3,250 pounds sterling was paid for the advance sheets of Charles Dickens's last three works'. In the *American Literary Gazette*, T. B. Peterson listed their twenty-two editions of Charles Dickens's works.[81] The *American Literary Gazette* reported: 'Ticknor and Fields Diamond editions have had an immense sale; so have Petersons' ... and now Hurd and Houghton are in the field with three [sets of Dickens]'.[82]

Before an exclusive publishing agreement was established between Dickens and Ticknor & Fields, the Boston firm, by arrangement with Chapman & Hall, distributed a Library Edition of twenty-six volumes from 1858 to 1861. Some 3,500 volumes were sent to them at two shillings per volume in January of 1858. There were 2,000 more volumes sent by December 1858. Fields imported 5,700 copies in 1859. The Boston firm was sent 100 volumes each of *Pickwick*, I and II by December 1860 and in December 1863 made available 1,650 volumes. James Fields 'had long been ambitious to get Dickens on his list'.[83] As of 1866, he began actively seeking Dickens, offering him his company's sponsorship of a reading tour of American cities and a 10 per cent royalty. As the reading tour was beginning in 1867, Fields negotiated a deal for £1,000 for a short story, 'A Holiday Romance' for *Our Young Folks: An Illustrated Magazine for Boys and Girls*. Clearly, Fields saw a market for young readers. Ticknor & Fields began 1867 with 300 volumes of Dickens without illustrations. By December, there were another 26,000 volumes. Paying $1,000 to Dickens, Fields also published Dickens's short story 'George Silverman's Explanation' in three instalments in the *Atlantic Monthly*. Ticknor & Fields's volumes of Dickens's works appeared in three editions: deluxe, moderate and cheap. They absorbed much of the Dickens trade for the next few years. According to Tebbel, 'these sets sold in the thousands'.[84]

In 1867, Hurd & Houghton followed with its own collection of Dickens's works. In response to Dickens's reading tour, Appletons, in 1868–70, likewise felt compelled to produce an eighteen-volume set. Ticknor & Fields responded with a letter to Dickens, saying that Appleton's volume of *Edwin Drood* had done 'incalculable damage'.[85] By 1873, Dickens was published by Appletons in a half dozen different editions, including, according to its catalogue, its 'best cheap edition' the seventy-five cents per copy, fourteen-volume cloth 'Handy Volume' edition.[86] Harpers, meanwhile, issued the illustrated 'Household Edition' in sixteen volumes and Lippincott produced deluxe and standard editions of Dickens and Thackeray.[87] J. Applegate, following the demise of George Conclin Publishing of Cincinnati, succeeded that firm by issuing 10,000 copies of Dickens's works in two volumes. Tebbel claims, 'it was so easy to sell' Dickens.[88]

American publishers invested considerable effort in distributing and selling Dickens. While the constant reprinting of Dickens's works makes it difficult to quantify the overall circulation of Dickens in America, it is obvious that his works became a site of intense commercial competition. In 1837, the public response to the serialization of the *Pickwick Papers* indicated the emergence of a mass readership that would revolutionize publishing in the United States of America.

Within the tensions of competitive commerce and American nationalism, fierce competition among publishers over Dickens's works reflects the extraordinary popular demand for Dickens's fiction. In the 1840s, men like George Palmer Putnam, James Cephas Derby and the Harper brothers looked toward Dickens's works to enhance the financial potential of their publishing businesses and to meet the rising demand and social promise of America's growing readership. The novels of Charles Dickens, so popular among American readers, launched by many publishers in a variety of ways, certainly fulfilled that promise. Meanwhile, Dickens's readers, like his character David Copperfield, continued actualizing their potential as 'heroes of their lives'.[89] With Dickens as a model, one could tell his or her own story and recognize his or her self in time. Like Oliver, who regains his inheritance, or Esther Summerson, who discovers hers, Dickens's readers, each in his or her own way, could grow and learn lessons. These readers were ones who picked up and read the book at home, or on the train, even as the landscape hurtled by. Life beyond the window, that large landscape of America, had its own enchantments. However, as the American nation grew larger, according to one critic, print had to supply 'some of the affectional needs formerly fulfilled locally'.[90] Fiction, including Dickens's portraits of groups of people interacting, his cast of many characters, offered people images of human interconnection. These fictional relations could act as a reminder of the dimensions of mutual life that people lived within. The self-constructing readers of Dickens's novels appear to have used Dickens's novels as a mirror in which they saw the people around them, especially the more eccentric and curious characters they encountered in their lives. It was often these persons, or images of people seen through the lens of Dickens, who struck their imaginations and found their way into the pages of their recollections and autobiographies.

8 VICTORIAN PANTOMIME LIBRETTI AND THE READING AUDIENCE

Jill A. Sullivan

The nineteenth-century pantomime was a complex theatrical event.[1] Each production ran for several months and whilst as a genre it was continually developing, responding to popular taste, and incorporating new theatrical trends and technological developments, its complexity lay in the additional mutability of the individual performances of any one production. Pantomime success relied on regular changes during a run, for example, updating topical references, adding new jokes and physical comic 'business' or introducing new novelty acts. Success also depended (as it still does) on a successful and participatory engagement with each audience.

Over the last twenty years there has been an increasing body of work that addresses the concept and definition of an audience and, more especially, the role that that audience plays during a theatrical performance.[2] Those discussions invariably address the relationship of the audience with a performance text, that which has been created by a multiple authorship of directors, designers and performers, plus the audience themselves in terms of responses and reactions. Audience responses are therefore addressed primarily in relation to a predominantly verbal, visualized spectacle. For theorists writing on recent productions, audience responses can be researched via reports but also, advantageously, in direct interviews with audience members. For the historian of the theatre, establishing audiences for past productions is a more problematic issue and yet we still acknowledge the essential difference between an author's text (the initial written dramatic text) and a performance text, always assuming that those distant theatre audiences were responding to a transient performance: the visual not the written text. However, in the nineteenth- and early twentieth-century British theatre, audiences attending the Christmas pantomime were regularly faced with the performance text *and* a version of the written author's text produced in the 'book of words'. By focusing on a selection of those produced in the mid- to late nineteenth century for the Theatre Royal, Nottingham, this paper sets out to explore the rationale for printing the book of words, and the potential effects of combining reading and spectatorial audiences at a performance of the annual pantomime.[3]

For nineteenth-century audiences, the book of words was a tradition aligned firmly with the annual pantomime, but the concept of producing a plot summary or libretti for theatre productions dates from a much earlier period. In *Theatre of the Book 1480–1880: Print, Text, and Performance in Europe* (2000), Julie Stone Peters describes the emergence in the seventeenth century of manuscript libretti, programmes and books of play texts that were occasionally produced for distribution in the theatre, the books intended more especially for 'eminent spectators or potential patrons as presentation copies'.[4] By the eighteenth century the practice was becoming more widespread, theatre '[c]ompanies regularly ... distributed libretti, printed plots, or separately printed prologues and epilogues at the theatre as programmes' and 'the sale of "books" in the theatre – primarily opera and masque libretti – was becoming a normal part of theatrical business'.[5] Peters's identification of opera and masque libretti illustrates how the combination of written text and visual spectacle has a long history, a point identified by John O'Brien in his study of eighteenth-century pantomime.[6] O'Brien and the theatre historian David Mayer, in *Harlequin in His Element: The English Pantomime 1806–1836* both establish that by 1800 accompanying libretti for pantomime, a popular genre that responded to developments in theatrical and cultural spectacle, were produced on a regular basis. In the early years of the nineteenth century these libretti – by this stage more often referred to as the book of words – took the form of a small booklet that was on sale to the audience at the time of performance, alongside the printed handbills and, from the late nineteenth century, the programme. Mayer describes how, in the 1800s, the book of words was on sale for between 6*d.* and 10*d.* in the West End Theatres Royal of Drury Lane and Covent Garden in London, but in the provinces, for much of the nineteenth century they more frequently sold for one or two pence. Around 1800, a book of words would have included the speeches, songs (occasionally the music) and brief descriptions of the scenes and actions of both the spoken and purely visual parts of the productions.[7] By the 1860s, the pantomime book of words comprised, on average, twenty-four pages which contained most of the scripted dialogue with a few of the briefer stage directions (such as exits and entrances), scene titles, a cast list, song titles and airs. Increasingly the full text and music of the songs were indicated in the text only by their titles, the name of the air to which it was set, together with the composer's name in parenthesis. This exclusion of the full libretto and music of songs may have been related to developments in copyright restrictions in the second half of the century, but there is some evidence that they could be printed separately in an accompanying 'book of the songs'.[8] In addition to the dramatic text, the book of words of mid-century usually contained half- or third-page advertisements on the coloured (predominantly pink, blue or green) inside and back covers, an initiative that had begun in the 1820s.[9] By the 1890s the book of words had become a sizeable commodity, comprising as many as fifty or sixty pages, often with full page advertisements either on facing pages or interspersing the text, as well as line drawn illustrations – artists' impressions – of the pantomime characters. Twentieth-century critics who have written on pantomime, such as Mayer and M. R. Booth have recognized that the book of words did not represent the whole script as produced in performance; it did not include detailed stage directions, nor the comic 'business', nor even all the song titles, and certainly not the additional material, the *ad libs* and updated topical references for which pantomime was well known.[10] Discounting the advertisements, essentially the text in the book of words represented the pantomime prior to the first night performance: it was closer to the author's text than to the performance text that the audience witnessed. However, despite the fact that sections of the book of words could become redundant during a production run of one to two months, the book continued to be produced and sold each year, with sparse evidence that reprints occurred to accommodate changes.[11] For the theatre management, it was primarily a practical concern; it was another opportunity to create income and, in this sense, the book reflects the commercial nature of what was the most important production of the year in financial terms: income from the annual pantomime has regularly funded the remainder of the theatre season, especially in the provinces.[12] Produced and printed prior to the opening night along with handbills and posters, the book of words 'met the customary need for a souvenir programme'.[13] Mayer's phrase engages with two aspects of the book of words' use: as a souvenir for the theatre-going audience and a necessity for the pantomime audience. I will return to the issue of necessity later in this paper, but as a souvenir, the book of words signified not only the financial importance but also the social importance of the pantomime, especially for first night audiences. The first night of a pantomime traditionally took place on Boxing Night, 26 December (or 27 if Boxing Day fell on a Sunday). This particular performance usually attracted the largest house and the longest reviews; it is the night most frequently recalled in pantomime histories, illustrations and memoirs. The Boxing Night performance and the book of words (only available in the theatre and to audiences for the first time on this occasion) were consequently bound up in what Auslander refers to as the 'cultural value' of a special event. In other words, for those members of a first night audience there was a specific sense of occasion: 'being able to say that you were physically present at a particular event constitutes valuable symbolic capital'.[14] Peters also comments on the use of libretti as souvenirs for masques and spectacles in the seventeenth and eighteenth centuries,[15] and there is a clear link between the two concepts of occasion and souvenir in performances of spectacular theatre that culminate in the nineteenth-century pantomime event. If the book of words is regarded solely as a souvenir, this sense of occasion was reflected in their appearance. The covers of the books of words became more decorative as the century progressed: from simply announcing the title and production details, to ornate line drawings of characters and – in the 1890s – photographs of the principal performers. In 1891 the management of the Theatre Royal, Nottingham produced an extremely elaborate book of words for their production of *Robinson Crusoe*. Larger than other versions, in this edition both covers and each inside page are in full colour, incorporating the text within elaborate pictures and designs. It was printed by Stafford & Sons of Nottingham, an important national producer of theatrical advertising. On closer inspection, however, the illustrations bear no resemblance to the story of the pantomime. The pictures and abstract designs are all fashionably Japanese in style, each illustration apparently telling a separate and specifically Japanese tale irrespective of the textual story of Robinson Crusoe who, in this particular pantomime production, ends up on a Cannibal Island somewhere near Africa. Whether the illustrations signify a lack of communication between the theatre management and the printers, or an economy drive by the printers, using standing print from another publication, the item remains a beautiful example of the book of words as souvenir. The advertisements feature on the back and inside cover or are inserted as full-page entries, separated from the text of the pantomime; the advertisements do not punctuate the artistry, and while the text answers any requirements of necessity, the book exists as an elaborate souvenir, an item to be admired for itself rather than something which is purely necessary to the appreciation of the pantomime in performance. Here the book clearly forms part of the consumer experience of going to the pantomime. For the theatre audience, or for those who purchased the book of words, a souvenir suggests that the book of words is optional, fun and perhaps a little frivolous. If even the simpler versions were regarded as souvenirs, they may indicate what the theatre management perceived as an ideal audience, one that could appreciate the trappings of the theatrical event and who were not concerned by the expenditure of a couple of extra pence in addition to the programme and the theatre ticket; an audience by definition middle class.

The increasing number of advertisements contained in the book of words certainly reflected an assumed middle-class audience, appealing to the family group, in, for example advertisements for perambulators, cordials and medicines for children, even 'Godwin's Amber Ale ... A delicate light taste for families, of absolute purity',[16] as well as to the individual adult. (Advertisements never appealed directly to the child; despite ongoing debates about the extent to which nineteenth-century pantomime was a children's genre, the consumer experience was distinctly that of the adult.) Advertisements in the period 1860 to 1900 featured, for example, pianos, photographic studios, high-class tailors, house furnishers, handmade boots, restaurants, opera glasses, respectable furniture removers, wines and spirits. In part, these advertisements signify a specific relationship to the theatre. In the 1865 book of words for the production of *The House That Jack Built* at the Theatre Royal, Nottingham, the advertisers included Allen's stationers and printers (who had also printed the book of words), Henry Farmer, music and instrument shop, who frequently sold sheet music and songs from productions at the theatre, and Mr Hart, the 'Wine and Spirit Merchant', who also rented the refreshment rooms at the theatre, and whose sandwiches and drinks even warranted a mention in the script: 'Here in this house, the best you can obtain, / Supplied by Mr. Hart, 14, Peck Lane'.[17] In the provincial towns and suburban areas, businesses that advertised in the book of words were always local to that area and detailed services and goods with which the reader in the audience could identify themselves, either as an active customer (and in this action thereby connecting the theatre with their personal choice of shopping), or as a potential customer (the advertisement acting on this occasion independently of its printed location, in other words, the customer isolating their desire for a product from the reading or perusal of the pantomime text), or as a participant in a local community beyond, but still including, the theatre, for example in their recognition of the business name and location: the restaurant around the corner, or the butcher's shop their neighbour used. The placing of many of the advertisements appears to be arbitrary in relation to the pantomime text: the plotting of the *Forty Thieves* opposite an advertisement for 'Artistic Bordered Victoria Quilts' or a scene set in 'The Magician's Tryst in the Mountains of the Moon' accompanied by an advertisement for Hyam's winter overcoats.[18] Occasionally advertisements did – whether intentionally or not – carry aspirational connotations. In the book of words for an 1892 production of *Cinderella*, a drawing of the glamorous and elaborately coiffured Principal Boy, Prince Paragon is placed opposite an advertisement in which Mr Thomas Parker announces that he has just returned from London with the latest fashions in hairdressing, and has engaged a first-class court hairdresser to assist in this department. Similarly, in the same book of words, opposite a scene in the text featuring the Fairy Godmother an advertisement promoted the latest fashionable corsets, thus aligning in the female reader's eyes a desire to appear fairylike with the means of achieving it.[19]

Thematic suitability aside, the range of advertisements and the type of goods detailed both confirmed and appealed to the respectable nature of local businesses and their customers. The appearance of such advertisements within the theatrical event satisfied the reader that their personal consumer choices and knowledge were recognized by the theatre and, similarly, that the consumer's decision to attend the theatre had been correct. The book of words effectively appealed to and confirmed the status of the audience member in their role as sanctioning consumer. The integration of consumer desire and purchase power with a consumer's decision to frequent the theatre – even if it was only for the children – also inferred approval of that theatre and, consequently, the production that they were attending. More particularly, that decision implicitly conferred respectability on the pantomime, a genre which was so often a cause for rebuke by the nineteenth-century critic for the inclusion of *risqué* music hall songs and dancers who displayed their legs.

In reading the advertisements and accepting the additional cost of a book of words, I have defined a middle-class consumer. However, it is of course possible that members of the artisan or working class also purchased copies, especially with the rise in literacy as the century progressed. Recent research has shown clearly that nineteenth-century theatre audiences cannot be divided neatly by areas in the auditorium, for example the middle class in the dress circle, the lower-middle class and artisan workers in the pit, and the poorest members of the audience up in the gallery.[20] Therefore, potentially, copies of the book of words could have been seen in all parts of the house; instead of an image of a single section of the audience – the middle-class dress circle occupants – carefully reading their book of words, reading and subsequent engagement with the performance could have been occurring throughout the house. Furthermore, as I have mentioned, the price of a book of words varied. Mayer cites 6*d*. in the 1820s at the Theatres Royal of Covent Garden and Drury Lane in London,[21] but in a small industrial town like Nottingham in the 1860s, a gallery seat cost 6*d*. and the book of words was 1*d*. The variation in price, as with seat prices, surely reflected alertness by theatre managements to the different wage levels of the local population. It is possible that the orange-peel throwing, disorderly gallery-ites of legend and newspaper reviews had at least a couple of books for reference. Therefore, whatever our retrospective assumptions – or those of the nineteenth-century theatre managers – regarding the middle-class consumer, we (and they) cannot be certain as to the specific purchasing practices of pantomime audiences

As noted above, in addition to the book of words acting as a souvenir, it has also been described as a necessity for pantomime audiences, where the relationship between pantomime and the production of libretti highlights more practical issues regarding costume and acoustics. Rather than the economic divisions suggested by regarding the book as a souvenir and the optional nature of the consumer experience, a more complex set of divisions occur when considering the book of words as a necessity. In other words, divisions created in the actual reading practices and the uses to which the text was put, which depended on individual and group choices.[22]

Mayer's definition of the book of words as a necessity for the pantomime audience is an argument linked closely to the format of the early nineteenth-century pantomime.[23] In this version of the genre, the production comprised two parts: the opening, which told the story of a classical legend or fairy tale in rhyming verse, and the much longer harlequinade – the main part of the pantomime – which contained the knockabout, generally silent antics of the Clown, Pantaloon, Harlequin and Columbine. At the end of the opening, the main characters were transformed into the harlequinade characters, for example the hero into Harlequin, and his lover, the heroine, into Columbine. The transformation, brought about by a good fairy, not only changed the setting and style of performance, but also required the shedding of large masks and outsized costumes for the male performers to reveal the traditional costumes of the harlequinade characters. Because of these masks, the spoken element of the pantomime in the opening could be difficult to hear for an audience, the words muffled by the large masks, and made more indistinct by the size of the large two or three thousand seat auditoriums of the period.[24] Copies of the dialogue were therefore necessary for members of the audience to understand what was being said on stage in the first part of the production. However, changes in the genre, as well as in theatrical licensing, meant that after the 1840s the spoken opening became the dominant feature of productions and separate casts were engaged for the different sets of characters in the opening and harlequinade. Therefore the transformation of costumes became unnecessary and by mid-century the large, elaborate masks were increasingly worn only by extras or minor characters with little to say.

However, there were occasions where acoustics remained a problem: theatres were still large, some actors did not speak loudly enough, and audiences could be noisy. In his essay 'Popular Theatre in Victorian Birmingham', Reid defines three different 'categories of noise and disturbance' present in a theatre: what he calls 'the normal noisy reflection of the theatre's role as a social centre', in other words talking, joking, laughing amongst groups and individuals (not as a direct result of what was happening on stage) as well as eating and drinking, but this category could also include the rustle of people getting to their seats or turning the pages of the book of words.[25] Reid also defines the 'ritualized' noise which 'punctuated the course of a play or marked the significance of an evening', to which he aligns, for example, the whistles and banter by some members of the audience that formed a tradition, along with the development of the *claque*.[26] Reid highlights this type of noise as participatory and, of course, pantomime in performance, which demands active participation and response from its audience would create a further level of 'ritualized' noise. Reid finally defines the 'objectionable noise of disorder and deliberate disturbance', which would have probably resulted in police action and forcible removal from the premises.[27]

In 1879, the *Nottingham Journal* expressed concern when a book of words was not made available for the audience. In a January review of the pantomime, the critic mentioned that the lack of a book of words created a significant problem as the pantomime could only be imperfectly followed amid the social noise which continued for some time after the curtain rose.[28] However, a shorter review published the day before had made the lack of a book of words the central focus of the report, stating that:

> We would venture to hint that a little clearer enunciation of the words, more particularly by some of the ladies, is very desirable, especially as for some mysterious reason no 'book of the words' is published ... Such publication was earnestly desired last year, and it is again wished for this year. Its denial is a mistake. It is not probable that any loss [of income] would accrue, but if such a loss should arise it would be a very small matter compared with the advantage and pleasure which it would afford to many frequenters of the Theatre. The libretto is one of the best ever produced at the Theatre, and it is but justice to the authors that the public should be able to hear it or read it in its integrity.[29]

Not only does the critic request the actors to speak up, but he defines an audience that needs to refer to a book of words. In this instance, the book of words is seen not simply as an optional and decorative souvenir of the theatre-going experience, but rather is necessary, even integral, to the appreciation of the pantomime itself at the moment of performance. However, in the final sentence, the reviewer implicitly separates those who would follow the spoken words in the book from those viewing or listening to the performance, to be able to *'hear it or read it in its integrity'*. The distinction between hearing and reading the pantomime performance is not as clear as may be presumed; the book of words here potentially played a more complex role in relation to the interaction between performers and audience. For example, instead of considering the book of words as helping to distance the performance from interference (whether due to acoustics or noise) as suggested by our Nottingham theatre critic, it potentially becomes part of that noise, of effectively 'cueing' the audience for certain songs and jokes. It did not contain the traditional pantomime catchphrases, such as 'He's behind you!' (a phrase established by the 1870s and probably in use much earlier) but traditions such as these would be known and expected by most in the audience and those new to the genre could be cued by their neighbours in the auditorium. Instead the songs and jokes printed in the book of words were more recent additions to that particular production. Copies of the book of words were sent to local newspapers prior to the opening night and recommended speeches – especially those of a topical nature – were copied into the newspaper previews, thus preparing the audience member for speeches in the performance; that person could then look out for those lines in performance, with the book of words as an *aide-memoire*. In this instance, the book effectively links the social with the ritual or participatory noise, but it further indicates the creation of an apprecia-tive audience member. By choosing (or having the ability) to purchase the book of words, that action reflected a desire, not simply the desire to consume, but a desire for knowledge. The purchase represented the theatre-goer who, not con-tent with viewing/listening, wanted to ensure comprehension and appreciation of the words. Whilst this desire recalls the complaint by our Nottingham theatre critic, a complaint made by a reporter at the Exeter Theatre Royal pantomime in 1881 more clearly indicates the parallel activities of reading and participation when he commented that 'I have not read the [book of words] and I pitied those who were conscientiously striving last night to make out what was going on by references to the printed story'.[30] Indeed, in this context the book of words acts as a singular example of a perceived need to read rather than just view – of par-ticular interest at a time when pantomime scripts were generally condemned by the *literati*, and the visuals and technology were regarded as the main focus of pantomime productions – and a desire to know and not just to watch and join in the songs if one knew them; of needing to understand the performance as well as engaging with it.

The book of words could further fragment audience cohesion. For example, among those audience members who had copies of the book of words, no doubt some exchanged comments with their neighbours, telling them a joke they had missed or even pre-empting the end of a scene. According to Reid's definition, this would be classed as the 'normal' social noise in a theatre, but if the audience member's comments were made from a personal observation and not requested as part of the regulated ritual of response in pantomime, they were engaging with the pantomime but creating an individual response, made possible only by the book of words. Modern critical debates around the concept of an audi-ence have focused on the influence of the audience collective on the individual as well as that of the individual on the whole.[31] Millie Taylor's recent work on modern British pantomime engages with the idea of the pantomime audience as a temporary, artificially created community through the linked activities of singing and responding with catchphrases.[32] However, for nineteenth-century audiences, this idea does not work fully if we add the book of words into the equation. The book of words, if actively used, potentially separated and delayed activity by the individual from the group. Even if only referred to momentarily, the book of words both obstructed and engaged with the performance and its audience/community. Similarly, a desire to comprehend as the primary motiva-tion behind purchasing a book of words potentially further divided an audience: between those who followed the book of words in part – to clarify or to par-ticipate at particular moments, requiring an occasional glance therefore – from those who followed the book of words in detail (enabled by the fully-lit auditori-ums for much of the period). Also, if noise or poor acting made the performance inaudible, this act of reading the book of words separated those audience members who could follow the plot in the book from those who relied on the visuals for their storytelling, and those who were not reading or listening/watching but were busy chatting to their friends. Inevitably, the situation created by the book of words highlights the distinction that the critic Susan Bennett makes, that 'the theatre audience is ... a social gathering' whereas '[r]eading is, by and large, a private experience'.[33] For those people reading the book of words, the written text effectively supplanted the performance text in front of them on the stage. The reader was diverted not only away from the on-stage activities, but also from the intended vocalizations of the script in performance. Referring to the book of words, albeit for a few moments, distanced the reader from the action on stage, diverting them to a script that may not, later in the run of the pantomime, match the words lost through noise or poor acoustics.

Audience members entered the theatre with different expectations, based on factors such as their experience of the genre, knowledge of the actors in the production, the reviews and the 'pre-production' material such as handbills and posters, plus of course the book of words, purchased once inside the theatre.[34] As audience engagement would have varied according to those expectations and the shifting observations natural in a three or four hour performance (the usual length of Victorian pantomimes) the book of words may have maintained interest for some; an alternative diversion in an already diverse visual extravaganza. However, audience expectations could be both established and changed by the book of words. It was a well-known fact that people frequently went to see more than one pantomime production each season, and also re-visited the same production later in the run. As previously mentioned, pantomime had always been a very mutable genre, not only in its evolution, but also in performance and during the run of a production. New gags, business and novelties were added, line changes were made, scenes were cut and songs were updated, especially those with topical references. The book of words, however, was a largely static text. With little evidence of altered reprints, we must assume that in general they more closely represented – and continued to represent for the remainder of the run – the first night version of the author's text. Therefore, for all audiences viewing a particular pantomime in one Christmas season, including the first-nighters, the cuts, changes and different audience reactions natural to any theatrical production in performance, as well as those intrinsic to pantomime potentially acted to increasingly distance those audiences from the written text in the book of words.[35] It still had a use as many of the speeches would have stayed the same, but the developing differences between the text and elements of the performance physically re-engaged later audiences with the events on stage and attention had to be drawn away from the book to listen to and/or watch the latest additions. The book of words was not solely an item produced to instil audience expectation of the impending performance. It could, indeed was, intended to be read during the performance, thus creating but also, by virtue of being a relatively static text, confounding expectation during the process of performance.

In addition to purchasing the theatre ticket to attend the performance, the book of words allowed the theatre-goer to engage in another aspect of the consumer experience. Susan Bennett has argued that the purchase of a theatre ticket enables a theatre-goer to both buy access to a show, plus the experience of being in a theatre.[36] Similarly, Tracy C. Davis, in acknowledging the commodity of theatre, allows that the more ephemeral commodity known as the performance ceases to be once that performance has finished.[37] The Victorian book of words, however, presents a further twist to the concept of transient commodification in that its purchase equated to buying a version – potentially another performance – of the pantomime. Combining the idea of the book of words as a souvenir and as a mode of engagement, Mayer suggests that '[w]ith such a booklet, someone who had seen the pantomime and who could recall the music might reconstruct the pantomime, describing the activity and singing the airs for his own or others' pleasure'.[38] He reiterates the point that the books of words do not contain the full script, and also emphasizes that they are separate from the scripts that were provided along with toy theatres for children to stage shows at home. Similarly, in his discussion of the eighteenth century pantomime libretti, John O'Brien suggests that 'such texts ... seemed designed not to replace the live performance but to serve as an *aide-memoire* for those who have already seen it'.[39] In terms of distraction such as I have outlined in this paper, O'Brien does not address the implicit issues of a libretti potentially replacing a performance, but his comment regarding memory, together with Mayer's suggestion of domestic re-creations of productions highlights another facet of the book of words. Using it in this way extends the pantomime performance beyond the theatre, and further enables a new version, according to the reader's preferences. Indeed, it may have been that such selective reading, defined by times and places beyond the theatre, gave the book greater literary qualities for that reader (and their immediate audience). The book of words was frequently cited in newspaper previews and later reviews, the wittiest, cleverest and most satirical puns or poetic lines being picked out for commendation. Similarly, reading the book of words beyond the theatre enabled a different reading audience to emphasize chosen lines and demonstrate their knowledgeable appreciation of a political pun or a reference to Tennyson or Shakespeare.

Despite its cultural and critical history, nineteenth-century pantomime did not have the *éclat* of other theatrical genres and was rarely printed for sale in collections such as Lacy's Acting editions.[40] Whilst some manuscript copies exist, our understanding of the genre is based largely on the books of words that have survived through being kept by audience members, sent to the Lord Chamberlain's office for licensing, or passed between provincial theatres for adaptation. Despite what they represented in the eyes of the *literati*, many of the books of words for pantomimes produced throughout the country and for a period of nearly a hundred years have survived. They have become the principal research tool for nineteenth-century pantomime and yet they are in many ways a problematic text, not wholly representative of the author's text, nor of the production and certainly not of the ephemeral performance. It was essentially a commercial text, compiled and created by the theatre management responding to both immediate need and consumer desire. However, even though it was an additional source of income for the theatre management, at a penny a time it did not add vastly to a theatre exchequer and problems of poor annunciation and noise must have been issues for other dramatic genres where books of words were not produced. Furthermore, as an item of pre-production for an overtly participatory genre, the book of words did not necessarily unite an audience; it enabled rather than dictated participation but it was a varied participation at different levels and for separate members of the audience. Participation related to when the book was read and for what purpose: to acquire knowledge; to aid with acoustics; to know the songs; or to know, hear and appreciate the jokes and references. Historically, pantomime audiences have never been passive or silent and, whilst the book of words did not instigate activity, which existed through the traditions of performer–audience interactions, it did provide a further level of engagement and diversion.

9 MATERIAL MODERNISM AND YEATS

Alex Davis

In his volume in the *Oxford English Literary History, 1910–1940: The Modern Movement*, Chris Baldick argues forcefully that we need to revise our conception of a period often unquestioningly identified *in toto* with, in his eyes, a relatively small group of writers, those whom, retrospectively, we have learned to label 'modernist'. 'In their own time', he states, 'the writers we call the modernists ... regarded themselves as participants in a rather larger and looser enterprise which was then more commonly known as "the modern movement" ... [We must not] forget that there are many ways of being modern'.[1] For Baldick, recent scholarship has expanded the modernist canon 'beyond credibility', and is driven, he believes, by the 'undeclared assumption that other writers are worthy of notice only insofar as they resemble that central avant-garde'.[2] It is true that a monolithic conception of 'international modernism' has seceded to an understanding of the period as intricately variegated; that modernism, in short, has given way to modernism*s*. The reductive versions of the modernist movement and the modernist text constructed by a number of critics in the 1980s and early '90s, especially certain theorists of a putative postmodernism, increasingly have the air of T. S. Eliot's hollow men, 'filled with straw'.[3] Few would now maintain that modernism is definable simply through the employment of certain structural, formal and stylistic devices, such as stream of consciousness, fragmentation, collage, etc. And neither would we isolate a specific series of themes and preoccupations as inherently modernist. In these respects, the delimiting of modernism at the hands of the so-called 'new modernist studies' has, from one perspective, brought the enormously varied contours of modernist literature into view, even as they recede into the literary historical distance; from another, however, it has produced a miasma. As Carla Kaplan observed as early as 1995, 'What many are calling the "new modernist studies" would seem, then, to be at a conceptual impasse, caught between expansion and erasure. How can we reconstruct modernism while simultaneously calling into question its categorical status?'[4] Baldick's remapping of English modernism within the context of a broader 'modern movement' suggests one way to negotiate this critical cul-de-sac in a specific national context, but, while of heuristic value, it is by no means conceptually unproblematic. The stability of the category of 'modernism' is preserved from erasure by Baldick through its being reserved for those few 'central avant-garde' works which have been unquestioningly recognized as such. However, as our knowledge of modernism is derived empirically from the relevant cultural evidence – it could hardly be known *a priori* or by reason alone – Kaplan's own suggestion as to how research in this area should proceed strikes me as more fruitful than Baldick's. Kaplan urges us to undertake 'thick description[,] upon which any new understanding of the field necessarily will depend'.[5]

In the current reappraisal of modernism, an example of this kind of thick description is Helen Carr's comprehensive study of Imagism, *The Verse Revolutionaries* (2009). Carr's history of the movement enriches the familiar account by paying close attention to the work not only of its self-proclaimed instigator, Ezra Pound, but that of his avant-garde fellow travellers, including Amy Lowell, Joseph Campbell, John Gould Fletcher and F. S. Flint.[6] Complementing this kind of literary historical carpet-bombing is a new concentration on the modernist work's material conditions of construction, reproduction and dissemination – on that which George Bornstein describes as 'its original sites of production and ... the continually shifting physicality of its texts and transmissions'.[7] An extreme instance – in conception if not actuality – of the importance of a modernist text's physical form and transmission to its imagined audience is the bizarre tactility envisioned by Christopher Isherwood and Edward Upward for their early collaborations, the Mortmere writings (*c.* 1923–7). These playful narratives, largely written while their authors were undergraduates at Cambridge, distantly recall, on the thematic level, the Brontës's youthful gothic extravaganzas depicting the make-believe kingdoms of Angria and Gondal.[8] Whereas the Brontës's narratives are touched by contemporary events, however, Mortmere and its collection of outlandish denizens constitute a literary fantasy that, in the authors' words, has no 'starting-point in sanity or objective reality'.[9] Irreverent and escapist, largely surviving in fragmentary form, the Mortmere stories might be read as a parodic version of the unrealizable Mallarméan *Livre*, in that each work exists as – in Sam Slote's comment on Stéphane Mallarmé's – 'a pretext bereft of a final text'.[10] Mallarmé intended his *Grand Oeuvre* to be encyclopedic (it would contain the sum of all books); but, as Slote observes, Mallarmé's surviving notes and essays on the project deal more with the material form and the prospective readers' reception of the projected book than any putative content.[11] The authors of the abandoned Mortmere project would also seem to have been deeply, even overly, preoccupied with the format of their envisaged text: a de luxe edition, we learn, was to be published as a volume containing oil paintings, brasses, intaglios, pressed flowers, mirrors and harmless bombs to emphasise points in the story. The dialogue was actually spoken by a concealed gramophone. A musical box played emotional airs. The pages would smell, according to their subject-matter, of grave-clothes, manure or expensive scent. Within a pocket of the cover there would be a valuable gold present for each reader.[12]

Though begun when Isherwood and Upward had yet fully to absorb, and thence react against, modernism (the authors, at this date, 'endorsed every word of the *London Mercury*'s review of *The Waste Land*'),[13] the stories' wilful disruption of realist forms is itself a ludic variation on the revolution of the word in the contemporaneous fiction of James Joyce and Virginia Woolf. Subsequent to Mortmere, Upward would abandon Gothic-surrealism in favour of a pellucid prose influenced by his Marxist convictions, as in the documentary realism of *The Spiral Ascent* (1962–77) trilogy. Isherwood too, after tinkering with the device of stream of consciousness in *All the Conspirators* (1928), gravitated towards a realist mode of writing, one which would achieve its most memorable expression in the autobiographically-inflected stories in *Goodbye to Berlin* (1939) and *Down There on a Visit* (1962).

Yet the example of Mortmere, despite its authors' protestations, illustrates that texts – modernist or otherwise and regardless of their grotesquerie – necessarily have their 'starting-point[s] in ... objective reality', if by that we comprehend their historical horizon of production (and reception), and their manifestations over time as a material text (imagined or real) or indeed as a number of texts. For as Bornstein insists, in line with all verbal artworks, the modernist text has two codes: a 'bibliographic code' deriving from such aspects as its design, layout, binding, etc., and a 'linguistic code', that is, its semantic content.[14] Critical work on modernism, from its canonization at the hands of I. A. Richards and the New Criticism, has primarily laboured to unpack the linguistic code of texts which are, in many cases, perceived as 'difficult' if not, on occasion, opaque. Such quite necessary explication has often gone hand-in-hand with a relative neglect of the text's multiple sites of production and reception and, in many cases, its several incarnations as manuscript and/or typescript, in periodical and/or book publication, as a reprint (owing to popularity or for institutional reasons) and as an anthologised work (owing to its fame or because judged institutionally significant/representative).

Given the non-existence of the de luxe edition of the Mortmere stories, a published modernist sequence of short fiction, W. B. Yeats's *The Secret Rose* (1897), provides a germane but more palpable example of the interrelationship of a text's linguistic and bibliographic codes. The extraordinarily beautiful cover of *The Secret Rose* was the fruit of Yeats's collaboration with the artist Althea Gyles. Its design derives from a passage Yeats added to one of the volume's stories, 'Rosa

Alchemica', after its initial publication in *The Savoy*, but which, on reflection, he chose to delete from the proofs of the 1897 collection. The relevant passage describes the bound manuscript of the history, doctrine and symbolism of the Order of the Alchemical Rose:

> In the box was a book bound in vellum, and having *a rose-tree growing from an armed anatomy, and enclosing the faces of two lovers painted on the one side, to symbolize certainly the coming of beauty out of corruption, and probably much else*; and upon the other, the alchemical rose with many spears thrusting against it, but in vain, as was shown by the shattered points of those nearest.[15]

The cover design of *The Secret Rose* closely matches the deleted words (italicized) and subsequent passage. Yeats's own book thus becomes analogous to the occult work described therein, and its fictional contents, it is implied, equally embody occult truths. Furthermore, in partially erasing this correspondence at proof stage, Yeats adds to the secrecy of such hermetic knowledge, obscuring a full realization of the parallel from the (non-adept) reader. Crucially, it is the convergence of the bibliographic code and the linguistic code that produce this intensely self-reflexive moment, as a glance at the 1995 Penguin edition of Yeats's *Short Fiction* (which includes the stories of *The Secret Rose* in their 1897 versions) illustrates all too vividly. Usefully annotated, and competitively priced, the cover of the latter reproduces not Gyles's design but a painting by Jack B. Yeats, the new bibliographical encoding effectively denuding the linguistic code of its original suggestiveness.[16]

The cover to the first edition of *The Secret Rose* is an example of how Yeats, in attending to the material composition of his book, seeks to shape his readers – granting his audience a trembling of the veil of the Temple, the spiritual truths of which he is cognisant from his membership of the Hermetic Order of the Golden Dawn.[17] A less esoteric, though more imperative, instance of Yeats's attempt to make an audience can be seen in his editorship of the magazines and pamphlets associated with the creation of a national theatre and the production of plays fundamental to that which Yeats would later call '[t]he modern literature of Ireland'.[18]

Of the many sites of modernism, and the modern movement, that of the magazine is crucial.[19] Modernism was disseminated through a large network of periodicals that appeared in the wake of the vast increase in the number of print-outlets in the late nineteenth century, an expansion fuelled by developments in print-technology and the availability of inexpensive paper. In the early twentieth century modernism finds outlets not only in the 'little magazines' with which it is so often associated – *The Egoist*, the *Little Review*, *Poetry* (Chicago), *Blast* and the like – but also in mass-market magazines: *Vanity Fair*, for instance, seriously considered publishing *The Waste Land*, and Eliot and Pound seriously entertained the prospect. Pound's Herculean labours on behalf of Eliot's poem are well documented – that he negotiated the initial American publication of *The Waste Land* in *The Dial* on terms which included Eliot's receipt of the Dial Award *without* the editors having read the award-winning poem is eloquent testimony to his role as modernism's chief impresario.[20] Yet Pound was not unique in his ability to manipulate the marketplace for modernism. At the turn of the century, Yeats (whom Pound had come to London in 1908 with, among other motives, the intention of meeting) had shown the importance of exerting control over the institutional matrices of his publication, reception and consumption; and he would continue to prove adept in this regard after Pound had begun to lose his grip on such matters in the late 1920s.

The performances of Yeats's *The Countess Cathleen* and Edward Martyn's *The Heather Field* in the Antient Concert Rooms, Dublin, in May 1899 were accompanied by the publication of the first issue of *Beltaine* (which ran for three issues, from May 1899 to April 1900), '*An Occasional Publication*', the title page informs its readers, constituting 'THE ORGAN OF THE IRISH LITERARY THEATRE'. In the pages of this 'ORGAN', and the other magazines associated with the early Irish dramatic movement, *Samhain* and *The Arrow*, Yeats would mount a case for a form of experimental, non-illusionistic drama in a medium which, as noted, would become a key vehicle for the dissemination of modernism in subsequent years.

Of the magazines with some claim to literary significance in Ireland in the 1890s, *Beltaine* is the most important; it was not, however, the first. In the seemingly unlikely pages of the Irish Agricultural Organization Society's weekly journal, the *Irish Homestead* (1895–1923), readers were sure to encounter some of the leading Irish writers of the day. Shaped by Æ from 1897, the magazine published work by, among others, Douglas Hyde, E. Œ. Somerville and Martin Ross, Katharine Tynan, Alice Milligan, Yeats and Æ himself. In the new century, short stories by Joyce, eventually destined for *Dubliners*, would disturb at least some of its readers. Nevertheless, while paleo-modernist and early modernist texts are a fitful presence in the *Irish Homestead*, *Beltaine*, it has been argued, can lay claim to being the first instance in Ireland of the modernist little magazine. In his invaluable study of Irish literary magazines, Tom Clyde advances the argument that *Beltaine* comports with the basic criteria of this form of periodical: espousing radicalism in art and politics, such magazines aimed at a small but relatively homogenous readership, and, in both content and physical format, sought to produce 'a unified artistic statement'.[21] Furthermore, Clyde maintains, in contrast to the great Victorian reviews, the little magazine's courting of a select audience indicates a contempt for commercialism of a piece with the avant-garde pretensions entertained by its editor(s) and contributors. As a general description, Clyde's received account of the little magazine – and of *Beltaine* as an exemplum of this medium – is not without validity, yet it requires significant qualification.

As Mark S. Morrisson has convincingly demonstrated, the modernist magazine of the early twentieth century possesses a complicated relationship with 'the explosion of mass market print publications and advertising' at the end of the nineteenth.[22] Morrisson contends that interpretations of the avant-garde which depict it as resolutely opposed to the supposed degradations of mass culture fail to note the extent to which certain modernists interacted with and manipulated 'the new institutions of culture of the period to create a prominent public role for their art and literature'.[23] As editors, such modernists, far from showing the kind of 'lack of, and disdain for, commercial sense' attributed to them by Clyde,[24] seized upon the relative affordability of the periodical as a means of, in Morrisson's words, 'making their voices and their art prominent in the vibrant and exciting new print venues of the public sphere that the commercial culture had helped to create and sustain'.[25] *Beltaine* inaugurated Yeats's attempt, at the turn of the century, to employ the little magazine to promote and critically justify the modern dramatic literature of Ireland in a public print forum. In this attempt, as Paige Reynolds has contended, Yeats faced a conundrum. Seeking to 'assemble a broad Irish audience for national culture', *Beltaine* and the theatre's succeeding periodicals, *Samhain* (October 1901–November 1908) and *The Arrow* (October 1906–August 1909), were catering to both 'a small reading public which would support an experimental theater and a large theater audience which would attend their native plays'.[26]

The irresolvable tension at the heart of Yeats's many contributions to the Abbey's theatrical pamphlets is the fact that, on the one hand, Yeats plainly seeks a national drama that is, in some sense, *representative*, while on the other, his 'antithetical nationalism' (in Hazard Adam's fine phrase)[27] constantly rebels at the thought of a crudely committed theatre and literature. Yeats, in short, is divided over the *instrumentality* of art. As Terry Eagleton comments of the Irish Literary Revival's cultural nationalism: 'Art must revive the nation, but this suggests a utility at odds with its own autonomy. Culture as political means is at odds with culture as utopian end'.[28] As a result, Yeats came into inevitable conflict with *both* ultra-nationalist opinion, including that of Arthur Griffith and the *United Irishman*, and the iconoclastic views of free-thinkers such as John Eglinton (the pseudonym of William Kirkpatrick Magee), who trenchantly demanded a theatre that engaged directly with contemporary Irish problems, specifically that of religion.[29]

In the 1906 issue of *Samhain*, Yeats lays down a number of general principles in an essay reprinted from the *Contemporary Review*, 'Literature and the Living Voice'. The importance of the theatre's work, he states, lies in the fact that a literature belongs to 'a whole people' when it is experienced 'without the mediation of print and paper'.[30] Irish literary culture possesses such immediacy to the extent that its poetry and narratives 'were made to be spoken or sung, while English literature, alone of great literatures because the newest of them all, has all but completely shaped itself in the printing press'.[31] As early as 1889, in a piece for the Boston *Pilot*, Yeats had described Ireland as 'the country where poetry has been a living voice among the people'.[32] Yet over the course of the

1890s, the artifice and hermeticism – the 'purity' or autonomy – of the Symbolist movement increasingly attracted him, as is evident in several essays of this period, most notably 'The Autumn of the Body' (1898). In another essay later collected in *Ideas of Good and Evil*, 'What is "Popular Poetry"?' (1902), Yeats can be seen attempting to square this aesthetic circle by bringing together 'the poetry of the coteries, which presupposes the written tradition', and 'the true poetry of the people, which presupposes the unwritten tradition': '[b]oth are alike strange and obscure, and unreal to all who have not understanding'.[33] By the time of 'Literature and the Living Voice', on which he was working in mid-April 1905, the significance of the 'unwritten tradition' had altered for Yeats: for his current dramatic purposes that tradition dictates principles of clarity and variety both in composition and performance, rather than imparting an estranging obscurity. But this 'tradition' is still in the service of an avant-garde anti-mimetic 'wonder', as an essay in the fourth issue of *Samhain*, 'The Play, the Player, and the Scene', makes apparent. For plays to be 'literature' (and they 'must be literature') speech must 'cherish the musical lineaments of verse or prose'; movement must be 'decorative and rhythmical'; and scenery must be minimal and non-naturalistic.[34]

In attempting to conjoin 'antithetical nationalism' to a modernist experimental drama coloured by his earlier Aestheticism, Yeats argues in the pages of the seventh and final number of *Samhain* that 'it is the presence of a personal element alone that can give it [literature] nationality in a fine sense, the nationality of its maker'.[35] According to this dictum, not only is J. M. Synge's *The Playboy of the Western World* – 'so full of the temperament of a unique man' – demonstrably more Irish than the novels of Michael Banim, Gerald Griffin, Charles Kickham and the stories of William Carleton, but, by the same token, the poetry of the Young Irelanders is actually less Irish than that of Kentishman Lionel Johnson.[36] Bedevilling the creation of a national literature in Ireland, Yeats continues, is the pervasive belief that the artist must surrender his or her personality to a collective cause; and it is precisely that, to his mind, erroneous view of the relationship between art and nationality that has caused difficulties for the theatre.

The foregoing discussion of the linguistic code of these occasional publications is usefully supplemented by attending to aspects of their bibliographic code. The first issue of *Beltaine* includes the theatre's first programme at the Antient Concert Rooms, followed by a poem by Johnson, which presents the programme's two plays as dramatic offerings on the night of festival after which the periodical is named. The succeeding contribution, by the 'Editor of "Beltaine"',[37] outlines the 'Plans and Methods' of the theatre, which are complemented by brief commentaries on *The Countess Cathleen* and *The Heather Field* by Johnson and George Moore, respectively. Yeats's presence in the periodical's brief run increases with the second number. This issue is longer than the first and its price accordingly had doubled from threepence to sixpence, and differs from the first in including a table of contents, on which Yeats is identified as the periodical's editor. (The final issue, which also has a similar content's page, would be disappointingly brief, but could be had for a ha'penny.) Subsequent to the third and final issue, all three were, 'in their original wrappers', rebound 'simply encased in boards, for preservation on the bookshelf, with no addition save that of a Table of Contents to Number One', which now follows the format of the second and third numbers. There is, however, a further addition which this notice overlooks: an inserted title page which foregrounds Yeats as editor of the entire series. *Beltaine* number two has another editorial piece on 'Plans and Methods'; of the six other pieces, Yeats has contributed two; the other contributors, one a piece. Of Yeats's two essays, that on 'Maive; and Certain Irish Beliefs' sits oddly in a periodical devoted to theatre business: it is an exercise in ethnology, discussing an aspect of Irish folklore. But its inclusion is representative of Yeats's growing ascendancy in the magazine; a dominance not confined to editorials and essays, but equally visible in other elements of its bibliographic code. *Beltaine* is typical of little magazines in advertising cultural products including other magazines and books. In the first issue, there are four advertisements which mention Yeats: his *Poems* of 1895 is advertised as one of 'Mr T. Fisher Unwin's Books', and is typographically indistinguishable from Douglas Hyde's *A Literary History of Ireland* and George Sigerson's *Bards of the Gael and the Gall*, which immediately precede and follow it in Fisher Unwin's list. Yeats is further mentioned as a contributor to the *Daily Express* (Dublin), co-publisher of the first issue of the magazine, and *The Dome*, and there is even advertised a lithograph of W. B. Yeats ('A few remain', we learn). In the second issue of *Beltaine*, Yeats's visibility is still higher. Announced as '*JUST PUBLISHED*' is 'A Song by W. B. YEATS. / Set to Music by THOS. F. DUNHILL' (See Figure 9.1). The advertisement for sheet-music, 'Boldly printed and full music size', takes up a third of the page; adverts for five other works take up the remaining space on the page. The typographical layout of the advertisement is itself '[b]oldly printed' – firmly distinguishing the sheet-music from the works offered for sale below. All these works, including that of Yeats, have been published in '*LONDON: AT THE SIGN OF THE UNICORN*', that is, published by Ernest James Oldmeadow, who was also the co-publisher (with the *Express*) of the first issue of *Beltaine* and sole publisher of numbers two and three. He was also the publisher of *The Dome*, advertised on the facing page, which, as in issue one, lists Yeats first among its contributors. Indeed, Oldmeadow had printed the lithograph of Yeats touted on the back page of that first number. Oldmeadow's advertisements would appear to seize increasingly on Yeats's marketability, his commodity status (in this context) reinforced by the growing identification of the magazine with Yeats, through his editorship and increased presence among the contents.

JUST PUBLISHED.

'AODH TO DECTORA.'

A Song by

W. B. YEATS.

Set to Music by THOS. F. DUNHILL.

Boldly printed and full music size.   PRICE ONE SHILLING NET.

LONDON: AT THE SIGN OF THE UNICORN.

Sixpenny Belles Lettres

1. OTHER PEOPLE'S WINGS.

By T. W. H. CROSLAND.

The Manchester Guardian.— 'These parodies, like all good things of their kind, have a decided critical value.'

2. FIFTY FABLES.

By T. W. H. CROSLAND.

London Letter.— 'One of the wittiest little books that we remember for some time.'

2. THE ABSENT-MINDED MULE.

By T. W. H. CROSLAND.

Just ready.

Feap. 8vo. paper, Sixpence net. In buckram, gilt, One Shilling net.

Hand & Soul.

By D. G. ROSSETTI.

IN the belief that many persons will be glad to possess Rossetti's 'Hand and Soul' (reprinted in *The Dome*, New Series, No. 13) as a separate volume, the Proprietors of The Unicorn Press have produced a Small Edition of the work. This Edition differs from its predecessors (now out of print and enhanced in price) in that it contains no borders, initials, or other decoration. It has been printed at the Chiswick Press, on hand-made Van Gelder paper (imperial 32mo.).

The price is Two Shillings and Sixpence net. Copies can also be supplied by arrangement, in choice bindings, at prices ranging from Five Shillings to Five Guineas net.

The Little Christian Year

New and Cheaper Edition.

In white cloth, with Hand-by-de coration in blue, suitable for a present. One Shilling Net.

The Church Review (Dec. 21, 1899) says; 'In this little volume, excellently printed and daintily bound, we welcome a real contribution—and one which strikes a new note—to the literature of the devotional life.

'A miniature in every sense, the "Little Christian Year" is worthy of its title. To each of nineteen chosen Christian seasons four pages are devoted; the first contains the title, the second a text of Holy Scripture, the third a short poem of from four to twelve lines, and the last a little prayer of a single sentence at once allusive in its language and direct in its point of appeal. The poems—and here is the note of novelty—are in the main not directly religious, but are meant to illustrate sketches of some aspect of life or nature, duly connected with their subject by an invisible yet none the less real link. And sometimes the connexion is only by force of contrast—to the poem on the Annunciation, a daring but illuminating contrast. The work has not the theology of the greater "Christian Year," and is marked by far intensely personal and often paradoxical method of the new school than by the "follies of the Tractarian.'

THE 'CHORD.'

A QUARTERLY DEVOTED TO MUSIC.

** THE CHORD is not a Paper-covered Magazine, but a Bound Book (Pott Quarto) on Antique Paper, with Full-page Plates and Facsimiles. No. 1 was received with enthusiasm by Musicians and the Press everywhere in reviews ranging from one to six columns in length. No. 1 will not be reprinted, and the Proprietors reserve the right to increase the price without notice.

THE CHORD, No. 2, contained Articles by John F. Runciman (on 'The Regeneration of the Orchestra'), Ernest Newman (on 'The Prose Works of Berlioz'), E. A. Baughan ('A Plea for the Symphony'), H. A. Scott (on 'Brahms'), and other important papers.

THE CHORD, No. 3, contains the following Plates and Articles :—'Two Groups of Angels,' from an Altar-piece by Jan and Hubert Van Eyck ; The Universal Pitch'; 'Music in the Roman Church,' by Vernon Blackburn ; 'Anglican Church Music,' by R. R. Terry ; 'The Decay of the Organ,' by John F. Runciman ; 'The Angels of Jan and Hubert Van Eyck,' by L. A. Corbeille ; 'The Decline of Bayreuth,' by Vernon Blackburn ; 'Bayreuth from an American Point of View,' by E. E. Ziegler ; 'As Others Don't See Us,' and 'The Provincial Festivals of 1899,' by B. W. Findon.

Price One Shilling net. ;

Annual Subscription, post free, Five Shillings net.

THE 'DOME.'

AN ILLUSTRATED MONTHLY MAGAZINE OF LITERATURE, MUSIC, ARCHITECTURE, AND THE GRAPHIC ARTS.

The *Dome* has won for itself, during the last three years, a world-wide reputation as an organ of artistic opinion.

Among the contributors are W. B. Yeats, Fiona Macleod, Arthur Symons, Stephen Phillips, Francis Thompson, Laurence Binyon, Laurence Housman, J. F. Runciman, Vernon Blackburn, William Strang, Liza Lehmann, Arnold Dolmetsch, Edward Elgar, and other well-known artists.

The *Pall Mall Gazette* says : 'No one of an artistic taste can afford to ignore this unique publication.'

Monthly—One Shilling net.

Figure 9.1: Advertisements in *Beltaine*, 2 (February 1900).

Yeats's marked profile in *Beltaine*, by means of his own offices or those of its publisher, is part of the complex story whereby Yeats seeks to become – in the words of the subtitle to the periodical – 'THE ORGAN OF THE IRISH LITERARY THEATRE'. Yeats's attempt to write the history of what, for convenience's sake, we call the Abbey are well known, and culminate in his 1923 Nobel speech, in which he concentrates on the Irish dramatic movement at the expense of his poetry.[38] His involvement with *Beltaine*, and its successors *Samhain* and *The Arrow*, are an important chapter in that story, and attending to the magazines' bibliographic codes is important to its fuller understanding.[39]

It remains only to consider the afterlife of these ephemeral publications. As early as 1905, it would seem, Yeats sought to collect a selection of his contributions to *Samhain* and *The Arrow* in a more permanent form. A 1907 letter to his publisher, A. H. Bullen, shows Yeats actively preparing to integrate his occasional dramatic criticism into his projected *Collected Works in Verse and Prose*, a handsome multi-volume edition that would eventually appear in 1908.[40] Yeats wanted to call the pieces culled from the periodicals *Friends and Enemies*, but he settled on *The Irish Dramatic Movement*, probably at Bullen's request. What had been occasional contributions to a communal endeavour was now to be collected as a discrete section (in volume four) of a canonical body of work by an increasingly lionized author – for the *Collected Works* represented, to Yeats and many reviewers, the establishment of the poet and dramatist as a major literary presence. As Yeats wrote to John Quinn, the American collector and patron of the arts: 'This collected edition is going to be a beautiful thing. I have seen the first specimen volume and am well content with my share of it and with Bullen's. I think I am better in the mass than in fragments'.[41]

However, the 'mass' of the 1908 *Collected Works* was always conceived as an interim marshalling of Yeats's work to date. As early as 1913, the restless author wanted a revised collected edition assembled. In 1922 he proposed a new collected works including a volume entitled *Plays Written in Prose for an Irish Theatre; and The Irish Dramatic Movement*. In 1923, he had to compromise, re-collecting the dramatic criticism in *Plays and Controversies*. In the 1930s, an Edition de Luxe was planned by Yeats and his then publisher, Macmillan, the second volume of which would include *The Irish Dramatic Movement*; an American edition, by Scribner, was also to include this work. The Edition de Luxe and the Scribner collected works would flounder amid the Depression's impact on the world of publishing, but would resurface after Yeats's death in 1939 as the now-renamed Coole Edition, in the tenth volume of which *The Irish Dramatic Movement* was now placed. With the Second World War, this edition also went into abeyance. *The Irish Dramatic Movement* was eventually republished in 1962, in a volume of Yeats's work called *Explorations*, the contents of which were '[s]elected', the dust jacket and title page inform the reader, 'by Mrs

W. B. Yeats'.[42] Until recently, this has been the edition scholars and readers have usually consulted and quoted from, rather then *Plays and Controversies*, despite the fact the latter was published in Yeats's lifetime and thus arguably has greater authority. *Exploration*'s own authority, as a posthumous collection, is problematic, if one cedes the determination of a final text to what one can construct as or construe to be an author's final intention.[43] Indeed, there is a lively debate in Yeats's textual scholarship as to which text one should base a definitive edition of *The Irish Dramatic Movement* on. The copy text of the 2003 Scribner edition of the work, edited by Mary FitzGerald and Richard J. Finneran,[44] is the marked-up proofs of the volume of *Mythologies* (which includes *The Irish Dramatic Movement*) in the never-published Edition de Luxe of 1931–2 – a decision stemming from the editors' belief that this base-text records Yeats's last-known intentions. Against this decision stand the editors of the most recent edition of *Mythologies* (2005), Warwick Gould and Deirdre Toomy,[45] who accord both Yeats's reader for Macmillan, Thomas Mark, and the poet's wife, George Yeats, authority in determining Yeats's *expectations* regarding his final text.[46] Yeats is notoriously poor in both his spelling and grammar, and, in preparing the Edition de Luxe, deferred much to Mark's judgement and to George's proofreading. FitzGerald and Finneran choose, in their edition, to discount what they take to be Mark's pencilled corrections to the proofs as not sanctioned by the author. Gould and Toomy, by way of contrast, argue that Mark's alterations have Yeats's implicit authorization, given Yeats's reiterated approval of his reader's skill with his proof. Without adjudicating between the merits of these two approaches, it seems clear that we have here an instance of the further multiplication of a modernist text, one which, in this instance, involves more than the proliferation of editions resulting from Yeats's habit of revision and re-collecting his work. A textual crux in *The Irish Dramatic Movement* illustrates what is at stake here. In her fine study on the Irish and Harlem Renaissances, Tracy Mishkin states:

> In the 1905 edition of the Abbey publication *Samhain,* Yeats complained about the harsh reception of the company's plays in Ireland. Searching for a way to explain this phenomenon, he suggested that the Irish people's loss of self-confidence, which he connected to the decline of the Irish language, caused their reluctance to accept humorous, imaginative, or critical presentations of Irish life. 'If Ireland had not lost the Gaelic', he wrote, 'she never would have had this sensitiveness as of a *parvenu* when presented at Court for the first time, or of a negro newspaper.'[47]

In fact, in the 1905 issue of *Samhain* to which Mishkin refers, Yeats did not exactly make this complaint. He actually wrote 'nigger newspaper.'[48] Correcting proof copy in the early 1960s, Mark had queried Yeats's vocabulary in the margin, and, presumably with George Yeats's approval, the word was altered for the text of *Explorations*. FitzGerald and Finneran, following their intentionalist principles, revert to the earlier reading, their choice of text firmly governed by Yeats's last-completed corrections. Against this decision, one might observe that *Explorations* is of course a belated modernist text, one published on the brink of the Civil Rights Act in the United States of America (1964); and, in this political context, Mark and George Yeats understandably felt queasy about Yeats's casual racism. In its new site of publication and dissemination, a different, more politically-correct text is required. Is it permissible to justify this change through recourse to authorial *expectation*? Would Yeats have allowed the word to stand if he had lived into an age of Civil Rights? Obviously, the question cannot be answered; but it makes one think again of W. H. Auden's great elegy on Yeats, and his reflection that '[T]he words of a dead man / Are modified in the guts of the living'.[49]

10 CHANGING AUDIENCES: THE CASE OF THE PENGUIN *ULYSSES*[1]

Alistair McCleery

Introduction

A book is a machine for generating meaning; the material form of the book itself contributes to the creation of meaning and, in so doing, shapes the reader. Often statements like this are produced as if the book historian or textual critic were discovering new truths rather than restating shared knowledge in a new vocabulary. The Royal Engineers conducting the Ordnance Survey in Brian Friel's *Translations* (1981) rename the places of Donegal; they give the authority of print and lend the status of officialdom to the new names. Yet the people of Donegal have known, and worked and lived in, these places for countless years under their original names. Publishers, who take the decisions about the material form that the text will take, can be relegated to the same status. Their role in making calculated and calculating judgements is ignored in the renaming of paratext and in the analysis of its generation or qualification of meaning. This essay attempts to reinstate publishers as active agents in making books and shaping readers, through a case study of the 1969 Penguin edition of *Ulysses*.

The establishment of Joyce's novel in the academy in the UK, the essay will argue, was a deliberate result of the marketing of that 1969 paperback edition, Penguin number 3,000. The date is significant. It falls at the close of the decade that saw what Geert Lernout termed 'the institutionalization of Joyce studies', that is, the ghettoization of Joyce within the academy, particularly but not exclusively the US academy.[2] It also falls at the close of ten years of rapid expansion, and the striving for a distinctive modern and progressive identity, within UK higher education. This essay examines the publishing decisions that influenced the reception of *Ulysses* in the UK through the 1969 edition. The Penguin edition of *Ulysses* represents the key moment in the novel's transition in terms of reception: at the risk of making an over-generalized assertion, before Penguin 3,000, *Ulysses* was perceived in the UK as an avant-garde work, with a minority readership found chiefly amongst the literati; or as a select art object suitable for collection (a viewpoint stressed by Lawrence Rainey); or as a notorious work celebrated for its pornographic passages, or as any combination of these three perspectives. After the Penguin paperback edition, and its volume sales, *Ulysses* was regarded as a 'safe' classic of modern literature taking its place as canon-fodder for the expanding number of students in a burgeoning UK higher education system.[3]

Cultural Capital

For the period prior to 1969, the avant-garde, as both creators and audience, can be defined in terms of minority challenges to the majority culture. In the case of Joyce's *Ulysses* those challenges were both aesthetic and sexual (in the earlier case of *Dubliners* the printers interpreted the challenge as political).[4] The conjunction of these two was characteristic of little magazines such as the *Little Review*. However, in challenging the majority view of how explicit a writer could be in sexual matters, Joyce was also aligning himself, albeit unwillingly, with those writers who did that solely for profit, who targeted what Lawrence called 'the "improper" public'.[5] The term 'the targeted reader' was used by Edward L. Bishop in his ground-clearing article on '[T]he "Garbled History" of the First-edition *Ulysses*'. Bishop drew on archival evidence from a number of sources to stress that there was no homogeneous group of readers for the 1922 *Ulysses* but rather a number of different types, often found in the one individual, 'like the overlapping coloured circles in a sociology text'.[6] This linked and limited number of readers and markets, avant-garde and pornographic, are implicit in the questions posed by Charles Duff in 1932: 'Is *Ulysses* often bought and kept merely because it is a forbidden book? Or because of the scatological and sexual passages? Are they all bought as a sop to the intellectual snobbery of their purchasers?'[7] The mere fact that Duff's book has to make a persistent special pleading that the novel can be tackled by the 'plain reader' is itself indicative that he/she was doing no such thing (if only because of its relative unavailability in 1932). Indeed, the publicity for the Random House edition of 1934 did its best to advance simultaneously the modernity of *Ulysses* and the use of guidance to allow successful navigation through its pages.[8] Random House presented *How to Enjoy James Joyce's 'Ulysses'* with the first edition to act as such a navigation aid and a similar full-page advertisement appeared in the *Saturday Review of Literature*. It succeeded. The 1934 edition went through multiple printings and sold some fifty thousand copies before 1940.

However, in the post-war period, William Powell Jones could still write in the opening sentence of *James Joyce and the Common Reader* that 'James Joyce is much talked about but too little read for a writer of his importance'.[9]

If he was describing the situation in the US, then it will not have differed much from that in the UK. Purchasers of the novel, as opposed to readers, were still attracted to it by what Hugh Kenner pithily termed its 'gameyness' and/ or by the expectation that its possession might indicate membership of a rather exclusive intellectual club.[10] John Carey rails against just that aspect of Modernism: that it deliberately shut out the plain or common reader. 'The principle around which modernist literature and culture fashioned themselves was the exclusion of the masses'.[11] The paradox of *Ulysses*, a novel that has at its centre a 'common' man whose inner life is rendered in as much intimate detail as any Proustian character, lies in its exclusion of a reader like Bloom himself through 'the complexity of the novel, its avant-garde technique, its obscurity ... More than any other twentieth-century novel, it is for intellectuals only.'[12] Of course, the more elite an institution appears, the more enthusiastic are its would-be members to join. Even at a banal commercial level, the sale of 'limited edition' objects by the Franklin Mint represents a much-diluted form of this aspiration (coupled with the hope of a rise in resale value, the motivation Rainey pinpointed for purchasers of the 1922 edition of *Ulysses*).

The desire to acquire 'cultural capital', to use Bourdieu's term, through purchase and knowledge of particular texts, should not be underestimated.[13] After all, its acquisition results in status and distinction. Although Bourdieu's work was based on the 1960s, and therefore doubly germane to this essay, and remains fairly undifferentiating between different forms of cultural capital, the application of the general principle seems sound throughout the period from 1922 to 1969 as *Ulysses* moves from avant-garde to classic.

> The boundary of the [literary] field is a stake of struggles, and the social scientist's task is not to draw a dividing line between the agents involved in it by imposing a so-called operational definition, which is most likely to be imposed on him by his own prejudices or presuppositions, but to describe a *state* (long-lasting or temporary) of these struggles and therefore of the frontier delimiting the territory held by the competing agents.[14]

The struggles are between cultural forms and activities that are: avant-garde, legitimized initially by a formative critical coterie and then further validated by adoption within education; 'bourgeois', where other forms of legitimization operate such as reviews in particular newspapers or book club adoption; and popular, such as *Tit-Bits* or *Sweets of Sin*. It is the avant-garde that contributes most in terms of cultural capital. It is the avant-garde that is consecrated within the academy.

What John Carey does not factor sufficiently into his account of Modernism, that Bourdieu (and the whole field of book history) underlines, is the role of publishers: the latter wish to cash in on that desire to acquire cultural capital;

they respond to and stimulate the market for the avant-garde. 'For book historians ... the most important implication of Bourdieu's analysis is that these contests between rival positions do not involve only writers.'[15] Joseph Kelly too, while writing from a predominantly American perspective, offers an emphasis upon 'the packaging of the book' as an influence on the differing reception of *Ulysses*, while not going the full length of crediting the publishers with the calculated knowledge of particular markets that enabled them to design the packaging best targeted to those very markets.[16] Penguin in the UK deliberately transformed *Ulysses* into a classic institutionalized within higher education; its status was underpinned by the nature of the material book – its binding, cover, size, price, series, pagination guide, afterword, its promotion and publicity.

Contracts I

Penguin 3,000 in 1969 was the fourth major UK incarnation of Joyce's novel. The first three, the Bodley Head editions of 1936 and 1937 and the Bodley Head edition of 1960, as expensive hardbacks with a clear emphasis upon design, were more clearly targeted at the members or aspirant members of the avant-garde club. In other words, the physical books themselves, and the circumstances of their publication, illustrate the movement from avant-garde work, and collectable art object, to classic deriving its status from the academy.

The eventual contract for these initial Bodley Head editions was issued in May 1936, signed by Joyce in the presence of the British Pro-Consul in Paris. This contract licensed the Bodley Head to issue a limited edition of *Ulysses* but Joyce was insistent that the phrase 'for private circulation only' should not appear anywhere in the book. This phrase could be interpreted, from the other pornographic contexts in which it was found, as an acknowledgement of the similarity of *Ulysses* to such salacious material and that Joyce could not countenance. Indeed, the contract, signed by Joyce at the British Embassy in Paris on 22 May 1936, further specifies in clause three, at the author's instigation, the respectable newspapers in which *Ulysses* was to be advertised.[17] This list for the Bodley Head edition of 1936 – *Times Literary Supplement*, *New Statesman*, *Observer* and *Sunday Times* – can be compared to the list detailed by the Penguin marketing department in 1968 and discussed below.

For Lane, the production of a limited rather than a general edition was an act of expediency in order to facilitate a publication in which he had invested so much personal effort and money. It also reinforced the appeal to the interlinked and targeted markets, of the avant-garde and prurient, through its very price and limited nature. The return from the limited edition alone would cover his family's risk and he had confidence in the nature of those markets to lead to a profit over and above his investment.

Joyce, for his part, was adamant in his desire to avoid harmful association, the implication that this was a surreptitious, under-the-counter publication, but he was won over by the argument that the limited edition was a necessary manoeuvre to minimize the risk of legal action. Joyce was unwilling to make any compromises, either to the integrity or the presentation of his work, in order to accomplish UK publication and remained throughout the negotiations conscious of the need to retain control over all aspects of the publishing process. Yet Joyce had also been shaken by Roth's pirating of *Ulysses* in the US; he was afraid of a UK pirated edition being produced and reacted testily to any overtures from 'non-established' publishers; and he was concerned that copyright could not be claimed in a book found obscene. Paul Léon, his secretary and *de facto* business manager, acted as the mouthpiece for Joyce's concerns:

> Whilst all these [established] publishers are waiting to see the weather change, it seems some enterprising plagiator [*sic*] will succeed in bringing out an edition which will frustrate Mr Joyce as well as his publishers from their deserved earnings. This is a situation which cannot be tolerated any longer, you will I'm sure agree with me. I am instructed and will do my best to prevent such an eventuality and will stop before nothing to frighten people unscrupulous to attempt it. But I am not sure I can achieve it. It seems to me it is high time for a British publisher to [word deleted] his courage and attempt to do finally what he has not dared to do yet.[18]

For both parties, however, only a trade edition of *Ulysses* would be the culmination of their long-held ambitions. Although Joyce was creatively engrossed in the work-in-progress that was to lead to *Finnegans Wake*, he was still eager to see the novel appear legitimately in the UK as a standard publication under a reputable imprint. The 1936 contract had bound the Bodley Head to an ordinary trade edition no later than 1 October 1937 with a penalty of £10 for each day's delay in publication payable to Joyce up to a maximum of £1,000. The financial situation of the Bodley Head had, in the meantime, deteriorated to the point of receivership in November 1936 before voluntary liquidation in January 1937. Allen Lane and his brothers lost all links with the Bodley Head, carrying away from the wreckage the two projects for which they had had to take personal responsibility: Penguin Books and the limited edition of *Ulysses*. The former went from success to success; the latter quickly sold out.

The contract for the trade edition remained one of the assets of the Bodley Head and was reaffirmed in a further contract between the company and Joyce in July 1937. The irony of the situation would not have been lost on Lane. When the trade edition appeared in September 1937, no prosecution took place. A hastily-convened meeting between the Home Office, the Director of Public Prosecutions, and the Attorney-General in November 1936 had concluded with a decision that no action should be taken.[19] In other words, Lane's last gamble for the Bodley Head proved to be a winning bet and, moreover, the profits from the trade edition helped to re-float a restored Bodley Head and bring it back to financial solvency. Joyce's royalty account with John Lane, the Bodley Head, dated 25 August 1937 reveals that sales from 1 February 1937 to 30 June 1937 of eighty-six copies of *Ulysses* sold at three guineas brought in an income of £270.18.0. A royalty of 15 per cent equalled £40.12.8 which, less a 10 per cent commission paid to Pinker of £4.1.3, resulted in a net payment to Joyce of £36.11.5.[20]

Yet a trade edition should not, and did not from these figures, imply a mass or popular market. The price being charged effectively put the novel beyond the pockets of the majority and its dubious status led to a reluctance on the part of public libraries to stock it. *Ulysses* remained the purchase of the avant-garde, the aspirant intellectuals and those interested in pornography. If this satisfied Joyce (and there is no reason to suggest it did), it did not sit well with Lane's drive to democratize culture and learning. His primary vehicle for this was Penguin Books, established in 1935:

> imbued with the ideal that everyman should be able to make an enlightened rational decision, [Penguin] strove to disseminate knowledge and ideas to a wider public ... [Allen Lane's] development of the quality paperback, promotional skills, and appetite for ideas converted the hopes of idealists into a marketable commodity.[21]

The whole thrust of Lane's career in publishing was to make the best available to the mass. 'There can be little doubt that the Penguin Book group of publications is the most important and influential British publishing venture of this century, for it has penetrated various economic and sociological barriers to bring new reading to hundreds of thousands of people'.[22]

Contracts II

No wonder then that Lane should also wish to see *Ulysses* appear as a Penguin paperback. Penguin made an initial overture for the novel in 1958 to the Bodley Head which still held the UK rights, including paperback rights. Given Allen Lane's earlier connection with the book, Penguin thought it would be appropriate to issue a paperback *Ulysses* as part of the company's silver jubilee celebrations in 1960. Max Reinhardt, the then Managing Director of the Bodley Head, declined the offer politely as plans were afoot for a new re-designed and re-set Bodley Head edition which did in fact appear in 1960. Reinhardt suggested that the paperback rights might become available for Penguin's fiftieth birthday, that is, in 1985. Potential purchasers would have been limited for twenty-five years to those who could afford the hardback edition at 35*s*., many times the cost of any paperback (the 1960 *Lady Chatterley's Lover* cost 3*s*. 6*d*. and the 1961 Vintage paperback edition of *Ulysses* in the United States of America was $2.95). The request was renewed by Tony Godwin, Penguin's editor-in-chief, in 1961 and again rejected.[23]

However, the Bodley Head decided not to wait that long after all and in 1967 offered the British paperback rights in *Ulysses*, asking five interested paper-back houses, including Penguin, to make offers. Allen Lane had to have it and his final, successful offer was at that time the highest price to date ever paid for paperback rights. His was not the highest bid but Reinhardt decided to rec-ommend it to the Joyce Estate. The prestige of Penguin, compared to its rivals, was an unquantifiable but substantial consideration in this decision. Penguin's starting point in the negotiations had been an advance of £10,000 for the first year, followed by a guaranteed minimum of £3,000 per annum for ten years, set against a 10 per cent royalty: a total advance of £40,000 as opposed to the £75,000 eventually agreed. Reinhardt's view was that this was a niggardly offer, particularly in the light of estimated sales of 200,000 in the first year of publica-tion and 75,000 in each of the subsequent ten years of the proposed agreement. Reinhardt initially held out for a royalty of 12.5 per cent that Penguin thought 'crippling'. By the end of 1967, however, the terms had been agreed: an advance of £15,000 upon signature of the contract, a further advance of £6,000 a year for a subsequent ten years, against a royalty of 10 per cent on the first 250,000 cop-ies sold and of 12.5 per cent above that.[24] If a classic, then a commercial classic.

Reinhardt waited until he had confirmed the approval of the Joyce Estate, then administered by the Society of Authors, before the contract was signed. It was probably at the urging of the Joyce Estate that the standard contract was altered so that 'the design of the jacket shall be at the approval of the Gran-tor which approval shall not unreasonably be withheld.'[25] It was further agreed to postpone publication until 23 April 1969 to match Lane's half-centenary in publishing. Publication of the paperback would be as a joint imprint with the Bodley Head. However, unlike the 1960 Bodley Head hardback edition, this Penguin would seek out the new market of 'the student'.

Size and Price Matters

In the initial negotiations with the Bodley Head, Allen Lane's concerns had been less about the amount of the advance and more about the level of royalty against which it was to be set. 12.5 per cent on every copy sold would add about 1*s.* to the selling price and 'since our sale is likely to be largely to students, a low price is essential'.[26] Lane won the argument: the 12.5 per cent royalty only took effect after the initial 250,000 copies had been sold, that is, when the point at which Penguin had covered its fixed costs had been reached and the price could be kept low. Indeed, in an internal production memo that same month, it was clearly stated that 'AL hopes that we shall be able to publish the book at 10/6'. The production staff at Penguin exercised their ingenuity to be able to stick to that target price and indeed brought it down to 10s. One immediate thought was to use the Bodley Head setting: this would be cheaper, even taking into account the fee payable to the Bodley Head; it would result in a standard-sized Penguin; and it would eliminate the need for meticulous proofreading. However, this would have created a very thick book (some 952 pages), one that the paperback bindings of the day would have found difficulty in handling. Besides which, and this was the key factor, a larger format publication would not only solve the practical production difficulties but it would provide the edition with greater status.

Penguin already had such a format that was used for their more upmarket, and academic, Peregrine imprint. The standard Penguin was 181 x 111 mm and the Peregrine format was 198 x 129 mm. Other titles published as Peregrines were non-fiction and included: published in 1969 *The World of the Shining Prince: Court Life in Ancient Japan* by Ivan Morris, *Social Origins of Dictatorship and Democracy: Lord and Peasant in the Making of the Modern World* by Barrington Moore, *Berkeley* by G. J. Warnock, *The Historical Novel* by Georg Lukács; in 1970 *The Liberal Imagination* by Lionel Trilling; and in 1971 *A Selection from 'Phoenix'* by D. H. Lawrence and *In the American Grain: Essays* by William Carlos Williams. The eventual extent of the Penguin edition of *Ulysses* in the Peregrine format was 720 pages. Hans Schmoller, the company's designer, provided four costings based on the different formats and on different type sizes. He also calculated for each costing the number of copies needing to be sold to recover the advance. For the format eventually chosen 753,000 copies had to be sold at 10s. to earn the total advance of £75,000.[27]

Large sales were anticipated: 250,000 copies were produced for initial publication; a further 70,000 after six months and a further 100,000 in two batches by the end of 1970 (420,000 copies in all). The estimated profit, after the initial royalty payments to the Bodley Head, was £19,926 if all 420,000 copies were sold. The principled stand on price for a student market could also lead to a modest profit for the company. If there was a risk attached to the Penguin publication of *Ulysses* in 1969, it was that the novel would be treated as *Lady Chatterley's Lover* had been after the famous trial in 1960, finding a public ready to purchase the book in expectation of sexual titillation rather than as a serious work of literature. To ensure the serious minded, and student, market would demand clear packaging and promotion of the status of the novel as a classic of world literature. Penguin had previously published a paperback edition of Stuart Gilbert's *James Joyce's 'Ulysses'*. This book, originally produced by Faber, had been of course an early attempt to provide the novel with a scholarly and respectable patina. In 1969 Penguin decided to re-issue it in the Peregrine format as a companion volume to the novel itself.

Academic Scaffolding

Greater status, as well as a clear pitch for the student market, could also be gained through use of a suitable academic to lend the edition a scholarly imprimatur. Richard Ellmann was the obvious candidate. Ellmann's biography of Joyce, first published in 1959, had been reissued in paperback in 1965 to further critical acclaim. Such was his prestige, and Penguin's desire to 'capture' him for the edition, that Oliver Caldecott, Penguin's editor-in-chief in London, actually phoned – at a time when transatlantic phone calls were still exceptional and expensive – Ellmann at Northwestern University where he was then working (in early 1968 just before his move to Yale). Ellmann agreed to write 7,000 words on the history of *Ulysses* at a rate of $200 per 1,000 words.[28] The deadline for the essay was 1 May; Ellmann delivered on 29 April. The material was incorporated into the new edition at the back. An account of the genesis of the novel is followed by a catalogue of the Homeric parallels and the afterword concludes with its erratic publishing history and official reception.[29]

Ellmann's approach to the origins of the novel yokes together fiction and biography, setting out the correspondences, the 'generative clusters', between the stories told in *Ulysses* and the recorded events of Joyce's life. The origin of Leopold Bloom lies in the 'Good Samaritan' act of kindness by Alfred Hunter to Joyce himself. The novel exemplifies Stephen/Joyce's view that literature is 'the eternal affirmation of the spirit of man'. In other words, Ellmann's afterword summarizes the material of and repeats the principles/practices of his earlier biography: chiefly, as Ira Nadel has commented, a movement from the novel to the life, the use of the fiction not just to understand but to mythologize the life.[30] Ellmann's belief that Joyce transformed the raw material of his life into something transcendental in fiction leads him to view that life as itself a form of fiction. Moreover, the life was an ahistorical fiction, concerned with the inner development of the self rather than its engagement with the history that had happened or was happening around it. Ellmann's Joyce, here in the Penguin edition as in the earlier biography, may have found a sympathetic readership in the post-1968 generation of students more concerned with development of their inner selves than with engagement, more interested in Herman Hesse or Jonathan Livingston Seagull or Robert Pirsig. Be that as it may, Ellmann's afterword provided Joyce's novel with suitable academic scaffolding. The purpose of such scaffolding is reinforced by Genette:

> The two functions of attributing high value and supplying critical commentary are by no means incompatible ... the second may be the most effective form of the first – most effective because indirect, the commentary bringing to light 'deep' meanings that are for that very reason rewarding.[31]

A fortuitous opportunity was presented for additional academic endorsement of the edition. Fritz Senn wrote to Penguin in 1969, sometime before the April publication date, in order to collect all the launch material for his archives in Zurich. He also asked Penguin to support the second James Joyce Symposium to be held that June in Dublin; in return, the Symposium would provide the occasion for Penguin to promote and sell its own publications, including the forthcoming *Ulysses*.[32] Penguin duly seized on the offer, promoting the edition and supporting the Symposium through advertising in the printed programme. Penguin was participating, as with its commissioning of Ellmann, in what Dr Senn was later to term 'the Joyce Industrial Evolution'.[33]

Ellmann's '*Ulysses*: a short history' also featured prominently in the carefully worked out and tightly controlled promotional plan for the launch of the Penguin edition. 30,000 additional and separate copies of this essay were printed and bound to promote the edition, particularly to an academic market. Penguin Education, a distinct imprint within the company, circulated copies to its mailing list of the influential, that is, to compilers of compulsory reading lists. The advertising campaign concentrated on the sort of respectable outlets that academics and even students might be expected to read: the *Guardian*, *The Times* (Saturday Review) and the *Sunday Times*, the *Daily Telegraph*, the *TLS*, *New Statesman*, *New Society*, *Listener* and *Spectator*.

Reception

Press reaction on publication was excellent from Penguin's perspective. Peter Fuller, writing in the *City Press*, echoed Ellmann in claiming that the novel's paperback publication indicated how far we had moved 'towards the liberal humanism of which he [Joyce] is literature's greatest advocate'. Fuller also noted that

> the acceptance of his [Joyce's] book by the mass marketers, and the nation-wide campaign which will back it up, means that the sensibility of the age has shifted ... the fact that it will be on sale on every railway bookstall, on every newspaper stand, and probably before long in vending machines as well, means that the climate has changed.[34]

Some qualification of this optimistic vision could be found in the *Liverpool Post* of 2 May 1969, which reported that *Ulysses* would not be obtained on the open shelves of the city's public libraries: 'Adults can borrow it upon request, but anyone under 21 is required to show that they have their parents' or teacher's approval for reading the book'.

Other newspapers picked up the spin of the Penguin publication of *Ulysses* bringing Allen Lane's career full-circle.[35] The anonymous reviewer in the *Scotsman* wrote a paean of fulsome praise to the novel's celebration of 'the commonness of the common man'. 'James Joyce's long, difficult and extraordinary novel is at last freely available in a shape and at a price which means that anyone can buy it who really wants it.'[36] The notice in *The Times* drew attention to the 'respectable clerical black' of the cover; it could also have noted – but did not – the use of the Augustus John drawing on the back cover complete with full pseudo-academic provenance.[37] *The Times* did remark other elements that reinforced the book's particularly academic respectability such as the table providing page correspondences to the Bodley Head edition of 1937. Ellmann had noted,

> how much consternation it causes in the cloistered halls of Joyce scholarship when the pagination of *Ulysses* is changed, thus putting out of date all references in all books up to the time of the new edition. I hope you are going to retain the 1960 pagination rather than disobliging pedantic readers.[38]

Penguin's solution was to offer a conversion table similar to that in the Bodley Head 1960 edition. In itself this must be an index of the predominance by then of the academic among the novel's readership.

Conclusion

For few, if any, reviewers were issues of obscenity or morality a concern. This may be seen by way of contrast with the Vintage edition of eight years previously where the reader, before encountering Joyce's text, was confronted by an introduction by Morris Ernst, the chief defence lawyer in the novel's prosecution twenty-seven years before, and by the reprinted decision in that case by Judge John M. Woolsey. In the Vintage edition, the trial is still being fought and *Ulysses* presented as a novel found not guilty of being obscene. The Penguin edition states that we have moved on from that old struggle and must approach *Ulysses* on different, reverential terms as a modern classic of Literature (with the capital L). With the publication of the 1969 Penguin edition of *Ulysses* a movement in the reception of the novel was confirmed: not by accident but by design, not as a result of factors external to that edition but as a consequence of a series of clearly framed publishing decisions.

The black-covered paperback sat comfortably alongside the similarly designed members of the Penguin Classics series that had been inaugurated in 1946 with E. V. Rieu's translation of Homer's *Odyssey*.[39] Joyce had achieved posthumously the mixture of respectability and wide circulation, if not readership, denied to him in the UK during his own lifetime. However, the 'targeted reader' had now become in the Penguin 1969 edition the academic and his or her students. The targeting involved the deliberate use of the non-textual elements of the material book to create a larger readership and a greater commercial opportunity than previous editions had recognized. If we deny to Penguin, and to publishers as a group, the understanding of the working of paratext (and the insight into interpretive communities of readers) that this case study (and others) reveals, then, like the Ordnance Survey in Donegal, we are guilty of an unjustified dismissal of those who have long known and shaped this territory.

11 THE SOUND OF LITERATURE: SECONDARY SCHOOL TEACHING ON READING ALOUD AND SILENT READING, 1880–1940[1]

Ton van Kalmthout

In his *History of Reading*, Steven Roger Fischer suggests that written communication of the type already familiar in increasingly large parts of the world will eventually eliminate traditional methods of oral information transfer in their entirety. Moreover, '[T]his may be soon'.[2] Where specifically *literary* texts are concerned, Fischer and other historians of Western reading habits believe that the switch to predominantly silent reading occurred as early as 1900. The latest historical example of this cited by Fischer and, before him, Alberto Manguel, is the use of lectors in North American cigar factories – people who were still being collectively paid to read aloud to labouring workers as late as the 1920s.[3] The question is, however, whether this was indeed the last brief revival of the custom. Where the teaching of Dutch literature is concerned, the preference for reading aloud certainly survived in the initial decades of the twentieth century and this was, after all, how a large proportion of the new and future readership was trained to consume literature.

This paper questions Fischer's interpretation of developments and shows that the custom of reading aloud, which flourished in the nineteenth century, remained alive and well throughout the whole first half of the twentieth century.[4] Indeed, it may even have remained the dominant practice. Surprisingly, it seems that the silent reading of literary texts was far from the general rule even as late as the beginning of the Second World War. Although my evidence relates to the situation in the Netherlands, I assume that this was not unrepresentative of practice in Europe generally.[5] The conclusions are based on the results of initial exploratory research which examines the main teaching journals of the period and textbooks designed for use in Dutch general secondary schools.[6] The pupils that used them were aged twelve to eighteen and would at that time have included some who were already training to be teachers.

I will begin with a brief discussion of the contemporary concept of the reader and then go on to talk about the practice of reading aloud and recitation of texts in schools between 1880 and 1940. In doing so, I will touch on certain circumstances which encouraged an oral approach to literature at that time. Finally, I will discuss the effect of attempts to introduce the silent reading of literary texts in schools. Needless to say, this is a somewhat broad and sometimes general account; there had been, of course, for centuries an intellectual elite who were accustomed to read silently. What I discuss here is the general public and what they were taught at school in the decades around 1900 as the best way to approach the reading of literary texts.[7]

The Reader as a Performer

As Robert Darnton has noted, 'for most people throughout most of history, books had audiences rather than readers. They were better heard than seen'.[8] Dutch educationalists of the nineteenth century and the first half of the twentieth century also knew this. They illustrate that the history and practice of reading in Holland has a material context that can reveal much regarding policy, audiences and cultural attitudes to literature. In other words, reading as a concept – specifically reading aloud – has a physical reality in textbooks, presumably requiring individual, silent absorption. That encounter with material theories of reading encourages a performance of reading that is unrecoverable unless it has been recorded technologically. What survives in the manuals, then, is evidence that formal reading both presumes and requires a physical audience (of viewers and listeners) in order to be successful.

As late as 1932, a manual on the mother-tongue teaching of Dutch stated that '[I]n schools, reading is still, although no longer exclusively, taken to mean first and foremost "reading aloud"'. Where a text was first learned by heart, 'reading' was sometimes also understood to mean reciting – an activity in which, according to the same teaching manual, teachers of Dutch trained their pupils 'more or less regularly'.[9] Viewed in this light, the teaching of reading also meant teaching pupils to speak and listen, since lessons usually required the class to listen to texts being read aloud. Indeed, some people felt that it should also include teaching pupils to write, since the texts that were read provided pupils *en passant* with examples for the composition of their own texts. In other words, the teaching of reading in secondary schools interfaced with virtually the entire field of mother-tongue teaching.

People also saw links to other disciplines. For example, they thought that reading aloud and recitation were closely related to acting, although clearly distinct from it: apart from the occasional expressive gesture, the reader was not expected to move around and was advised to concentrate entirely on the text.

Various experts on reading also identified a similarity between reading and singing, or music-making in general. Just as a musician transformed the notes written by the composer into an audible melody, so the reader turned the author's printed words into sound. According to one leading Dutch literary historian, poetry and music were alike in that 'similarly, a person has a full grasp of a beautiful poem only when he has heard the lines recited in the manner they deserve or, better still, has recited them himself'.[10]

The reader was seen as an intermediary between the author and his public. His or her job was to convey the author's thoughts and emotions. Since the author was thought to have literally 'translated' these, first into phonemes and then into the written word, the reader's task was to translate the written word back into phonemes in order to evoke in the audience the thoughts and feelings originally experienced by the author.[11] Only a good oral presentation of the text could allow it to 'show itself in its true form and reveal its full power'.[12] Accordingly, classroom anthologies had titles that explicitly urged pupils to listen: for example, Aafjes's *Buig de stem!* ('Modulate your Voice!') and Horsten's *Stemmen van verre en dichtebij* ('Voices from Far and Near').

Reading Aloud in Schools

A 'technical' mastery of the rudiments of reading and speaking was not, therefore, a sufficient preparation for the oral presentation of literary texts. Far from it; secondary schools had to teach their pupils how to read aloud or recite works of literature in the approved manner. Due attention had to be paid to matters like speed, emphasis, articulation, received pronunciation, phrasing and intonation, the volume and timbre of the voice and the reader's attitude and posture. The two last points were of particular concern in the originally German 'torso position' theory. This held that:

> the manner in which we write, speak, paint, walk etc. encompasses certain elements that are connected with our physical and mental selves and are reflected in the position of the muscles of the torso. To enter into another person's work, or to recite it, one must therefore necessarily assume the same torso position as that person, something which many people do without even realising it.[13]

A rough rule of thumb for the 'art of reading' was that the words being spoken should not sound like a written text. This involved more than simply literacy skills; in order to present the text well to an audience, the reader also needed empathy and some knowledge of the world. In this respect, the teacher usually helped his or her pupils by providing an oral introduction to the text. It was then read aloud or recited by members of the class, and perhaps also by the teacher himself. Finally, the pupils summarized the content of the text, analysed it, or elucidated it in response to various questions and assignments.[14] This approach was already customary in the nineteenth century[15] and its aim was to promote comprehension, which was regarded as an essential precondition for proper reading. The analysis always had to focus first and foremost on the aesthetic aspects of the text. To teach the subject properly and set a good example, the teacher needed to possess outstanding skills in public reading and recitation. Where such skills were lacking, schools might hire actors and other paid performers to fill the gap. The increasing professionalization of the practice of declamation from around 1900 led such performers to discover literature education in schools as a platform for their skills.[16] Even the most celebrated amongst them exploited this market, not only by performing in schools, but also by writing manuals[17] and by accepting private lectureships in the art of recitation at the universities of Leiden and Amsterdam (which then trained a proportion of the Dutch teaching corps). After World War I, moreover, great things were expected of that exciting new invention, the gramophone.

The gramophone offered a wonderful opportunity to produce exact voice recordings exemplifying the ideal oral delivery of prose and poetry. Edison had demonstrated this in the first sound recordings he made with the phonograph, an invention patented in 1878. The recordings included his own reading of popular rhymes, pieces of middlebrow poetry, some lines of Shakespeare's *Richard III* as well as passages from the Bible with funny interruptions.[18] In 1913, a Dutch specialist in Romance languages reported enthusiastically on the inventions and experiments being made at the phonetics institute of the Sorbonne, including the voice recordings being made on the Pathé company's new gramophone discs. He expected the gramophone to become an indispensable aid not only to modern language teaching, but also to the teaching of public reading and recitation. Pathé had already put together 'entire courses', complete with sample performances.[19] By that time, the professional stage circuit in the Netherlands had also spotted this gap in the market: professional performers had started producing recordings of recitations as far back as the turn of the century.

Teachers and pupils needing to know more about the art of reading and recitation could also refer to a host of books published in the Netherlands and elsewhere, ranging from scientific tomes on physiology and phonetics to handy manuals full of exercises and practical tips.[20] If they wanted concrete examples but had no access to sound recordings, they had to rely on experimental systems of notation, which used musical notes or other kinds of symbols to indicate how texts should be spoken (as in Figure 11.1).

Figure 11.1: Some experiments using notation from C. L. Merkel, *Physiologie der men-schlichen Sprache (physiologische Laletik)* (Leipzig: Otto Wigand, 1866), pp. 412–28, reproduced in J. B., 'De kunst van lezen', with a postscript by d.B. [= T. H. de Beer], in *Noord en Zuid*, 3 (1880), pp. 236–44, between pp. 243 and 243.

What kinds of texts were suitable for classroom use? Teachers were repeatedly urged to use complete texts, rather than the extracts often given in anthologies. This was probably to ensure maximum comprehension. For the same reason, they were advised to use texts that were not too difficult for their pupils, although they were told that this should not be a barrier to the use either of classics of the early modern period or of the most up-to-date contemporary literature. One school of thought held that prose was more suitable for novice readers than poetry, on the grounds that poetry was more difficult to understand and to speak. One option was to read contemporary verse as prose. But other experts opposed this, arguing that metre and rhyme should be given their full due and should not be glossed over. Moreover, they advised, certain types of poetry (especially lyric poetry) should be read in a rather musical way. Even so, pupils themselves tended to opt for more formal verse when they had to recite it or read it in public. However, one experienced teacher cautioned that it was better not to give pupils a completely free choice of texts, in view of the 'monstrosities' they sometimes selected.[21]

It is unclear whether there were differences in the kinds of text preferred by the two sexes, but there was certainly a view that women were particularly well-equipped to read literature aloud:

> Their organs are by nature more flexible and better suited to imitation than those of men ... What a pleasure it must be for a girl to soothe the afflictions of a sick father or sorrowing mother with a few well-read pages from a good book.[22]

However, it was equally important for boys to acquire such reading skills during their secondary education; they needed them for careers involving reading and speaking in public, for example in the church or the law. Indeed, such skills were even necessary for working-class boys with little prospect of entering such professions as they would help them fulfil their civic duties in a society that was becoming increasingly democratic. For example, they might need to address meetings of their own clubs and associations.[23]

It was generally thought that the best time to start acquiring a proper reading technique was during the initial years of secondary education, before children entered puberty and became self-conscious.[24] At that stage, literature was used as an aid to the teaching of reading skills. Later on, the emphasis switched and the reading skills that pupils had acquired were used as an aid to the study of literature. However, the aim was certainly not to produce professional performers: as one teacher wrote, '[A] secondary school pupil can be said to know how to read if he can understand a text of moderate difficulty and read it aloud reasonably well to other people'.[25]

A Time of Quiet Aesthetic Enjoyment

The continuing concentration on reading aloud was undoubtedly linked to the examination system. For example, the examination syllabus prescribed '*[A]ccurate* and *natural* reading with a cultivated accent': '[C]andidates must show that they understand what they have read and can express their thoughts about it with some degree of ease'.[26] To demonstrate this, each candidate was given one piece of prose and one piece of poetry. These had to be read aloud over a period of ten minutes and then the candidate had to answer questions about them. The examiner assessed both the candidate's understanding of the texts and the correctness of his intonation. Another reason for the continuing dominance of reading aloud lay in an educational reform movement known in the Netherlands as the *Nieuwe Richting* (or 'New Direction'). In part following the example of German educationalists and in part inspired by a group of reform-minded Dutch artists, this movement embraced the idea that language is not so much *written* as *spoken*: its adage was 'Language is sound'.

With this slogan in mind, one classroom anthology of this persuasion indicated not only the emphases to be placed on the words but also the pitch at which the texts were to be read. It even sought to perfect the reader's intonation by giving directions like 'robustly', 'diffidently', 'drawlingly', 'mockingly', 'scornfully', 'irritably', 'gaily', 'encouragingly' and 'fearfully'.[27] The pupils were expected to decide what the texts in the anthology should sound like in an ordinary speaking voice and in their own language.[28] In fact, there was the general emphasis on making texts sound like spoken language and not reading them too literally. 'Reading properly means getting away from the written word', noted one Dutch literature professor in 1940, adding that this involved 'restoring the intended sounds, the right emphasis, the natural rhythm and the authentic intonation'.[29] One of the anthologies designed to encourage pupils to do this was actually called *Los van de letter* (that is, 'Away from the Written Word').[30]

So the New Direction movement advocated a more natural delivery and opposed the declamatory style of reading and reciting which, it felt, dated from a past era in which poetry was also more rhetorical in nature. That style was now regarded as outmoded, inartistic and melodramatic. The movement also criticized professional performers: it was true that literary texts needed to be heard, but there were strong objections to the sometimes affected and unnaturally sonorous delivery of professional artistes. This was felt to call too much attention to the performance itself and to distract from the intrinsic beauty of the text.

Shortly after 1900, a Dutch literature specialist, Aleida Nijland, conducted a remarkable experiment aimed at encouraging pupils in the fifth year of a girls' non-classical grammar school to 'read properly'. Every week she had six or seven pupils copy out one or two pages from the first part of a recently published three-volume epic about Bragi, the Norse god of poetry.[31] For homework, they had to learn the extracts by heart and then come back and recite them in class. Between them, the girls eventually recited the entire 107-page volume. Nijland reported that she never heard any complaint that the task was too hard, and she immediately went on to set up a similar project for the third and fourth-year pupils. She felt that the text she had chosen was ideal for this kind of exercise: '[T]he entire work is permeated by something so healthily Germanic, so robust, it is so true, simple and sincerely felt and the language – it rings and sings with *joie de vivre*!'.[32]

Such verbal ecstasies were by no means extraordinary among disciples of the New Direction movement, who felt that an instinctive and emotional approach to literature produced a truer artistic appreciation of it than any purely intellectual analysis of its meaning. The most important thing was for the reader to share the mood and emotion conveyed by the beauties of the text. '[O]ur reading period should be a time of quiet aesthetic enjoyment' wrote one Dutch specialist on mother-tongue teaching in 1938.[33] This explains the emphasis on rhythm and sound at that period: the musicality of the text had a direct influence on the emotions of the individual reader. But this need not be a bar to a traditional study of fine literature. Then, wrote another specialist, 'moments may occur when a sacred silence falls over the class, when teacher and pupils are transported by a shared emotion and they are all absorbed in the enjoyment of the same happy moment'. When a piece of poetry or prose had moved pupils in this way, he added, 'it is almost sacrilege to bring them down to earth with objective comments or explanations of the text'. Lyric poetry, in particular, should not be interrupted by explanations or by correcting the reader; that would undermine 'the keenly felt emotion' of the moment. It was better for the teacher to postpone discussion of the text to a later lesson and only then to analyse 'the occasion for the feelings expressed and felt, the beauty of their expression, the aesthetic appeal, freshness and effectiveness of the imagery, the musicality of the language, features of the rhythm, etc'.[34]

A Bracing Plunge

When these recommendations were made in 1932, reading aloud had been a matter of debate for some years. One section of the educational world objected to the trend towards speaking contemporary lyric verse in the most poetic way possible, in order to intensify the experience of the author's mood and emotions. If the pupil was reading to himself, there was in any case a lurking danger of developing decadent reading habits. As one writer warned in 1889,

> Reading should be a pleasure, but an ... elevated and exhilarating pleasure, not a weakening and demoralising form of relaxation; a pleasure of the kind that follows a brisk

walk or a bracing plunge, in no way reminiscent of the torpor-inducing caress of a warm bed or the languor that follows some intoxicating titillation of the senses.[35]

Likewise, it was regarded as hysterical or histrionic to lose oneself in the moods and emotions of the author: the practice of reading aloud could all too easily lead to a superficial wallowing in the sound of the text. But whether a reader read aloud or to himself or herself, it was important to maintain an active attitude, physically as well as mentally. To lounge on the sofa with a book was to fail to show proper respect to the author. Moreover, an unhealthy and soporific attitude did the reader no favours, either physically or mentally. To keep a clear mind, he should be literally active in his reading; for example, in 1890 one writer suggested that readers might perform occasional gymnastic exercises with their arms and legs, but should in any case always have a pencil and paper to hand so that they could take notes for later consideration.[36]

The criticism of reading aloud that was voiced some forty years after that date was summed up by the educationalist Jacob Leest as follows. While it might be true that authors translated sounds into phonemes, they did so only in their minds. Since they did not physically produce the sounds while they were writing, there was no reason to do so when reading; it was merely an *idée reçue* that all literary texts needed to be spoken out loud. A text might have greater impact when declaimed by a professional but, even then, the physical declamation of the text distracted from the private experience of its beauty. It tended therefore to be a barrier to aesthetic enjoyment rather than an aid to it. It was fully accepted that professional artistes and teachers needed to be trained to recite texts well. But since the majority of pupils would go into other professions, there was no justification for spending valuable classroom time on reading aloud, especially when the results in the examinations were invariably so disappointing. A drastic reduction was needed in the time spent teaching the skill in schools. Reading aloud was useful as an exercise in reading technique, to improve pronunciation and to check comprehension but teachers should minimize the instructions they gave concerning intonation, phrasing and so on. Moreover, they should only ask pupils to read texts aloud if the material had been specifically written for that purpose, as in the case of extracts from stage works, perorations or poetry written for recitation.[37]

Opponents of the practice argued that readers who did not have to think about translating the text into sound were better able to concentrate on its content and so to empathize with it. Because it was a purely intellectual exercise, silent reading allowed the reader to think about the text at the same time: after all, understanding the content of the text required thought rather than action. This view was bolstered by recent developments in education. In 1929, following examples in the English-speaking world, silent reading was introduced in

Dutch elementary education, where it was found to encourage textual insight and understanding, as well as independent thought.[38] Even while it was being perfected,[39] the new method unleashed a debate in Dutch mother-tongue teaching as elsewhere.[40]

In 1934, a Dutch language specialist and educationalist called Langeveld advocated silent reading in *secondary* education.[41] He sometimes called it 'mental reading' but in the educational world of his day it also became known as 'active' reading, because the method aimed to activate the process of individual thought by making pupils answer lists of questions referring both to internal features of the text and to external references. It was hoped that this would teach them to ask themselves such questions when reading literature in later life. The new method of teaching reading and comprehension quickly proved to be a useful means of assessing intelligence, and hence a good means of selection. In 1938 it looked as if this fact would spell the end of the dominance of reading aloud in the education system. In that year, the minister of education decreed that the admission examinations for secondary schools were to include silent reading tests. A year later, silent reading had filtered through into the school-leaving examinations and by 1940 reading aloud no longer featured in the examinations for aspirant head teachers.[42] Such changes might be expected to have far-reaching consequences for the methods used to teach reading in schools. For the time being, however, this was only partly the case.

'Chewed Up and Spat Out'

Despite the Depression, the 1930s saw an explosion of new literacy textbooks, sometimes with explicit titles like *Actief lezen* ('Active Reading') and *Denkend lezen* ('Mental Reading').[43] These silent reading textbooks were a prelude to the eventual sidelining of reading aloud and recitation in the classroom. However, even around 1940, few teachers were keen to see the change. A year earlier, somebody moderately in favour of silent reading could detect 'no very great enthusiasm for the new method among teachers' and added that it was 'still far from generally accepted in our schools'[44] The main objection related to the quality and number of questions set on texts.

The silent reading method was thought to deluge pupils with questions and assignments, obscuring their view of the author and his work. Sometimes quite literally so: one writer complained that 'these questions proliferate like parasites around the fragment of prose or poetry on which they thrive, ruining the visual impression of the page'.[45] Another cited the example of a twenty-four-line Impressionist poem, about which one of the most popular silent reading textbooks of the time asked pupils no fewer than fifty-seven questions, some of which questions were furthermore so banal that they demonstrated a 'spinsterish nosiness'.[46] The more serious charge was that the questions frequently failed to elucidate the text; they referred merely to things the person setting them happened to know and therefore provided at most an insight into *his* mind, rather than that of the author. Some opponents felt that this was a presumptuous way to deal with the products of great minds. It only made pupils thumb through the text in search of answers and leave it 'chewed up and spat out'.[47] Nor was there any real hope that pupils would learn to ask themselves such questions spontaneously. This was partly because the silent reading method was thought to be too cerebral: because the questions emphasized abstract thought and logic, the method made the approach to literary texts too one-sidedly intellectual.

Conclusion

So what can we conclude from this quick overview of a piece of educational history? Certainly that the custom of reading aloud and recitation survived – in the Netherlands at least – for longer than recent historians of the subject have suggested. Throughout the first half of the twentieth century, future consumers of literature were still being taught a traditional, mainly oral way of relating to literature that had been passed down from previous centuries. Changing ideas in the arts and education at the end of the nineteenth century encouraged rather than threatened the survival of the practice, as (to some degree) did new technology like the gramophone. The resilience of this oral reading culture was put to the test around 1930 when educational reformers began to advocate the teaching of silent reading. Yet, if we are to believe one of my sources, their advocacy may actually at times have been counterproductive. 'It is a fortunate fact', he wrote, 'that the recent interest in the subject of reading aloud has prompted a resurgence of the practice. This forms a welcome counterweight to the overenthusiasm with which silent reading has been propagated.'[48]

It was not until some time in the second half of the twentieth century – I suspect during the 1960s[49] – that silent reading would finally gain the upper hand in the teaching of literature in Dutch secondary schools.

Could this be one reason why (at least in the Netherlands) there has been a steady decline in schoolchildren's interest in literature and hence why the reading of literature now occupies only a marginal position in the secondary school curriculum? There has certainly been no decline in the normal human desire for literary entertainment. Where the approach to literature in schools over recent decades has been almost entirely reduced to silent reading, potential readers *out* of school seem to be filling the gap in their cultural repertoire with oral presentations of literary works. These days there is a greater audience than ever before for stage and musical versions of the classics, professionally presented reading tours by authors, poetry slams, radio book readings and audio books on CD-Rom, and so on: in other words, a strong demand for literature translated into sound.

12 INTERMEDIALITY: EXPERIENCING THE VIRTUAL TEXT

Órla Murphy

text ... one word to rule them all and in the darkness bind them.[1]

The internet and electronic media are edited and in turn edit and shape our experience of reading texts today. At present there is much interplay of a variety of media within cultural practice, in particular within reading, shaping and editing text or texts in their multiplicity of forms. This vibrancy and activity is balanced with an earnest revaluation of early digital textual scholarship and its methodologies which can serve to inform and guide the humanities community in its efforts to pursue its contemporary intellectual agenda.

A recent call for papers for a scholarly journal reflects this engagement:

> [I]ntermediality is associated with the blurring of traditionally ascribed generic and formal boundaries through the incorporation of digital media into all forms of cultural practice and with the presence of one or more media in the space and form of another medium.[2]

I suggest that a reappraisal of our boundaries and of our definition of what it means to be an audience for and creators of these texts needs to occur so that the perceived separation between technology and the humanist disciplines merges into a more successful scholarly partnership.

Intermediality in contemporary culture has led to the creation of new sites of encounter between texts in their burgeoning multiplicity of forms and the media through which, by which, and on which, they are represented. However subjectively you may define text, ideas and neologisms abound as intertexts, hypertexts, acts of remediation, and multimediality erupt in neon in the corner of a web browser even though the reader thought the popup blocker was switched on.

Old divides no longer exist as they once did. The caricature of the luddite humanities scholar has dissipated. Humanities scholars are active participants in an ever more elaborate textual environment from libraries to museums, from textual analysis, through to natural language processing (NLP), philological and linguistic work. We are creating digital editions and theorizing the virtual text. Most of the audience reading this paper read and write from their mobile phone or email while away from their base. New pixellated pages are read from hand-held devices that hold our personal text messages, today's rune sticks, and emails that are the memoirs of the future. Scholarship 2.0 and the active engagement of the scholarly community with social networking sites redefine the communica-tion of the text outside of the 'ivory tower'. A more reflective experience of these technologies and, in particular, an awareness of how 'invisible' web editors are working behind the text visible on the screen, encoding the text we write and see written, limiting what we might perceive at first glance to be open, limitless searches, is necessary to engage fully both with the technology and the audience.

The word 'intermediality' in the title of this paper encapsulates much of the networked potential and challenge that is humanities scholarship within the digital realm. As a medievalist I was trained in the multivalent world of biblical exegesis, where a text is deliberately constructed with many layers of meaning, for a variety of audiences, for a wide range of 'end-users'. The manuscript text in a sacred codex, aesthetically rendered in purple and red, became performatively active as part of a liturgical ritual carried aloft in a procession of singers in incense smoke. These texts with a complex exegetical, liturgical and aesthetic relationship are foregrounded in textual scholarship and codicology today and provide a use-ful paradigm for the polyvalency of cybertexts in their variety of forms.

Multimedia is not new – the technology simply changes place with that which has gone before. The inherent intermediality of an *alpha* or *omega* sung aloud or inscribed on parchment, vellum, glass and stone over centuries is an example of a dynamic engagement with a radically intermedial text that resists stasis and engages with new technology as it arrives. If understanding is the apprehension of objects in their context, a true experience of such texts makes demands of many readers at many levels of experience. 'New digital media are not external agents that come to disrupt an unsuspecting culture. They emerge from within cultural contexts and refashion other media'.[3] Intermediality is not new, but it serves as a metaphor for the interdisciplinary scholarly endeavour required when editing texts; as part linguist, part palaeographer, part historian, part art-historian we endeavour to create a single unity from a multiplicity of sources – our new text, a new edition. This is nowhere more evident than in the need for an interdisciplinary approach to creating good, scholarly digital *e*-ditions, where we need to learn new skills to facilitate knowledge transfer and sustain our knowledge work collaboratively with others.

Our present experience of the text, when it is newly shaped for us by yet another machine, mediated through browsers, on a variety of screens, offers simultaneously a new instance of what it means to be a reader in a digital age, whilst holding onto familiar signs and signifiers, the words, and the narrative. It would be a mistake however to think that nothing has changed, that figure and ground remain constant, that what we see is what we get. Further examination reveals that that is not the case – and that yet again in a transgressive way – 'the medium is the message'.[4]

The very idea of 'experiencing' a text that is not wrapped in the familiar and comforting surroundings of a cover, with flyleaves, perhaps a bit of dust – and a vague musty smell that reminds us of particular situations, will be anathema to some, for whom curling up with a good book is the only way to enjoy or experience narrative, or to explore a scholarly argument. Much of the discussion in this collection has centred on very personal, private experiences of texts, manuscripts, discoveries. Of course a digital text cannot approximate those experiences nor does it attempt to. The machine may for many interfere with the pure response of the reader used to a book in their hand, but just like any new technology there are tremendous gains as well as losses. The previous polarity between cultures of reading, analogue or digital, no longer exists as the exponential potential for digital scholarship in areas of research, pedagogy, publication, conservation and preservation have been revealed.

Ever since the 1930s when Fr Robert Busa began his epic endeavour to create a wordlist of Thomistic material, when he heard about these new machines – computers – and thought they might be of help and called in to IBM and described his problem, asked for help and received it, much of the scholarship in this field has been concerned with the structure of the data: in this case the text.

Vannevar Bush, writing in 1945, and referred to in George Landow's book *Hypertext 3.0*, also saw that the problem lay with information retrieval, 'the matter of selection'[5] – and that the primary reason that those who need information and cannot find it lies in turn with inadequate means of storing – structuring, arranging and tagging information. Unstandardized, undocumented categorization is transient. Structures and standards are needed to fix in some form, on these new pages, the fluctuating concepts of meaning and context. Over fifty years later in the digital deluge that 'matter of selection' is still prescient. How do we negotiate a path through the digital silos of knowledge? How do we create meaningful links? As Azcárate and Tötösy ask: '[D]oes intermediality represent the potential for innovative artistic creation, publishing and education? Or, on the contrary is it an attack on aesthetic purity or academic rigour?'[6]

The virtual or digital text offers new ways of reading, searching, cataloguing, understanding, comparing, judging, and even intellectually enjoying the textual experience. Digital texts and the discoveries possible owing to the scholarship of others are made more accessible owing to machines, owing to technology. A new world of possible readings opens as texts are made available. As scholars within the discipline it is necessary then to try to understand what we require of our digital experiences so that we may engage in a meaningful way with new technologies. We have had millennia to equip ourselves with our understanding of the page, since the invention of the codex its *modi operandi* have been refined and are now intrinsic to our daily acts of reading. Within the print apparatus we know where the index is located, or where the table of contents will be, but stripped of its cover and made available online what structures exist to enable us to understand this new recension of the book on an unpaginated digital screen?

Fundamental to this endeavour is knowledge of how the digital world works, a fundamental e-literacy that goes beyond word processing and email and searching the world wide web. Without such a fundamental e-literacy beginning a digitization project is much like getting into a car without having had lessons – or taking the theory test! We may have seen cars, we may like the car and find it comfortable, but driving it is a different story. We need to understand about gears, indicators, the clutch, accelerator and brake, the steering wheel. Fortunately, we do not need to be able to build an internal combustion engine; we do not need as scholars to be able to program in Perl, or to understand the Unix environment. But we do need to understand the basics, so that we realize the difference perhaps between driving a small one-litre engine and one that is turbo-charged.

We are now in the next generation of humanities computing where the initial excitement about primary access to large resources and searchable CD-Roms is over. We all have had the experience of going to a site or database and expecting something other than what the site delivered. There are lessons to be learned also about sustainability and access: we can still read the text of the Ellesmere Chaucer, but cannot open a floppy disk on a new netbook. We can reclaim the scholarly experience of the text by looking again at editing. All of the issues raised for printed matter in this edition also persist for digital works. How do we edit? How best do we organize information in a meaningful way? What is the purpose of the newly remediated textual object? In a rush to get the good-looking, graphics-led websites up so that the funding body sees that the project is active, fundamental issues can remain unaddressed. The interface is important; how will the user navigate the space? Does it aesthetically communicate the vision of the project? These attributes of the text are outside the usual closed system of scholarly publishing. The scholar provides a text of their work. Publishers publish it. Digital scholarship and publishing call for a radical reengagement with that mode by both scholar and publisher. It has gains for both sides: in a digital environment an active engagement with readers who comment on the text in an online peer review – a realtime discussion forum or through a comments feature – is possible. A scholar can present a text to the publisher in extensible markup language (XML) ready for structuring through extensible stylesheet language [family] transformations XSLT removing an amount of work for the publishing editor. There are studies underway that measure the impact of free digital editions on their print analogues and, while not a constant, often the print edition benefits from an online freely available text.[7]

The most popular web editing/encoding language for the web is called HTML, hypertext markup language, and now the more robust XHTML.[8] A web page is most likely to be marked up in HTML, although readers will not see the code: it is embedded in the text that appears on screen, shaping the way in which that text is experienced. HTML describes a way in which an editor prepares or presents a page (marks it up) in order that the page may be read in a meaningful way by web browsers (it is machine readable text). This encoding embeds within the text 'tags' that tell the browser how to interpret the text. For example: there is a head element and a body element giving information about the different parts of the page as it will be seen by the viewer/reader, the head contains the title information, the body the information about the text – font size, type, colour, background, when a paragraph begins or ends, when to insert line breaks, when to insert links. HTML is very useful and easy to learn, but has proven to be insufficient for the demands of much scholarship. It is concerned with the appearance of the text on a page and not the meaning of the words displayed. There are not enough tags in it to support the detailed kind of retrieval and search functions required at a high level by scholars.

As a very simple example: take a look at any web page; click on 'view' in your toolbar, and view the page source in your browser. This is what the machine 'reads' and it is different to the page initially viewed. Note also the metadata tags for description and keyword: these tags are the tags most likely to be read by search engines 'checking' texts for keywords when someone performs a search, since search engines do not search the full text of a long document. 'Search engine optimisation' techniques have meant that this is no longer the case as search engines will also search a cascading style sheet or CSS if present, and also use the number of links on a page as a way of ascertaining its importance/rank in a hit list. These analyses are changing daily as engines seek to optimize their output.

What this means is that if a document is 'published' on the web, and that document is not adequately 'tagged' within the metadata, it may well be more or less invisible to search engines and only visible to those to who know the URL. If I were to publish this paper on the web, and not insert 'intermediality' anywhere in the meta tags (and not in the title), the paper might never be found! In other words, without understanding the embedded editing – the tagging and meta content – the page may never be open, accessible or read, a fruitless endeavour.

Given the demands of humanities computing, and through the collaborative work of many scholars, the Text Encoding Initiative (TEI) has answered many of the questions asked of encoding by subject specialists.[9] The TEI has an extensive list of tags compared to HTML, and most importantly that list is extensible. How does that make a difference? The TEI sets a standard – eliminating text and search inconsistencies across a variety of platforms, archives and databases as many things had developed in an ad hoc fashion without thinking of potential future linkages. The TEI aims to give the publisher and scholar alike a framework from which to draw, and in XML an extensible markup language that structures content in a variety of ways. There is freedom within the structure.

Sperberg-McQueen and Burnard's description of the TEI as preparing a pizza is often cited:

> The base – essential ingredients – tomato and cheese, and one or more toppings.
>
> The base is a tag set chosen from the following: prose, drama, verse, dictionaries, spoken texts, and terminological data. The essential ingredients are the core tags – a set of tags common to all text types and including features like abbreviations, names, quotations and bibliographic citations and the header tags that provide metadata for documenting the text...Toppings would be optional extras like links to other documents, critical apparatus, and transcription of primary sources, and simple forms of linguistic analysis[10]

Other new developments in markup language include XML, so that in order to future proof a database/archive/project it would probably be best to bear this in mind and use an XML compatible version of TEI best practice to TEI P5. The TEI is an international standard endorsed by a host of international scholarly projects as a way forward for publishing, for creating a new experience of the virtual text and a new audience for dynamic, collaborative engagement in the field of textual scholarship.

So how we experience the text, how it is presented to us by editors, how we might inform best practice in presenting material on the web requires a familiarity not just with the research subject but also with available technologies in order to judge suitability and serve our intellectual objectives. An excellent recent example is the quartos.org project where quarto versions of Shakespeare's plays may be compared online, side by side, even though physically they are held in repositories on different continents.[11] Another digital publication is at NINES. org where through rigorous peer review the online site is an example of best practice and has succeeded in achieving recognition from the Modern Language Association.[12] The online audience is encouraged to view the primary source material and make their own collection and comparison. This view of scholarship is fluid and different to a closed audience of a few readers of expensively produced short run texts. The possibilities are further explored by Rotunda Press's digital publication of Bryant's edition of Herman Melville's *Typee*, where the scholarly sites of interest are examined and exposed for critical assessment.[13] New technology using the TEI also allows for a variety of rescensions of a text to be made available online. Susan Schriebman's 'versioning machine' allows the viewing of many versions of a text, an image of the writer's notebook, an initial draft, the first publication, on one screen, complete with XML and TEI encoding, all visible, all documented, all available for exploration.[14]

With even a simple understanding of markup language – of what can be encoded in a text or texts so as to encourage them to reveal their mystery – a scholar becomes an active participant in an emerging editorial community, with broadband speeds, wireless access and laptops we are no longer confined to desks behind block walls. In defining their needs scholars shape the production of the technology that further enables them to enrich their research and teaching lives.

NOTES

The following abbreviations have been used throughout the notes:

ODNB   *Oxford Dictionary of National Biography*

Allen, Griffin and O'Connell, 'Introduction'

1. D. F. McKenzie, 'The Sociology of a Text: Orality, Literacy and Print in Early New Zealand', in *The Book History Reader*, ed. D. Finkelstein and A. McCleery (London: Routledge, 2002), pp. 189–215, on p. 190.
2. See the work of Gérard Genette, especially *The Architext: An Introduction* (Berkeley, CA: University of California Press, 1992); *Palimpsests: Literature in the Second Degree* (Lincoln, NE: University of Nebraska Press, 1997); and *Paratexts: Thresholds of Interpretation*, trans. J. Lewin (Cambridge: Cambridge University Press, 1997).
3. J. J. McGann, *The Textual Condition* (Princeton, NJ: Princeton University Press, 1991), p. 12
4. J. J. McGann, *Black Riders: The Visible Language of Modernism* (Princeton, NJ: Princeton University Press, 1993), p. xi.
5. S. Eliot and J. Rose (eds), *A Companion to the History of the Book* (Malden, MA: Blackwell, 2007), p. 1.
6. W. Iser, 'Interaction between Text and Reader', in Finkelstein and McCleery (eds) *The Book History Reader*, pp. 391–96; S. Fish, 'Interpreting the *Variorum*', in Finkelstein and McCleery (eds), *The Book History Reader*, pp. 450–8.
7. McGann, *The Textual Condition*, p. 15; J. J. McGann, *A Critique of Textual Criticism* (Charlottesville, VA, and London: University Press of Virginia, 1992), p. xxii.
8. Witness several important, discipline-shaping publications, including Eliot and Rose (eds), *A Companion to the History of the Book*, Finkelstein and McCleery (eds), *The Book History Reader* and its companion volume by the editors, *An Introduction to Book History* (New York: Routledge, 2005). Several important developments, such as the establishment of dedicated series on the history of the book by major publishing houses, the continued success of the journal *Book History* (Penn State Press), and the rapid growth in academic courses, have ensured that the history of the book is now recognized by the academy as a relevant field of inquiry across disciplines.
9. C. Tilley, et al. (eds), *Handbook of Material Culture* (London: Sage, 2006), p. 1.
10. Ibid.
11. Ibid., p. 3.

12. R. Darnton, 'What is the History of Books', in *The Book History Reader*, ed. Finkelstein and McCleery, p. 10.

13. Ibid., p. 12.

14. T. Adams and N. Barker, 'A New Model for the Study of the Book', in *A Potencie of Life: Books in Society*, ed. N. Barker (London: British Library, 1993), pp. 5–43.

15. Darnton, 'What is the History of Books?', p. 12.

16. J. Derrida, 'Some Statements and Truisms about Neologisms, Newisms, Postisms, Parasitisms, and Other Small Seismisms', in D. Carroll (ed.), *The States of Theory* (New York: Columbia University Press, 1989), pp. 63–94.

17. R. Altick, *The English Common Reader: A Social History of the Mass Reading Public, 1800–1900* (Chicago, IL: University of Chicago Press, 1957).

18. J. Radway, 'A Feeling for Books: The Book of the Month Club, Literary Taste and Middle Class Desire', in Finklestein and McCleery (eds), *The Book History Reader*, pp. 469–81.

19. J. Rose, 'Re-Reading the English Common Reader', in Finkelstein and McCleery (eds), *The Book History Reader*, pp. 324–39, on p. 333.

20. See http://www.open.ac.uk/Arts/RED/ [accessed 4 August 2010].

21. W. St Clair, *The Reading Nation in the Romantic Period* (Cambridge: Cambridge University Press, 2004), p. 5.

22. '"Thing to Mind": The Materialist Aesthetic of William Morris', in *Black Riders*, pp. 45–76, on p. 45.

23. McKenzie, 'The Sociology of a Text', pp. 205–31; P. Gaskell, *A New Introduction to Bibliography* (Oxford: Clarendon Press, 1972); D. Pearson, *Books as History: The Importance of Books Beyond their Text* (London: British Library, 2008); A. Rota, *Apart from the Text* (Middlesex: Private Libraries' Association, 1998).

24. The conferences were hosted in April 2007 and 2008 by the *Making Books, Shaping Readers* project at University College Cork's School of English.

25. *Independent*, Tuesday, 27 July 2010.

26. *Independent*, Friday, 30 July 2010.

27. D. Lodge, 'My Joyce', in *Write On: Occasional Essays, '65–'85* (London: Penguin, 1986), pp. 57–69, on p. 62.

1 Thompson, 'The Memory and Impact of Oral Performance'

1. For the roots of this development in the earlier Middle English period see M. T. Clanchy, *From Memory to Written Record* (Oxford: Oxford University Press, 1993); on the impact of literacy on primarily oral early literary cultures see W. J. Ong, *Orality and Literacy: The Technologizing of the Word* (New York: Routledge, 2002); for mnemonics as a tool for teaching and understanding in both oral and written medieval literary culture, see M. Carruthers, *The Book of Memory: a Study of Memory in Medieval Culture* (Cambridge: Cambridge University Press, 1990).

2. On this development generally, see J. Coleman, *Public Reading and the Reading Public in Late Medieval England and France* (Cambridge: Cambridge University Press, 1996).

3. The underlying motif is explored in many of the essays in L. Hellinga and J. B. Trapp (eds), *The Cambridge History of the Book in Britain, vol. 3, 1400–1557* (Cambridge: Cambridge University Press, 1998); see also E. Eisenstein, *The Printing Press as an Agent*

of Change: Communications and Cultural Transformations in Early Modern Europe, 2 vols (Cambridge: Cambridge University Press, 1979).

4. The issue is explored in some detail in the provocatively-entitled *Book Production and Publishing in Britain, 1375–1475*, edited by J. Griffiths and D. Pearsall (Cambridge: Cambridge University Press, 1989); for the slightly earlier period where things are much less clear cut, see N. Morgan and R. M. Thomson (eds), *The Cambridge History of the Book in Britain, vol. 2, 1100–1400* (Cambridge: Cambridge University Press, 2007).

5. For a recent stimulating attempt to challenge the traditional paradigm, see J. Simpson, *Reform and Cultural Revolution, 1350–1547* (Oxford: Oxford University Press, 2002).

6. General Prologue, l. 25; all quotations and line references from L. D. Benson (gen. ed.), *The Riverside Chaucer*, 3rd edn (Oxford: Oxford University Press, 2008).

7. See K. J. Harty, 'Chaucer in Performance', in S. Ellis (ed.), *Chaucer, An Oxford Guide* (Oxford: Oxford University Press, 2005), pp. 560–75. Other essays in this volume explore methodologically-diverse and up-to-date critical approaches to reading Chaucer in the twenty-first century.

8. *Canterbury Tales*, 1 (A) l. 3171.

9. On the presumed dialogue between authorial intention and reader response that this interpretation implies, see R. Chartier, 'Figures of the Author', in *The Order of Books: Readers, Authors, and Libraries in Europe Between the Fourteenth and Eighteenth Centuries*, trans. L. G. Cochrane (Stanford, CA: Stanford University Press, 1992), quoted in R. Evans, 'Chaucer's Life', in Ellis (ed.), *Chaucer, an Oxford Guide* (Oxford: Oxford University Press, 2005), pp. 9–25, on p. 10. On the social relationship of the earliest English audiences to the poet, see P. Strohm, *Social Chaucer* (Cambridge, MA: Harvard University Press, 1989).

10. See also J. Coleman, 'Aurality', in P. Strohm (ed), *Middle English, Oxford Twenty-First Century Approaches to Literature* (Oxford: Oxford University Press, 2007), pp. 68–85.

11. General Prologue, ll. 672–3.

12. See the bibliographical gloss on these lines in M. Andrew, *A Variorum Edition of the Works of Geoffrey Chaucer, II: The Canterbury Tales, The General Prologue, Part One B, Explanatory Notes* (Norman, OK: University of Oklahoma Press, 1992), pp. 538–41.

13. For a sensible overview of this aspect of the transmission of short courtly verse see J. Boffey, *Manuscripts of English Courtly Love Lyrics in the Later Middle Ages* (Woodbridge, Suffolk: D. S. Brewer, 1985); also J. Boffey, 'Middle English Lyrics and Manuscripts', in T. G. Duncan (ed.), *A Companion to the Middle English Lyric* (Woodbridge, Suffolk: D. S. Brewer, 2005), pp. 1–18.

14. Useful bibliographical survey and further extensive references in A. S. G. Edwards, 'Middle English Inscriptional Verse texts', in J. Scattergood and J. Boffey (eds), *Texts and Their Contexts, Papers from the Early Book Society* (Dublin: Four Courts, 1997), pp. 26–43.

15. See, for example, A. Taylor, 'Fragmentation, Corruption, and Minstrel Narration: the Question of the Middle English Romances', *Yearbook of English Studies*, 22 (1992), pp. 38–62, and J. J. Thompson, 'Popular Reading Tastes in Middle English Religious and Didactic Literature', in J. Simons (ed.), *From Medieval to Medievalism* (Basingstoke: Macmillan, 1992), pp. 82–100.

16. Seminal discussion and references in R. Hanna, 'Analytical Survey 4, Middle English Manuscripts and the Study of Literature', *New Medieval Literatures*, 4 (2001), pp. 243–64; see also see the recent stimulating comments on the practice and study of western palaeography in M. B. Parkes, *Their Hands Before Our Eyes, a Closer Look at Scribes* (Aldershot: Ashgate, 2008).

17. See S. Nichols, 'Philology and its Discontents', in W. D. Paden (ed.) *The Future of the Middle Ages: Medieval Literature in the 1990s* (Gainesville, FL: University Press of Florida, 1994), pp. 113–41. My usage of this useful term to assist in this exercise does not endorse the attempts that have been made to totalize the experience of such an event as a power discourse. For discussion of the utility of mapping manuscript culture through micro-historical study, see J. J. Thompson, 'The Middle English Prose *Brut* and the Possibilities of Cultural Mapping', in M. Connolly and L. R. Mooney (eds), *Design and Distribution of Late Medieval Manuscripts in England* (Woodbridge, Suffolk: D. S. Brewer, 2008), pp. 245–60.

18. For the best such recent approach to this problem, dealing with large-corpus texts that enjoyed wide circulation in late medieval manuscript culture, see M. G. Sargent, 'What do the Numbers Mean? Observations on Some Patters of Middle English Manuscript Transmission', in Connolly and Mooney (eds), *Design and Distribution*, pp. 205–44. For the challenge manuscript cultures of all ages can pose to definitions of book history, see Darnton, 'What is the History of Books?', pp. 3–26.

19. See W. Scase, 'Imagining Alternatives to the Book: The Transmission of Political Poetry in Late Medieval England', in S. Kelly and J. J. Thompson (eds) *Imagining the Book* (Turnhout: Brepols, 2005), pp. 237–50; also W. Scase, *Literature and Complaint in England, 1272–1553* (Oxford: Oxford University Press, 2007).

20. See discussion and references in J. Boffey, '"Cy ensuent trios chanunceons": Groups and Sequences of Middle English Lyrics', in G. D. Caie and D. Renevey (eds), *Medieval Texts in Context* (Turnhout: Brepols, 2008), pp. 85–95.

21. J. Boffey and J. J. Thompson, 'Anthologies and Miscellanies: Production and Choice of Text', in Griffiths and Pearsall (eds), *Book Production*, pp. 279–315; see also A. Gillespie, *Print Culture and the Medieval Author: Chaucer, Lydgate, and their Books, 1473–1557* (Oxford: Oxford University Press, 2006).

22. All references and quotations of the different extant versions of this material are taken from H. M. R. Murray (ed.), *The Middle English Poem, Erthe upon Erthe, Printed from Twenty-Four Manuscripts*, Early English Text Society o.s. 141 (London: Kegan Paul Trench Truebner, 1911).

23. 'Remember O man that thou art dust and unto dust thou shalt return.'

24. Murray, *Erthe upon Erthe*, pp. xiv–xxxviii.

25. For a facsimile see Murray, *Erthe upon Erthe*, unnumbered plate opposite title page (where the folio is erroneously numbered); also N. Ker, intro., *Facsimile of British Museum MS. Harley 2253*, Early English Texts Society o.s. 255 (London, 1965), fol. 59v.

26. For bibliographical references and discussion of these items in the broader context of the other manuscript contents, see the essays by M. Kuczynski, J. Scattergood and S. Fein, in S. Fein (ed.), *Studies in the Harley Manuscript, the Scribes, Contents, and Social Contexts of British Library MS Harley 2253* (Kalamazoo MI: Medieval Institute Publications 2000).

27. *contra* Murray, *Erthe upon Erthe*, p. xv.

28. Murray, *Erthe upon Erthe*, pp. xxxv–xxxviii.

29. See J. J. Thompson, 'Mapping Points West of West Midlands Manuscripts and Texts: Irishness(es) and Middle English Literary Culture', in Scase (ed.), *Essays in Manuscript Geography*), pp. 113–28.

30. All quotations and line references to the Harley 913 texts are to W. Heuser (ed.), *Die Kildare-Gedichte: die Ältesten Mittelenglischen Denkmäler in Anglo-Irischen Überlieferung*

(1904; Darmstadt, 1967). For more up-to-date bibliographical discussion, see A Lucas (ed.), *Anglo-Irish Poems of the Middle Ages* (Blackrock, Dublin: Columbia Press, 1995).

31. Thus Heuser, *Die Kildare-Gedichte*, p. 167.

32. For extensive development of this idea, see Lucas, *Anglo-Irish Poems*, pp. 187–94. On the idea of granting pardon by privilege rather than more formally through authorised church procedures see R. N. Swanson, 'Pardons for Every Occasion', in R. N. Swanson, *Indulgences in Late Medieval England* (Cambridge: Cambridge University Press, 2007), pp. 23–76.

33. S. Wenzel (ed.), *Fasciculus Morum: A Fourteenth-Century Preacher's Handbook* (Philadelphia, PA: Pennsylvania State University Press, 1989).

34. S. Wenzel, *Preachers, Poets, and the Early English Lyric* (Guilford, NJ: Princeton University Press, 1986); also the more nuanced account in Marilyn Corrie's essay in Fein, *Studies*, pp. 427–44.

35. Murray, *Erthe upon Erthe*, p. 49.

36. Brief description of the very miscellaneous religious and didactic items in the manuscript in R. Hanna, *The English Manuscripts of Richard Rolle: A Descriptive Catalogue* (Exeter: Exeter University Press, 2010), pp. 34–6. MS Ii.4.9 also contains several extracts from Nicholas Love's *Mirror of the Blessed Life of Jesus Christ* and from the opening chapter of the Middle English *Meditationes de Passion,* so it is not difficult to appreciate that, in this part of the manuscript, a premium has been set on the meditative value for early readers of contemplating the material reality of their own mortality and of Christ's passion through a spectacular recognition of corporeal frailty set alongside the assurance of Christ's continuing bodily presence through the blessed sacrament.

37. On Hill's deployment of a variety of sources for the items he copied, including printed material, see H. Collier, 'Richard Hill – a London Compiler', in E. Mullally and J. J. Thompson (eds), *The Court and Cultural Diversity* (Woodbridge, Suffolk: D. S. Brewer, 1997), pp. 319–29; also A. Gillespie, 'Balliol MS 354: Histories of the Book at the End of the Middle Ages', *Poetica* (Tokyo), 60 (2003), pp. 47–63.

38. Quoted from the 1598 edition by Murray, *Erthe upon Erthe*, p. 38; see also J. Stow, *A Survey of London*, ed. C. L. Kingsford, 2 vols (London, 1925), vol. 1, p. 327, and recent discussion in A. Appleford, 'The Dance of Death in London: John Carpenter, John Lydgate, and the *Daunce of Poulys*', *Journal of Medieval and Early Modern Studies*, 38 (2008), pp. 285–314.

39. See F. Warren and B. White (eds), *The Dance of Death, Early English Text Society o.s. 181* (London: H. Milford 1931).

40. The main scribe of MS R.3.21 also copied the bulk of Cambridge, Trinity College MS R.3.21; see L. R. Mooney, 'Scribes and Booklets of Trinity College, Cambridge, MSS R.3.19 and R.3.21', in A. J. Minnis (ed.), *Middle English Poetry: Texts and Traditions, Essays in Honour of Derek Pearsall* (Woodbridge, Suffolk: D. S. Brewer, 2001), pp. 241–66.

2 Connolly, 'Print, Miscellaneity and the Reader in Robert Herrick's *Hesperides*'

1. I am grateful to Tom Cain, Meiko O'Halloran and the anonymous reader at Pickering & Chatto for their comments on earlier drafts of this essay.

2. R. Herrick, *Hesperides: or, The Works both Humane & Divine of Robert Herrick Esq* (1648; Menston: Scolar Press Facsimiles, 1968), sig. C2r. All quotations are taken from this edition, a copy of BL E.1090. All quotations have been checked against the collation of all existing copies carried out for the new edition of Herrick's works. See T. Cain and R. Connolly (eds), *The Complete Works of Robert Herrick*, 2 vols (Oxford: Oxford University Press, forthcoming).

3. Gaskell, *A New Introduction to Bibliography*, p. 131; J. Moxon, *Mechanick Exercises on the Whole Art of Printing*, ed. H. Davis and H. Carter (1683–4; London: Oxford University Press, 1962), p. 350.

4. Herrick, 'To a Friend', sig. Z3r.

5. I am grateful to the reader for Pickering & Chatto who drew my attention to these puns.

6. See for example, 'To Vulcan', sig. R6r; 'To his booke', Sig Y2r; 'To his Booke', sig. Aa2r.

7. T. S. Eliot, 'What is Minor Poetry', *Of Poets and Poetry* (London: Faber & Faber, 1957), pp. 39–52.

8. J. Creaser, '"Times Trans-shifting:" Chronology and the Misshaping of Herrick', *English Literary Renaissance*, 39:1 (2009), p. 171.

9. A. B. Coiro, *Robert Herrick and the Epigram Book Tradition* (Baltimore, MD: Johns Hopkins University Press, 1988) and more recently S. Pugh, 'Ovidian Exile in the *Hesperides*: Herrick's Politics of Intertextuality', *Review of English Studies* 57 (2006), pp. 733–65.

10. For an account of how the search for a similar narrative has distorted the critical reception of the work of another Royalist, occasional poet, see M.-L. Coolahan, '"We Live by Chance, and Slip into Events": Occasionality and the Manuscript Verse of Katherine Philips', *Eighteenth-Century Ireland/iris an dá chultúr*, 18 (2003), pp. 9–23.

11. Dobranski argues that Herrick was unable to guarantee 'the precise ordering of his poems' and was unlikely to have overseen the printing process. Nonetheless there are clear signs of authorial involvement, such as the deliberate separation of obvious companion poems like the 'Sack' poems and the 'Oberon' poems. The dedications to the Oberon poems also play on their placement in the volume. Herrick tells the dedicatee of 'Oberon's Feast' (sig. K4v), Thomas Shapcott that 'we'll see the Fairy Court anon', a reference to 'Oberon's Palace' on sig. N8v. 'Oberon's Palace' is immediately followed by a third poem to Shapcott that remarks 'I've paid thee, what I promis'd', a sequence of poems whose narrative of promise and deferral points to authorial involvement in the collection's organization and incidentally to mini-narratives within the collection that both recreate poetic occasions and removes the poems from their original context of composition as a dialogue with Simeon Steward. See S. Dobranski, *Readers and Authorship in Early Modern England* (Cambridge: Cambridge University Press, 2005), pp. 155–63, 159.

12. L. C. Martin (ed.), *The Poetical Works of Robert Herrick* (Oxford: Clarendon Press, 1956), pp. xv–xvi

13. For Herrick's history within manuscript-based literary coteries see M. O'Callaghan, '"Those Lyrick Feasts, made at the *Sun*, the *Dog*, the triple *Tunne*": Going Clubbing with Ben Jonson', in T. Cain and R. Connolly (eds), *Lords of Wine and Oile: Community and Conviviality in the Work of Robert Herrick* (Oxford: Oxford University Press, forthcoming); N. McDowell, 'Herrick and the Order of the Black Riband: Literary Community in Civil War London and the Publication of *Hesperides* (1648)', in Cain and Connolly (eds), *Lords of Wine and Oile*, (Oxford: Oxford University Press, forthcoming). T. Raylor, *Cavaliers, Clubs and Literary Culture: Sir John Mennes, James Smith, and the Order*

of the Fancy (Newark, NJ: University of Delaware Press, 1993); Creaser, "'Time's Trans-shifting'". On manuscript culture more generally see H. R. Woudhuysen, *Sir Philip Sidney and the Circulation of Manuscripts, 1558–1640* (Oxford: Clarendon Press, 1996).

14. Coolahan, 'We Live by Chance', p. 12. I am using the term relatively loosely here to argue that Herrick's poetry is prompted by the literary values of such environments rather than to suggest that every poem he composes is intended to commemorate a specific occasion or event.

15. W. Wall, *The Imprint of Gender* (Ithaca, NY: Cornell University Press, 1993), p. 25.

16. See A. Marotti, *Manuscript, Print and the English Renaissance Lyric* (Ithaca, NY: Cornell University Press, 1995), p. 2.

17. This formulation is influenced by Creaser's argument about the relationship between tenor and vehicle in Herrick's poetry in his 'Herrick at Play', *Essays in Criticism*, 56 (2006), pp. 324–50.

18. Wall, *The Imprint of Gender*, pp. 1–22; M. T. Crane, *Framing Authority: Sayings, Self and Society in Sixteenth-Century England* (Princeton, NJ: Princeton University Press, 1993); A. Marotti, *John Donne: Coterie Poet* (Madison, WI: University of Wisconsin Press, 1986).

19. A. Marotti and M. Bristol (eds), *Print, Manuscript and Performance: The Changing Relations of the Media in Early Modern England* (Columbus, OH: Ohio State University Press, 2000); J. Lowenstein, *The Author's Due: Printing and the Prehistory of Copyright* (Chicago, IL: Chicago University Press, 2002).

20. Crane, *Framing Authority*, p.175.

21. Although he does not read Herrick's practices within this tradition, Gordon Braden's account of Herrick's treatment of classical sources describe in detail how Herrick uses fragments of his source texts within his poems. G. Braden, *The Classics and English Renaissance Poetry: Three Case Studies* (New Haven, CT: Yale University Press, 1978).

22. R. Ingram, 'Robert Herrick and the Making of *Hesperides*', *Studies in English Literature 1500–1900*, 38:1 (1998), pp. 127–47.

23. Dobranski, *Readers and Authorship in Early Modern England*, pp. 170–3. Dobranski does not note that such tags are used in manuscript miscellanies to indicate incomplete poems. A truncated version of Herrick's 'A Country Life: To his Brother Master Thomas Herrick' subscribed 'caetera desunt' is contained in John Cave's miscellany, New York Public Library MS Arents S 191, ff. 18–20 (rev).

24. A. Smyth, *'Profit and Delight': Printed Miscellanies in England, 1640–1682* (Detroit, MI: Wayne State University Press, 2004).

25. See for example the kinds of readers depicted in 'To his Book', sig. N2r.

26. This also complicates the position proposed in Creaser's recent article, 'Chronology and the Misshaping of Herrick' which focuses on the dating of Herrick's poems. It does not invalidate his contention that reading Herrick's poems primarily as works of the late 1630s and 1640s has produced a distorted reading of his work, but it does complicate the seemingly straightforward claim that poems written in the 1620s should be interpreted in their context of composition and not their context of print publication. Clearly, however, any interpretation of what the volume as a whole and its individual poems are intended to signify to a late 1640s reading public requires precisely the kind of nuanced and careful reading of the poetry.

27. Peter Calfe, Poetic Miscellany, Harley MS 6918, British Library, London, f. 49v.

28. Like Weekes, all of these probably are friends of Herrick from Cambridge. Two can be confidently identified. Richard Hind took his BA from St John's College in 1614–15,

becoming a fellow in 1616 and obtaining his MA in 1618. Martin Nansogg graduated with a BA from Trinity Hall in 1613 and an MA in 1617. He was a fellow of the college from 1616–28. For Hind, see J. Venn and J. A. Venn (comp. and eds), *Alumni Cantabrigiensis Part 1*, 3 vols (Cambridge: Cambridge University Press, 1922–4), vol. 2, p. 376, and for Nansogg see vol. 3, p. 232. Herrick matriculated at St John's in 1613 but migrated to Trinity Hall in 1615 taking his BA in 1617 and his MA in 1620.

29. These voices are not only those of Herrick's contemporaries but also of earlier poets, a relationship established by allusion and imitation, which can be partly drawn out by editorial annotation. For an illuminating discussion of Herrick's debt to one classical poet, see Pugh, 'Ovidian Exile'.

30. The volume was bound in a badly damaged nineteenth-century calf binding when it was first acquired by the Beinecke Library, Yale University. I am grateful to Diane Ducharme for her assistance with this query.

31. Cresswell, L., *Stemmata Alstoniana: A Collection of Genealogical Tables relating to the ancient family of Alston* (privately printed, 1898), p. 10.

32. Herrick, *Hesperides*, sig. X5v–6r.

33. Venn and Venn, *Alumni Cantabrigiensis*, vol. 1, p. 24.

34. Ibid., p. 25.

35. Henry Glisson stood surety for Tabor when he entered the college. Tabor's father, also James, was a contemporary of Herrick's at Trinity Hall, and later registrar of the university. These repeated connections point to at least two generations of readers for Herrick's work so he clearly sustained a significant reputation at Cambridge during this period. See J. Venn (comp.), *Biographical History of Gonville and Caius College 1349–1897 Volume 1: Admissions 1349–1713* (Cambridge: Cambridge University Press, 1897), p. 312.

36. A poem on p. 158 of Alston entitled 'On the death of Dr. Stubbins' (incipit: 'What means all these that sorrow's livery wear') appears to be a unique copy. Samuel Stubbin (matriculated from Emmanuel in 1606) was born at Naughton where his father was the rector, and this poem may come from Stubbin via Norton.

37. This is a pair of poems: 'Upon Doctor Peirse of Caius College in Cambridge' ('Ten in the hundred lies under this hearse') and 'Another' ('Doctor Peirse before his dying day'), on p. 219. The first amends a more widely circulated epitaph but the other may be unique.

38. See pp. 76–83 and for Whaley, p. 155.

39. See pp. 227 of Alston for Hills, pp. 169 for the masque song and for the Ipswich libels, p. 177.

40. In her accounts of manuscript miscellanies, Hobbs describes the phenomenon of 'associated composition,' where mutual acquaintances and a shared classical education system meant poets regularly produced poems using the same theme or title or using a common incipit. See M. Hobbs, *Early Seventeenth-Century Verse Miscellany Manuscripts* (London: Scolar, 1992), pp. 30–1.

41. One of the problems with reading poems in miscellanies sequentially or chronologically is that after filling up a blank book with poems, compilers often squeezed short poems into any remaining space.

42. J. Eckhardt, *Manuscript Verse Collectors and the Politics of Anti-Courtly Love Poetry* (Oxford: Oxford University Press, 2009), p. 6. Although Eckhardt's work applies only to the practices of manuscript compilers, Herrick's presentation of his printed poems in a manner which allows for their piecemeal transcription suggests he expects such habits to at the very least co-exist alongside other ways of reading and using his printed book. It is worth noting that many of Herrick's poems are excerpted, recontextualised and repro-

duced without attribution in these ways in the 1650s, but in printed miscellanies. See Martin, pp. xxiv–xxvii.

43. For the uses of the paratext, see W. H. Sherman, 'On the Threshold: Architecture, Paratext, and Early Print Culture', in S. A. Baron, E. N. Lindquist and E. F. Shevlin (eds), *Agent of Change: Print Culture after Elizabeth L. Eisenstein* (Amherst, MA: University of Massachusetts Press, 2007), pp. 67–82, on p. 71.

44. In contrast, Lovelace's *Lucasta* was printed the following year accompanied by eighteen poems including one written by the only poet to commend *Hesperides*, John Harmar, who tells Lovelace that. 'Herrico succede meo: dedit Ille priora/Carmina, carminibus non meliora Tuis.' sig. A3v.

45. This point has been fully documented by Tom Cain and he provides a detailed analysis of the political motivations of Eglesfield and Williams in *The Complete Works of Robert Herrick*.

46. Perhaps pointedly, the same emblem was used only twice by Williams in 1647, for Fuller's *A Sermon of Assurance* and his *Good Thoughts in Worse Times*.

47. Corns notes that 1 January was used as the start of the year for the purposes of the imprint and it seems reasonable to assume that the volume as a whole appeared relatively early in 1648, given that the date on the collection's second title page is 1647. See T. Corns, *Uncloistered Virtue: English Political Literature 1640–1660* (Oxford: Clarendon Press, 1992), pp. 307–8.

48. 'Our songs may escape the greedy funeral pyres'.

49. I owe this point to Tom Cain.

50. For the volume's status as monument, see Ingram, 'Robert Herrick and the Making of *Hesperides*', pp. 132–3.

51. Randle Holme comments that esquires are courtesy titles for men of ancient families and automatically applied to the sons of titled aristocrats but notes 'Councellors at Law, Batchelors of Divinity, Law and Physick, who take upon them the Title of Esquire, are reputed Esquires, or equal to Esquires, although none of them are really so'. See R. Holme, *The Academy of Armory* (London, 1688), p.66.

52. This summoning and extinguishing of authorial presence plays with early modern print conventions that sought to create such presence through the use of a variety of manuscript features. See C. Shrank, '"These Few Scribled Rules": Representing Scribal Intimacy in Early Modern Print', *Huntington Library Quarterly*, 67:2 (2004), pp. 295–316.

53. Herrick, sig. A2r–v.

54. The lines also recall the appearance of Hesperus, the evening star, after Charles's birth on 29 May 1630. Herrick's celebratory poem on the event, 'A Pastoral upon the Birth of Prince Charles, Presented to the King, and set by Master Nicholas Lanier' (sig G8r–Sig H1r) was performed at court, a fact Herrick touches on in another poem 'To his Muse' (sig. R5v).

55. Herrick, sig. B1r.

56. A. Moss, 'Theories of Poetry: Latin Writers', in G. P. Norton (ed.), *The Cambridge History of Literary Criticism: Volume III The Renaissance* (Cambridge: Cambridge University Press, 1999), pp. 98–105, on p. 98; Horatius Flaccus, *De Arte Poetica*; trans. B. Jonson as 'Horace, His Art of Poetrie', in C. H. Herford Percy and E. Simpson (eds), *Ben Jonson Vol. VIII: The Poems. The Prose Works* (Oxford: Clarendon Press, 1947), pp. 304–55. Herrick's knowledge of this text and specifically of Jonson's translation is indicated in his reworking of Jonson's lines 'But neither men, not gods, nor Pillars meant/Poets should

ever be indifferent' (ll. 555–6) in his epigram 'Parcell-gilt-poetry' as 'Let's strive to be the best, the Gods, we know it,/Pillars, and men, hate an indifferent poet' (H-1000; 309.5) and the final line of Herrick's 'To the Generous Reader:' 'Homer himself, in a long work, may sleep' (H-95; 32.2.6) is a line translated by Jonson as 'Sometimes, I heare good Homer snore. / But, I confesse, that, in a longe work, sleep/May, with some right, upon an Author creepe.' (ll. 535–7).

57. See, for example, 'Upon Julia's Voice': 'So smooth, so sweet, so silv'ry is thy voice, / As, could they hear, the Damn'd would make no noise, / But listen to thee, (walking in thy chamber)/ Melting melodious words, to Lutes of Amber.' (sig. C3r).

58. Colie, cited in M. Swann, *Curiosities and Texts: The Culture of Collecting in Early Modern England* (Philadelphia, PA: University of Pennsylvania Press, 2001), p. 187. On these hierarchies which placed epic at the top and epigram at the bottom see A. Fowler, *Kinds of Literature* (Cambridge, MA: Harvard University Press, 1982), pp. 216–21. For an examination of the relationship between sonnet and epigram which focuses on 'The Argument of his Book,' see Coiro, *Robert Herrick*, pp. 30–42.

59. Swann, *Curiosities and Texts*, p. 193.

60. 'To his Muse', sig. B1v.

61. See A. Fox, *Oral and Literate Culture in England, 1500–1700* (Oxford: Clarendon Press, 2000).

62. Coiro, *Robert Herrick*, p. 6.

63. Herrick, sig. Q8v–R1r.

64. Pugh, 'Ovidian Exile,' p. 758. See also Corns's discussion of Herrick's treatment of time in Corns, *Uncloistered Virtue*, pp. 96–102.

3 Lenihan, 'Searching for Spectators'

1. Leonardo da Vinci, *Leonardo on Painting*, ed. and trans. M. Kemp and M. Walker (New Haven, CT: Yale University Press, 1989), p. 46.

2. J. Barry, 'Third Lecture on Painting', in *The Works of James Barry*, ed. E. Fryer, 2 vols (London, 1809), vol. 1, pp. 416–26, on p. 426.

3. Barry, *The Works*, ed. Fryer, vol. 2, p. 248.

4. From the *Universal Daily Register*, 2 May 1785, cited in M. Myrone, *Henry Fuseli* (London: Tate Gallery Publications, 2001), p. 36.

5. H. Fuseli, *Lectures on Painting*, 'Invention', in *The Life and Writings of Henry Fuseli*, ed. J. Knowles (London: H. Colburn & R. Bentley 1831), pp. 131–237, on p. 190.

6. L. Sterne, *The Life and Opinions of Tristram Shandy, Gentleman*, ed. M. New (London: Penguin, 2003), p. 309.

7. Barry, *The Works*, vol. 2, p. 319.

8. Michelangelo, *Life, Letters, and Poetry*, ed. and trans. G. Bull and P. Porter (Oxford: Oxford University Press, 1987), p. 142.

9. J. Brewer, *The Pleasures of the Imagination: English Culture in the Eighteenth Century* (London: HarperCollins, 1997), pp. 246–7.

10. P. de Bolla, N. Leask and D. Simpson, 'Introduction', in P. de Bolla, N. Leask and D. Simpson (eds), *Land, Nation and Culture, 1740–1840: Thinking the Republic of Taste* (Basingstoke and New York: Palgrave Macmillan, 2005), pp. 10, 11.

11. 'Book of Art' or 'Craftsman's Handbook'.

12. L. B. Alberti, *On Painting*, trans. J. R. Spencer (New Haven, CT, and London: Yale University Press, 1966), p. 59.

13. Ibid., p. 72.
14. D. Rosand, '*Ut pictor poeta*: Meaning in Titian's *Poesie*', *New Literary History*, 3 (1971–2), pp. 527–46, on p. 528. M. Baxandall, *Giotto and the Orators: Humanist Observers of Painting in Italy and the Discovery of Pictorial Composition, 1350–1450* (Oxford: Oxford-Warburg Studies, 1971), pp. 128–9.
15. *Leonardo on Painting*, p. 32.
16. M. C. Hall, *Michelangelo and the Reinvention of the Human Body* (New York: Farrar, Straus & Giroux, 2005), p. 225.
17. Ibid.
18. Ibid.
19. G. Vasari, *Lives of the Most Eminent Painters, Sculptors and Architects*, trans. G. du C. de Vere, 2 vols (London: George Bell, 1996), vol. 1, p. 742.
20. Fuseli, *The Life and Writings*, vol. 2, pp. 85, 87.
21. T. Puttfarken, *Titian and Tragic Painting: Painting Aristotle's Poetics and the Rise of the Modern Artist* (New Haven, CT, and London: Yale University Press, 2005), p. 25.
22. Ibid., pp. 53, 72.
23. Ibid., p. 62.
24. The Society received the prefix 'Royal' in 1908.
25. Barry, *The Works*, vol. 2, p. 405.
26. Ibid., vol. 2, p. 437.
27. Ibid.
28. Ibid., vol. 2, p. 438.
29. Ibid., vol. 2, p. 317.
30. Ibid.
31. C. Joost-Gaugier, *Raphael's Stanza della Segnatura: Meaning and Invention* (Cambridge: Cambridge University Press, 2002), p. 161. It is important to note that Joost-Gaugier has considered the influence notable figures like Bembo and Castiglione might have had on Raphael during his work on Julius II's private library. Yet she has offered a considerable amount of archival evidence to suggest that Inghirami was the only person with the position (i.e. proximity and authority) and learning to shape the Stanza della Segnatura.
32. Joost-Gaugier, *Raphael's Stanza*, p. 154.
33. P. de Man, *Allegories of Reading: Figural Language in Rousseau, Nietzsche, and Proust* (New Haven, CT, and London: Yale University Press, 1979), p. 14.
34. See note 29 above.
35. de Man, *Allegories of Reading*, p. 253. His italics.
36. Ibid.
37. Ibid., pp. 146, 150.
38. W. L. Pressly, *The Life and Art of James Barry* (New Haven, CT: Yale University Press, 1981), p. 118.
39. Ibid.
40. Ibid.
41. Barry, *The Works*, vol. 2, pp. 314–15.

4 Allen, 'Returning to the Text of *Frankenstein*'

1. A. A. Fisch, A. K. Mellor and E. H. Schor (eds), *The Other Mary Shelley: Beyond Frankenstein* (New York and Oxford: Oxford University Press, 1993). S. M. Conger, F. S. Frank and G. O'Dea, *Iconoclastic Departures: Mary Shelley after Frankenstein* (London: Associated University Presses, 1997).

2. Allen, G., 'Mary Shelley as Elegiac Poet: The Return and "The Choice"', *Romanticism*, 13:3 (2007), pp. 219–32; and 'Mary Shelley's Letter to Maria Gisborne', *La Questione Romantica*, 1 (2009), pp. 69–82.

3. St Clair, *The Reading Nation in the Romantic Period*, pp. 357–73. An earlier version of this essay can be found in W. St Clair, 'The Impact of *Frankenstein*', in B. T. Bennett and S Curran (eds), *Mary Shelley in Her Times* (Baltimore, MD, and London: Johns Hopkins University Press, 2000), pp. 38–63.

4. *The Frankenstein Notebooks. A Facsimile Edition of Mary Shelley's Manuscript Novel, 1816–17 (With Alterations in the Hand of Percy Bysshe Shelley) as it Survives in Draft and Fair Copy Deposited by Lord Abinger in the Bodleian Library, Oxford (Dep. c. 477/1 and Dep. c. 534/1–2)*, 2 vols, in C. E. Robinson (ed.), *Manuscripts of the Younger Romantics* (New York and London: Garland, 1996), vol. 9; hereafter *FN*. See also Mary Shelley (with Percy Shelley), *The Original Frankenstein*, ed. C. E. Robinson (University of Oxford: Bodleian Library, 2008).

5. See *FN*, vol. 1, p.xvi.

6. Ibid., vol. 1, p. xxvi.

7. Ibid., vol. 1, p. xxvi.

8. Ibid., vol. 1, p. xxvii.

9. That this consensus is being successfully revisited and revised can be seen, for example, in Nora Crook's discussion of the issue, 'In Defence of the 1831 *Frankenstein*', in M. Eberle-Sinatra (ed.), *Mary Shelley's Fictions: From Frankenstein to Falkner* (London: Macmillan, 2000), pp. 3–21.

10. G. Allen, *Mary Shelley* (London: Palgrave, 2008), pp. 29–36.

11. *FN*, vol. 1, p. lxviii.

12. Ibid., vol. 1, p. viii.

13. Ibid., vol. 1, p. lxvii.

14. Z. Leader, 'Parenting Frankenstein', in *Revision and Romantic Authorship* (Oxford: Clarendon Press, 1996), pp. 167–205, on p. 191.

15. Ibid., p. 198. Leader is referring to Anne K. Mellor's critique of P. B. Shelley's impact on Mary Shelley's style, in her *Mary Shelley: Her Life, Her Fiction, Her Monsters* (New York and London: Routledge, 1989).

16. J. Reiger, *Frankenstein or The Modern Prometheus: The 1818 Text (with variants, an Introduction, and Notes)* (1974; Chicago, IL: University of Chicago Press, 1984), originally published in the Library of Literature, Indianapolis by Bobbs-Merrill Company, Ltd. For Robinson's rebuttal of Reiger's claims see *FN*, vol. 1, p. lxvii.

17. As Robinson puts it: 'much of the criticism to date on *Frankenstein* will have to be re-evaluated in the light of the collaboration between MWS and PBS'. *FN*, vol. 1, p. xxvii).

18. Ibid., vol. 1, pp. 82–3.

19. Ibid., vol. 1, pp. 84–5.

20. Ibid., vol. 1, pp. 174–5.

21. Ibid., vol. 1, pp. 252–5.

22. Ibid., vol. 1, pp. 84–5.

23. Ibid., vol. 1, pp. 100–3.
24. Ibid., vol. 1, pp. 102–3.
25. Ibid. vol. 1, pp. 126–9.
26. Ibid., vol. 1, pp. 62–5.
27. See *FN*, pp. lxv–lxvi; and Mellor, *Mary Shelley*, pp. 54–5, 233.
28. *FN*, vol. 2, pp. 638–9.
29. Ibid., vol. 2, p. 639.
30. I am referring, of course, to Harold Bloom. See my G. Allen, *Harold Bloom: A Poetics of Conflict* (New York: Harvester Wheatsheaf, 1994); and R. Sellars and G. Allen (eds), *The Salt Companion to Harold Bloom* (Cambridge: Salt Press, 2007).
31. D. Reiman (ed.), *The Romantics Reviewed: Contemporary Reviews of British Romantic Writers*, Part C, *Shelley, Keats, and London Radical Writers*, 2 vols (New York and London: Garland, 1972), vol. 1, p.79.
32. *FN*, vol. 1, p. xciii; P. B. Shelley, *The Letters of Percy Bysshe Shelley*, ed. F. L. Jones, 2 vols (Oxford; Clarendon Press, 1964), vol. 1, p. 590. Mary Shelley was herself, later in the same year, to write from Italy to Walter Scott in thanks for his review and to correct him on his attribution of the novel to P. B. Shelley: see *FN*, vol. 1, p. xcvi; M. Wollstonecraft Shelley, *The Letters of Mary Wollstonecraft Shelley*, ed. B. T. Bennett, 3 vols (Baltimore, MD, and London: Johns Hopkins University Press, 1980–8), vol. 1, p. 71.
33. Reiman, *Romantics Reviewed*, Part C, vol. 1, p. 79.
34. Ibid.; P. B. Shelley, *The Poems of Shelley, Volume 1: 1804–1817*, ed. G. Matthews and K. Everest (London and New York: Longman, 1989), p. 457.
35. *FN*, vol. 1, pp. 250–1.

5 Crook, '"Casualty", Mrs Shelley and Seditious Libel'

1. W. Allingham, *Nightingale Valley*, comp. 'Giraldus' [W. Allingham] (London: Bell & Daldry, 1860), p. 282.
2. *Notes and Queries*, 4th series, 1 (15 February 1868), p. 152.
3. *Fortnightly Review*, 11 (May 1869), p. 539.
4. H. S. Salt, *A Shelley Primer*, Shelley Society Publications, 4th series, 4 (London: Reeves and Turner, 1887), p. 117.
5. P. B. Shelley, *The Poems of Shelley*, ed. G. M. Matthews, K. Everest, et al., 4 vols planned, 2 published to date (Harlow: Longman, 1989–) and *The Complete Poetry of Percy Bysshe Shelley*, ed. D. Reiman, N. Fraistat and (for vol. 3 onward) N. Crook, 8 vols planned, 3 published to date (Baltimore, MD: Johns Hopkins University Press, 2000–). Longer works for which the discredited 1904 Hutchinson's edition is still nominally the standard text include 'Fiordispina', 'The Woodman and the Nightingale', 'Ginevra', 'Charles the First', 'Fragments of an Unfinished Drama', 'Scenes from the Magico Prodigioso of Calderon' and 'Scenes from the Faust of Goethe'.
6. For Allingham's cordial relationship with Garnett, dating from 1858, see H. P. Allingham and E. B. Williams (eds), *Letters to William Allingham* (London: Longman, 1911), pp. 188–90.
7. Allingham, *Nightingale Valley*, p. 282.
8. Cf. 'Ode to the West Wind', where previously separate images of leaf, cloud and wave are united in the line 'O lift me as a wave, a leaf, a cloud!' (l. 53).
9. *Notes and Queries*, 4th series, 1 (25 January 1868), p. 81. I have not found this, but Shelley's *d* sometimes looks like a cursive *theta*. Byron's and Shelley's highly dubious sig-

natures were reported in 1819 (*Blackwood's Magazine*, 5 (April 1819), p. 13). Byron's is still pointed out, but Shelley's seems to have disappeared.

10. *Notes and Queries*, 4th series, 1 (15 February 1868), p. 152. 'A Cobbler' had been anticipated by *Bentley's Miscellany*, 33 (1853), p. 24 and F. C. Cook, *Sermons* (London: John Murray, 1863), p. 48.

11. *Notes and Queries*, 3rd series, 12 (27 December 1867), pp. 527–8.

12. *Notes and Queries*, 3rd series, 12 (7 December 1867), 467; 4th series, 1 (15 February 1868), p. 152.

13. *Notes and Queries*, 4th series, 1 (28 March 1868), p. 301.

14. A much-exaggerated inference from Peacock's 'Memoirs of Percy Bysshe Shelley' (pub. *Fraser's Magazine* in 1858 and 1860). L'Estrange passionately admired and corresponded with Peacock (1785–1866), though he was not a confidant. *Letters of Thomas Love Peacock*, ed. N. Joukovsky, 2 vols (Oxford: Oxford University Press, 2001), vol. 2, p. 391 and note.

15. For more details of Rossetti's transactions, see D. H. Reiman, *Romantic Texts and Contexts* (Columbia, MI: University of Missouri Press, 1987), pp. 86–9.

16. P. B. Shelley, *The Poetical Works of Percy Bysshe Shelley ... with Notes and a Memoir by William Michael Rossetti*, 2 vols (London: Moxon, 1870), vol. 1, pp. xi–xii.

17. Ibid., vol. 2, p. 598.

18. Photo-facsimiles with diplomatic transcripts of Shelley's notebooks and other manuscripts were issued between 1984 and 1997 by Garland Press in 31 volumes in two series, both under D. H. Reiman's general editorship: *Bodleian Shelley Manuscripts* (hereafter *BSM*) and *Manuscripts of the Younger Romantics: Shelley* (hereafter *MYR*). *Shelley and his Circle* (publication of the Carl H. Pforzheimer collection of the same name), is still proceeding (10 vols published to date, 13 planned; Cambridge MA: Harvard University Press, 1961–). More untraced manuscripts may yet turn up.

19. Charles H. Taylor, *The Early Collected Editions of Shelley's Poems* (New Haven, CT: Yale University Press, 1958).

20. 'Shelley's "Invocation to Misery", An Expanded Text', *Journal of English and Germanic Philology*, 65 (1966), pp. 65–74; 'Shelley's "Boat on the Serchio": the Evidence of the Manuscript', *Philological Quarterly*, 46 (1967), pp. 58–68. Raben showed that Mary Shelley suppressed sardonic and irreverent lines from the 'Boat on the Serchio' draft. However, his main arguments, based on a partial knowledge of the relevant manuscripts, have not been accepted.

21. I. Massey (ed.), *Posthumous Poems of Shelley: Mary Shelley's Fair Copy Book* (Montreal: McGill–Queen's University Press, 1969), p. 9 (hereafter Massey, *MWSd.9*); J. de Palacio, *Mary Shelley dans son œuvre* (Paris: Éditions Klincksieck, 1969), pp. 401–38.

22. Palacio, *Mary Shelley*, pp. 425–6, my translation.

23. S. Wolfson, 'Editorial Privilege: Mary Shelley and Percy Shelley's Audiences', in Fisch et al. (eds), *The Other Mary Shelley*, pp. 39–72; N. Fraistat, 'Illegitimate Shelley: Radical Piracy and the Textual Edition as Cultural Performance', *PMLA*, 110 (May 1994), pp. 409–23. An earlier version is 'Shelley Left and Right: The Rhetoric of the Early Textual Editions', reprinted in N. Fraistat, *Shelley's Poetry and Prose*, 2nd edn (New York: Norton, 2002), pp. 645–53 (hereafter *SPP*).

24. M. O'Neill, '"Trying to Make it as Good as I Can", Mary Shelley's Editing of P. B. Shelley's Poetry and Prose', in B. T. Bennett and S. Curran (eds), *Mary Shelley in Her Times* (Baltimore, MD: Johns Hopkins University Press, 2000), pp. 185–97; B. T. Bennett, 'Introduction', in *The Letters of Mary Wollstonecraft Shelley*, ed. B. T. Bennett, 3 vols (Bal-

timore, MD: Johns Hopkins University Press, 1980–8), vol. 2, pp. xvi–xvii (hereafter *MWSL*).

25. *MWSL*, vol. 1, pp. 299–300.

26. P. Feldman and D. Scott-Kilvert (eds), *The Journals of Mary Shelley*, 2 vols (Oxford: Clarendon Press, 1987), vol. 2, pp. 559.

27. 'Note on Poems Written in 1822', *The Poetical Works of Percy Bysshe Shelley*, vol. 4, p. 226.

28. The affected poems are 'To Constantia', 'To Jane. The Invitation' and 'To Jane. The Recollection'. With 'The Boat on the Serchio' and 'Rose leaves, when the rose is dead' her ordering of the fragments does not match that of the manuscript, but Shelley's fair copies often depart from rough draft order. She may have persuaded herself that she had realized his intentions; certainly her redactions are more coherent than the manuscript order.

29. 'Alfieri', in *Lives of the Most Eminent Literary and Scientific Men of Italy*, 2 vols (Longman: 1835), vol. 2, p. 294.

30. Compositors no doubt did this, too, because of their training in memorizing copy not word for word but in sentences, which maximizes speed and minimizes eye-skips. See C. F. Partington, *The Printer's Complete Guide* (London: Sherwood, Gilbert & Piper, 1825), p. 205. Some errors may be compositorial, but Mary Shelley overlooked them at proof-correction stage.

31. A. C. Swinburne, *Essays and Studies* (London: Chatto & Windus, 1875), pp. 229–30.

32. See Carlene Adamson's discussion in *BSM*, 6 (1992), pp. 39–41.

33. See, for instance, an abridged version of Smith's *The Printer's Grammar* (London: T. Evans, 1787), p. 104.

34. Examples (in italics) of words deciphered by Matthews and later editors include: 'Than the *undeceiving* sky' ('O Mary dear'); 'Veiled art thou like *a storm extinguished star*' ('The Zucca'); 'And frost in these performs what *fire* in those' ('Triumph of Life'). Corrections made by me (and perhaps by others, independently) include 'vulgar heads' for 'vulgar hands' ('Triumph of Life'); 'Were less obscurely fair' and 'rats in her breast' for 'Was less heavenly fair' and 'rats in her heart' ('Ginevra'). All are easily mistaken in the manuscripts concerned.

35. Fraistat, *SPP*, p. 648.

36. *MWSL*, vol. 1, pp. 261, 393, 396–7, 399.

37. Fraistat, *SPP*, p. 648.

38. It is unlikely that Mary Shelley approached Colburn, who published Procter, Godwin, and later herself, but his interests lay towards prose fiction and non-fiction; his magazines had given Shelley several bad reviews. Taylor & Hessey, publishers of Keats and Hazlitt, are unlikely to have been amenable. Taylor, a devout Christian, had refused to take on *Vision of Judgment*. As editor of the *London Magazine* he censored Hazlitt, Landor and Lamb, see E. Blunden, *Keats's Publisher: A Memoir of John Taylor* (London: Jonathan Cape, 1936), pp. 137–41, 161. For publishers who had in the past turned down Shelley, see C. E. Robinson, 'Percy Bysshe Shelley, Charles Ollier, and William Blackwood', in K. Everest (ed.), *Shelley Revalued* (Leicester: Leicester University Press, 1983), pp. 183–226, on p. 213.

39. See T. Webb, 'John Hunt', *ODNB*.

40. *MWSL*, vol. 1, p. 384.

41. They guaranteed only 250 copies of the print run of 500 copies that John Hunt thought necessary for financial viability. See R. Ingpen, *Shelley in England* (London: Kegan Paul, 1917), pp. 576–7.

42. For more details see Robinson, 'Percy Bysshe Shelley, Charles Ollier, and William Black-wood', pp. 208-12. Charles E. Robinson has generously communicated to me his later discovery of the numbers of the four Shelley titles in unbound quires offered for sale at the Ollier sale of 11 March 1823: 288 of *Prometheus Unbound* copies, 390 of *The Cenci*, 162 of *Hellas*, and 328 of *Rosalind and Helen*. These were the ones that made up *Poetical Pieces*. If all were bought by Simpkin, Marshall & Co., they would have made up a notional 162 copies of the four-volume *Poetical Pieces* and up to 126 copies of the three-volume one. The four-volume edition was still being offered for sale in 1824 (advertising leaf in *The Cambrian Plutarch*, also reissued in 1834). Most copies of the three-volume may have gone by 1829, when single remainder copies of *Rosalind and Helen* and *The Cenci* (possibly sold on by Simpkin, Marshall & Co. from the excess after the two *Poetical Pieces* had been bound up) and *Revolt of Islam* were offered for sale by the radical publisher John Brooks, who was still advertising them in 1832; see H. B. Forman, *The Shelley Library* (London: Reeves & Turner, 1886), pp. 55, 107–8.

43. *MWSL*, vol. 1, pp. 386–7; Robert Browning told Thomas Wise in 1886 that he had obtained Shelley titles from Hunt 'before 1830'. This would have been no earlier than 1825, the year that Browning became interested in Shelley; see *Letters of Robert Browning*, ed. T. Wise, 2 vols (privately printed, 1896), vol. 2, p. 53. The poetry titles offered singly by Hunt comprised *Epipsychidion, Hellas, Rosalind and Helen, Prometheus Unbound, The Cenci, Revolt of Islam, Adonais*.

44. 'A Ballad', a reversion to the genuinely 'vulgar' style of *The Devil's Walk* (1812), was not published until 1926. In 1839 Mary Shelley no doubt thought that it would detract from Shelley's poetic reputation, but she also appears to have lost both her fair copies by then. As late as 17 November 1823 she was still planning to include Shelley's irreverent 'On the Devil, and Devils' in a companion volume of Shelley's prose. (This was set up in type in 1839, but pulled at proof stage for fear of prosecution.)

45. See Massey, *MWSd.9*, pp. 11–14, 228. 'A New National Anthem' (never fair-copied by Shelley) and 'To S[idmouth] and C[astlereagh]' are absent. This last, however, was in another keeping-copy notebook.

46. O'Neill, '"Trying to make it as good as I can"', pp. 194–6. The rest of this paragraph and the next owe much to O'Neill's argument.

47. For more details of Hunt's prosecution see W. H. Marshall, *Byron, Shelley, Hunt and The Liberal* (Philadelphia, PA: University of Pennsylvania Press, 1960), pp. 126–31, 133, 205–6.

48. T. Webb, 'John Hunt to Edwin Atherstone: Seven Letters', *Keats–Shelley Journal*, 58 (2009), pp. 139–58, on pp. 154–5. The letters (discovered by Webb) show Hunt's stoicism, but also his suffering. Webb's essay of the same name in *Keats–Shelley Review*, 23 (2009), pp. 56–81 supplies extensive background and context. Hunt's circumspection may have paid off. The sentence, pronounced just after the publication of *Posthumous Poems*, was a fine, not imprisonment. Mary Shelley expressed relief (*MWSL*, vol. 1, p. 430).

49. Shelley, *The Poetical Works of Percy Bysshe Shelley*, vol. 3, p. 207. John Hunt's particular fear of being prosecuted for *blasphemy* could account for the omission of such an apparently innocuous line as 'Moans, shrieks and curses and blaspheming prayers' ('Julian and Maddalo', l. 218) from *Posthumous Poems*.

50. Hunt may also have talked over-sanguinely. Webb quotes Hobhouse's optimistic assurance to Byron of 23 February 1824, that he had inside knowledge that John Hunt's judges and prosecution 'seemed inclined to carry their joke no farther' (*Byron's Bulldog:*

The Letters of John Cam Hobhouse to Lord Byron, ed. P. Graham (Columbus, OH: Ohio State University Press, 1984), p. 347).

51. W. Hazlitt, *Table Talk, or, Original Essays* (London: John Warren, 1821), p. 357; *The Correspondence of Leigh Hunt*, ed. T. Hunt, 2 vols (London: Smith, Elder, 1862), vol. 1, p. 166.

52. *MWSL*, vol. 1, p. 452; *Edinburgh Review*, 40 (March–July, 1824), p. 505.

53. See her Schadenfreude upon learning that the Rev. W. B. Collyer, the most gloating rejoicer at Shelley's death, had been accused of paedophilia (*MWSL*, vol. 1, p. 380).

54. W. Godwin, *History of the Commonwealth of England*, 4 vols (London: Henry Colburn, 1824–8), vol. 2, p. 691. In *The Last Man* Mary Shelley similarly diverts Royalist poems to the purpose of lamenting the death of a republican ideal. Shelley's copy of *Eikon Basilike* is in the Pforzheimer Collection, New York Public Library.

55. *MWSL*, vol. 1, p. 411.

56. Advertising matter dated 1 July 1844, bound in with Mary Shelley's *Rambles* (1844).

57. Information from advertising matter in *Minor Poems*, dated 2 March 1846, personal copy. The 1845 *Essays, Letters* was priced at 5*s*. (Shelley's prose was always cheaper than his poetry). By 1861 the expurgated three-volume *Poetical Works* cost 15*s*. while the complete poetry and prose *Works* was 12*s*. Moxon's one-volume 1853 *Poetical Works* (7*s*.), which omitted the *Mab* Notes, may have partly met the demand for an expurgated *Mab*. (It also omitted Mrs Shelley's Notes.)

58. For instance, the correction of 'zone' to 'throne' in the lyric 'Liberty'. See also Mary Shelley to Edward Moxon, 30 January 1846, 'When do the Minor poems come out?' (*MWSL*, vol. 3, p. 275).

59. 'Prince Athanase', 'Mazenghi' and 'The Woodman and the Nightingale' were also excluded, perhaps because too fragmentary.

60. 'A Defence of Poetry' (*SPP*, p. 530).

61. MS PM MA 974 (*MYR*, vol. 8 (1997), pp. 218–19), with quotation marks regularized according to modern British norms. Quoted here by kind permission.

62. Bodleian MS. Shelley, adds.e.11, p. 84 (*BSM*, vol. 15 (1990), pp. 86–7).

63. See, for instance A. Wroe, *Being Shelley* (London: Jonathan Cape, 2007); M. Bradshaw, 'Reading as Flight: Fragment Poems from Shelley's Notebooks', in Webb and Weinberg (eds), *The Unfamiliar Shelley*, pp. 21–40; N. M. Goslee, 'Shelleyan Inspiration and the Sister Arts', in Webb and Weinberg (eds), *The Unfamiliar Shelley*, pp. 159–79. A forerunner of these is Lisa Vargo's 'Close Your Eyes and Think of Shelley: Versioning Mary Shelley's Triumph of Life', in T. Clark and J. E. Hogle (eds), *Evaluating Shelley* (Edinburgh: Edinburgh University Press, 1996), pp. 215–24.

64. N. M. Goslee, 'Dispersoning Emily: Drafting as Plot in *Epipsychidion*', *Keats-Shelley Journal*, 42 (1993), pp. 104–19; reprinted in *SPP* (2002), p. 738.

65. There would be advantages for conservation. One great advantage over the present black-and-white photo-facsimiles would be that the hue and depth of colour might be seen. But actual handling of the manuscript is still indispensable in determining whether pencil overwrites or is overwritten by ink; this can be crucial in dating Shelley's poetry.

66. There are important differences in policy and arrangement between the two editions, but here I wish to emphasize their common aims.

67. See St Clair, *The Reading Nation in the Romantic Period*, pp. 122–39.

68. The long-overdue completion of the Oxford Shelley *Prose Works*, interrupted by the death of E. B. Murray, is now proceeding under the editorship of Michael O'Neill and Timothy Webb.

6 Griffin and O'Connell, 'Writing Textual Materiality'

1. Charles Clark, Letter to the *Mechanics' Magazine*, 22 November 1822.
2. Letter to Thomas Frognall Dibdin, 10 June 1837, San Marino, Huntington Rare Book and Manuscript Library DI 105 (hereafter MS DI 105).
3. MS DI 105.
4. J. Bettley, 'Clark, Charles (1806–1880)', *ODNB*, available at: http://www.oxforddnb.com/view/article/5457 [accessed 20 May 2010].
5. MS DI 105.
6. The authors are currently compiling a scholarly publication on Clark's literary activities.
7. Johnson's Preface, cited in A. Brignull, *Charles Clark: The Bard of Totham* (Loughborough: Hedgehog Press, 1990), p. 2.
8. Based on work carried out on Clark to date, we have reason to believe that he also accumulated and sold books to Smith. A discussion of this is beyond the remit of this paper.
9. C. Clark, *Tiptree Races* (Maldon, Essex: P. H. Youngman, 1833), p. 41.
10. Ibid.
11. Friday, 14 June 1839, p. 3, col. 2.
12. Great Totham Press, 1846.
13. Clark's death was not noted in the press; see Brignull, *Charles Clark: The Bard*, p. 9.
14. H. A. Plomer, 'Some Private Presses of the Nineteenth Century', *The Library: Transactions of the Bibliographical Society*, 4:s2–1 (1899) p. 418.
15. Brignull, *Charles Clark: The Bard*, p. 9.
16. MS DI 105.
17. There are *c*. 300 letters from Clark to John Russell Smith preserved amongst Clark's papers at Essex Public Records Office, Chelmsford. The authors are very grateful for the support of The Bibliographical Society, which awarded them their Antiquarian Booksellers Association Award (2010), enabling them to undertake this research.
18. Brignull, *Charles Clark: The Bard*, p. 7.
19. Letter to John Russell Smith, 1839 (cited in Brignull, *Charles Clark: The Bard*, p. 6).
20. Brignull, *Charles Clark: The Bard*, p. 7.
21. Charles Long died in 1838, and his cousin in 1829.
22. MS DI 105.
23. Information on this manuscript can be found in the British Library's Online Manuscripts Catalogue at: http://www.bl.uk/catalogues/manuscripts/HITS0001.ASP?VPath=html/20072.htm&Search=2433&Highlight=F [accessed 18 January 2010].
24. The e-version is preserved in a letter to John Russell Smith, 10 February 1843; Chelmsford, Essex Public Records Office, MS D/DU 668/7.
25. C. Clark (alias 'Bookworm'), 'Whimsical Book-Plate', *Notes & Queries*, 141 (10 July 1852), pp. 32–3.
26. MS DI 105.
27. MS DI 105.

7 McParland, 'Charles Dickens's Readers and the Material Circulation of the Text'

1. I. I. Hayes, *An Arctic Boat Journey, in the Autumn of 1854* (Boston, MA: James Osgood & Company, 1871), ch. 21, p. 203.

2. Hayes, *An Arctic Boat Journey*, p. 203.

3. Jonathan Rose indicates the use of Dickens as a model by autobiographers. He writes that 'most working people had to struggle with the art of recording their lives, and they cited Dickens, more than anyone else, as the man who got it right'. See J. Rose, *The Intellectual Life of the British Working Classes* (New Haven, CT: Yale University Press, 2001) pp. 111–12.

4. Dickens's fiction appeared serialized in periodicals and in numerous book editions. This variety of formats is illustrated by *Hard Times*, which was serialized in *Household Words* and then appeared in the Cheap edition, Library edition, Illustrated Library edition, Household edition, Charles Dickens edition, American Diamond edition. See P. Schlicke, *The Oxford Companion to Charles Dickens* (Oxford: Oxford University Press, 1999). The Dickens book trade in Britain is amply documented by R. L. Patten, *Dickens and his Publishers* (Oxford: Oxford University Press, 1978). One may also consult, J. Eckel, *The First Editions of Charles Dickens* (1913; London: Haskell House, 1932), W. Smith, *Charles Dickens: A Bibliographical Catalog*, 2 vols (Los Angeles: Heritage Book Shop, 1982); and Sumner and Stillman, *Thirty Six First American Editions* from the Allan D. McGuire Collection. For an attempt to sort out pirated editions of Dickens, see W. G. Wilkins, *First and Early American Editions* (Cedar Rapids, 1910; reprinted by Burt Franklin, 1968).

5. Serialization of Dickens's stories in America began with the 'story papers,' such as Park Benjamin's *New World* and *Brother Jonathan*. With no International Copyright, Carey, Harpers, Putnams, and many others began to reprint Dickens's fiction. See M. McGill, *American Literature and the Culture of Reprinting, 1834–53* (Philadelphia, PA: University of Pennsylvania Press, 2003). A downturn in the US economy in the panic of 1837 appears to have coincided with the rise of the cheap story papers. *New World*'s version of *American Notes* (1842) competed with Harper & Brothers. These competed with the British, two-volume, 614-page book (see McGill, *American Literature*, p. 23). *Putnam's Monthly* circulation ranged from 12,000–20,000 and competed with *Harper's*, whose initial printing of 7,500 in 1850 catapulted to a print run of 50,000 within six months. Dickens's *Household Words* was also distributed in the United States of America.

6. McGill, *American Literature*, p. 26.

7. Ibid.

8. Recent work on common readers gives us useful methodological models for an investigation of Charles Dickens's audience. From studies such as Rose, *The Intellectual Life of the British Working Class* and K. Flint, *The Woman Reader 1837–1914* (Oxford: Clarendon Press, 1993), we are directed toward memoirs, autobiographies, letters and journals of nineteenth-century readers. Quantitative data may be obtained via publishers' records and library circulation records. One may investigate the minutes of reading circles, or the exchange in periodicals and the letters to their editors. In investigating Dickens, we may ask to what extent we may recover middle-class and working-class readers' responses and how these differed from each other. It is useful to compare the responses of male and female readers, blacks and whites, immigrants, and people of different occupations.

9. M. Lyons, 'New Readers in the Nineteenth Century', in G. Cavallo and R. Chartier (eds), *A History of Reading in the West* (Amherst, MA: University of Massachusetts Press, 1999).

10. R. Wittmann, 'Was There a Reading Revolution at the End of the Eighteenth Century?', in *A History of Reading in the West*, p. 300.

11. K. Tillotson. and J. Butt, *Dickens at Work* (London: Methuen, 1957), p. 21; L. K. Hughes and M. Lund, *The Victorian Serial* (Charlottesville, VA: University of Virginia Press, 1991), p.11.

12. Wednesday Club minutes, 24 February 1892, Onondaga Historical Association [hereafter OHA], Syracuse, New York.

13. Wednesday Club minutes, 24 February 1892, OHA.

14. Hughes and Lund, *The Victorian Serial*, p. 61.

15. K. Haltunnen, *Painted Women and Confidence Men* (New Haven, CT: Yale University Press, 1982), p. 35.

16. F. Willard, *The Living Age* (Spring 1852), pp. 154–8.

17. R. E. Broome, Federal Writers Project, 'How Branson's Bulldog Courage Won', Manuscript Division Library of Congress, Stiles M. Scruggs, South Carolina Writer's Project (28 February 1939), at http://memory.loc.gov/wpaintro Item No. 2>, p. 3.

18. Rose, *The Intellectual Life of the British Working Class*, p. 48.

19. A. N. Ward and M. Ward (eds), *The Husband in Utah: Sights and Scenes Among the Mormons* (New York: Derby & Jackson, 1857), p. 267.

20. C. Dickens, *Oliver Twist*, Great Illustrated Classics Series (New York: Dodd & Mead, 1941).

21. Mr Micawber's phrase 'something will turn up' is pervasive in Dickens's novel *David Copperfield*. For example, Chapter 17 is entitled 'Somebody turns up'. See *David Copperfield*, Great Illustrated Classics (New York: Dodd & Mead, 1943).

22. E. M. McPherson, *The Political History of the United States During the Period of Reconstruction* (Washington, DC.: Solomons & Chapman, 1875), p. 295.

23. Proceedings, p. 429.

24. H. B. Stowe, *Sunny Memories of Foreign Lands* (Boston, MA: Phillips, Samson & Company, 1854), p. 317.

25. J. F. Rusling, *The Great West and Pacific Coast* (New York: Sheldon & Company, 1877), p. 82.

26. O. Brownson, *The Spirit Rapper, An Autobiography* (Boston, MA: Little Brown, 1854), p.111.

27. C. A. Warfield, *Miriam Montfort* (New York: D. Appleton, 1873).

28. J. Holbrook, *Ten Years among the Mail Bags* (Philadelphia, PA: H. Cowperthwait & Company, 1855), p. 122.

29. R. B. Roosevelt, *Five Acres Too Much* (New York: O. Judd, 1885), p. 135.

30. D. S. Miall, E. Greenspan and J. Rose (eds), *Book History*, (Philadelphia, PA: University of Pennsylvania Press, 2006), vol. 9, p. 296.

31. Cited in Miall et al., *Book History*, vol. 9, p. 294.

32. H. R. Helper, *The Impending Crisis of the South: How to Meet It* (New York: A.B. Burdick, 1860), p. 257.

33. E. Sweet, *The Future Life* (Boston, MA, and New York: W. White, 1869), p. 172.

34. Miall et al., *Book History*, vol. 9, p. 304.

35. J. H. Browne, *The Great Metropolis: A Mirror of New York* (Hartford, CT: American Publishing Company, 1869).

36. Browne, *The Great Metropolis*, p. 195. See *Oliver Twist*, Chapter 1, pp. 1–4; *Oliver Twist* (1941).

37. Browne, *The Great Metropolis*, p. 195–6.

38. M. C. Cabell, *Sketches and Recollections of Lynchburg by the Oldest Inhabitant* (Richmond: C. H Wynne, 1858), p. 333.

39. I. L. Nascher, *The Wretches of Povertyville: A Sociological Study of the Bowery* (Chicago, IL: J. J. Lawzit), p. 49.
40. H. Coppee, *English Literature Considered as an Interpreter of English History, Designed as a Manual of Instruction* (Philadelphia, PA: Claxton, Remsen & Haffelfinger, 1873).
41. Hughes and Lund, *The Victorian Serial,* p. 61.
42. Ibid.
43. Wednesday Club minutes, 4 February 1892, OHA.
44. Ibid.
45. Ibid.
46. Ibid.
47. Ibid.
48. Ibid.
49. Ibid.
50. Truxton Club minutes, 2 February 1886, Cortland Historical Society.
51. C. Pawley, *Reading on the Middle Border – The Culture of Print in Late-Nineteenth Century Osage, Iowa* (Amherst, MA: University of Massachusetts Press, 2001), pp. 6–7
52. C. Ostrowski, *Books, Maps and Politics: A Cultural History of the Library of Congress, 1783–1861* (Amherst, MA: University of Massachusetts Press, 2004).
53. Mercantile Library of Philadelphia, p. 8, cited in A. Abbot, *Catalogue of the Mercantile Library of Philadelphia, Annual Report* (1867), in 'A Village Library', *Harper's New Monthly Magazine,* 1:26 (May 1868), pp. 774–7.
54. Ibid., p. 776.
55. Ibid.
56. Ibid., p. 774.
57. *Public Libraries* (Washington, DC: US Library of Congress, 1876).
58. C. A. Cutter, 'New Catalogue of Harvard College Library', *North American Review,* 108:222 (January 1869), p. 99.
59. Patten, *Dickens and His Publishers,* p. 136.
60. Ibid.
61. Ibid.
62. 'Letter to John Bull', *Putnam's Monthly,* 1:2 (February, 1853), p. 225
63. Ibid.
64. Ibid.
65. Ibid., p. 226.
66. Ibid.
67. E. Exman, *The Brothers Harper* (New York: Harper & Row, 1965), p. 310.
68. C. Dickens, *Pilgrim Letters,* ed. K. Tillotson and N. Burgis, (Oxford: Oxford University Press, 1978), vol. 4 (1844–6), p. 483.
69. Patten, *Dickens and His Publishers,* p. 227.
70. *Ladies Repository,* 14:14 (May 1854), p. 236.
71. J. Tebbel, *A History of Book Publishing in the United States* (New York: R. R. Bowker, 1972), vol. 1, p. 247.
72. E. T. Freedley, *Philadelphia and its Manufacturers* (Philadelphia, PA: Edwin Young, 1859), p. 166.
73. Exman, *The Brothers Harper,* p. 89.
74. Patten, *Dickens and His Publishers,* p. 403.
75. Ibid.
76. Tebbel, *A History of Book Publishing in the United States,* p. 411.

77. Ibid., p. 376.
78. Patten, *Dickens and His Publishers*, p. 389n.
79. Tebbel, *A History of Book Publishing in the United States*, pp. 544–5.
80. S. Moss, *Dickens' Quarrel with America* (Troy, NY: Whitson, 1984), p. 215.
81. Ibid., pp. 215–17.
82. Ibid.
83. J. T. Fields, *Yesterday's With Authors* (Boston, MA: Houghton, Osgood, 1879).
84. Tebbel, *A History of Book Publishing in the United States*, p. 402.
85. M. B. Stern (ed.), *Publishers for Mass Entertainment in Nineteenth Century America* (Boston, MA: G. K Hall, 1980), p. 22.
86. Ibid., pp. 22–3.
87. Tebbel, *A History of Book Publishing in the United States*, p.376.
88. Ibid., p. 483.
89. Dickens, *David Copperfield* (London: Bradbury & Evans, 1850), p. 1.
90. R. J. Zboray, *A Fictive People: Antebellum Economic Development and the American Reading Public* (Oxford: Oxford University Press, 1993), p. 80.

8 Sullivan, 'Victorian Pantomime Libretti and the Reading Audience'

1. My opening description draws on T. Postlewait, 'Constructing Events in Theatre History: A Matter of Credibility', in V. A. Cremona et al. (eds), *Theatrical Events Borders Dynamics Frames*, pp. 33–52, in which he emphasizes the need to apply the historian's definitions of 'complex' or 'discrete' to theatre events (pp. 42, 49, n. 13).

2. This is an extensive body of work. For an overview of developments in the field as well as influential theories on audience expectations, see S. Bennett, *Theatre Audiences: A Theory of Production and Reception* (London: Routledge, 1994); interpretations of the concept of the event and audience engagement both in aesthetic and practical terms can be found in V. A. Cremona, P. Eversmann, H. van Maanen, W. Sauter and J. Tulloch (eds), *Theatrical Events Borders Dynamics Frames* (Amsterdam: Rodolpi, 2004). The particular relationship between audiences and modern pantomime is discussed in M. Taylor, *British Pantomime Performance* (Bristol and Chicago, IL: Intellect Books, 2007).

3. The collection held at the Nottingham Central Library comprises books of words for the majority of the pantomimes produced each year at the Theatre Royal between 1860 and 1900. Such collections exist at other public libraries, for example in Birmingham and Manchester, as well as examples in the Lord Chamberlain's Collection at the British Library.

4. J. S. Peters, *Theatre of the Book, 1480–1880: Print, Text, and Performance in Europe* (Oxford: Oxford University Press, 2000), p. 32.

5. Ibid., pp. 48–9.

6. J. O'Brien, *Harlequin Britain: Pantomime and Entertainment 1690–1760* (Baltimore, MD: Johns Hopkins University Press, 2004), p. 113. I have not engaged with opera libretti in this paper, as they require a different argument, but again, the links with spectacular theatre are apparent.

7. O'Brien, *Harlequin Britian*, p. 113; D. Mayer, *Harlequin in His Element: The English Pantomime 1806–1836* (Cambridge, MA: Harvard University Press, 1969), p. 365.

8. The only example of a 'book of the songs' that I have found is from the Theatre Royal, Nottingham, pantomime of 1890, *Puss in Boots*. (All Nottingham books listed are held at the Nottingham City Council Local Studies Library, L78.9).

9. Mayer notes that the inclusion of advertisements in the 1820s reduced the price from 10*d.* to 6*d.* (*Harlequin in his Element*, p. 365).

10. Mayer, *Harlequin in his Element*, p. 367; M. R. Booth, *English Plays of the Nineteenth Century*, 5 vols (Oxford: Clarendon Press, 1969–76), vol. 5 (1976), p. 86.

11. I have come across only two examples of re-printed versions of a book of words: those for *Little Red Riding Hood* (1885) and *Babes in the Wood* (1887) (both at the Theatre Royal, Nottingham). It is unclear when in the run the second version of each was produced, but it remains unlikely that regularly updated versions were printed during a single run of any one pantomime. There is financial evidence that the book of words for *The House That Jack Built* was re-printed for the end of the pantomime season at the Nottingham theatre in February 1866 when a reduced pantomime opening was added to the main post-pantomime season programme for six performances (Nottinghamshire Archives, M8807).

12. This fact has been emphasized by nineteenth- and twentieth-century critics, the latter including T. C. Davis, *The Economics of the British Stage 1800–1914* (Cambridge: Cambridge University Press, 2000), pp. 342–3, and Booth, *English Plays of the Nineteenth Century*, vol. 1, pp. 1, 55. For further details of the historical discussion, see J. A. Sullivan, 'Managing the Pantomime: Productions at the Theatre Royal Nottingham in the 1860s', *Theatre Notebook*, 60:2 (2006), pp. 98–116, on pp. 98, 114.

13. Mayer, *Harlequin in his Element*, p. 365.

14. P. Auslander, *Liveness: Performance in a Mediatized Culture* (London: Routledge, 1999), p. 57.

15. Peters, cited in O'Brien, *Harlequin Britain*, p. 113.

16. *Cinderella*, Theatre Royal, Nottingham, 1892, back cover.

17. *The House That Jack Built*, Theatre Royal, Nottingham, 1865, p. 21.

18. *The Forty Thieves*, Theatre Royal, Manchester, 1888, pp. 4–5 and *Aladdin*, Alexandra Theatre, Liverpool, 1884, pp. 10–11 (both copies kindly loaned to the author by David Mayer).

19. *Cinderella*, Theatre Royal, Nottingham, 1892, pp. 26–7 and 20–1, respectively.

20. The most important recent work on this area is J. Davis and V. Emeljanow, *Reflecting the Audience: London Theatregoing 1840–1880* (Hatfield: University of Hertfordshire Press, 2001).

21. Mayer, *Harlequin in his Element*, p. 365.

22. In part this idea develops Carlson's argument in which he extends Umberto Eco's concept of the model reader, regarding the assumptions made by a play's producers as to how an audience reads a text, and how that audience, through the diversity of its inherent communities, in actual fact provides a greater variety of interpretations; M. Carlson, 'Theatre Audiences and the Reading of Performance', in T. Postlewait and B. A. McConachie (eds), *Interpreting the Theatrical Past: Essays in the Historiography of Performance* (Iowa City, IA: University of Iowa Press, 1989), pp. 85–6.

23. Mayer, *Harlequin in his Element*, p. 365.

24. Ibid., p. 21.

25. D. A. Reid, 'Popular Theatre in Victorian Birmingham', in D. Bradby, L. James and B. Sharratt (eds), *Performance and Politics in Popular Drama: Aspects of Popular Entertainment in Theatre, Film and Television 1800–1976. Papers given at a Conference at the*

University of Kent at Canterbury, September 1977 (Cambridge: Cambridge University Press, 1980), pp. 65–89, on p. 74.

26. Ibid., p. 75.
27. Ibid., p. 76.
28. 'Footlights', *Nottingham Journal*, 8 January 1879, p. 3.
29. 'Theatre Royal', *Nottingham Journal*, 7 January 1879, p. 3.
30. 'City Chat', *Exeter and Plymouth Gazette Daily Telegram*, Wednesday, 28 December, 1881, p. 3.
31. Generally speaking theorists accept that an audience is not comprised of a single community but multiple communities. See Bennett's discussion of the work of Ann Ubersfeld and Keir Elam on the influences of the individual and the collective on audience responses (*Theatre Audiences* pp. 71–2, 153–5). Carlson and Taylor both discuss the social impact of audiences on the individual, whilst Peter Eversmann addresses the notion of the 'collective' response as being influenced by the individual.
32. Taylor, *British Pantomime*, pp. 125–6, 131–3.
33. Bennett, *Theatre Audiences*, p. 21.
34. The various potential horizons of expectation experienced by theatre audiences are succinctly discussed by Bennett, *Theatre Audiences*, ch. 3 (esp. p. 99). Her phrase 'pre-production' occurs on p. 136 specifically in relation to theatre programmes. See also Carlson on playbills as pre-production tools (pp. 92–3). For a re-reading of nineteenth-century playbills for implicit audience expectations, see J. Bratton, *New Readings in Theatre History* (Cambridge: Cambridge University Press, 2003), pp. 38–66.
35. The most succinct discussion of changes to performance texts and the potential effects also made by an audience on the author's text is made by Bennett, *Theatre Audiences*, pp. 18–19, although she does not address pantomime.
36. Bennett, *Theatre Audiences*, p. 118.
37. Davis, *The Economics of the British Stage*, p. 6.
38. Mayer, *Harlequin in his Element*, p. 365.
39. O'Brien, *Harlequin Britain*, p. 113.
40. The Victorian Plays Project at the University of Worcester lists three pantomimes in the digitized collection of Lacy's Acting Editions (see http://victorian.worc.ac.uk).

9 Davis, 'Material Modernism and Yeats'

1. C. Baldick, *The Modern Movement* (Oxford: Oxford University Press, 2004), pp. 4–5.
2. Ibid., p. 399.
3. T. S. Eliot, *The Complete Poems and Plays of T. S. Eliot* (London: Faber & Faber, 1969), p. 83. Ihab Hassan's tabular distinctions between modernist and postmodernist literary forms, in *The Dismemberment of Orpheus: Toward a Postmodern Literature*, 2nd edn (Madison, WI: University of Wisconsin Press, 1982), is one such instance of a misprision of modernism. The weakness of his approach is that many of the terms he ascribes to the postmodern – such as 'play', 'dispersal', 'anti-narrative' – are equally in evidence in texts we comfortably ascribe to literary modernism. Likewise, Brian McHale's differentiation in his *Postmodernist Fiction* (London: Routledge, 1987) between modernism's epistemological and postmodernism's ontological 'dominant' is another binarism that, arguably, does not withstand close scrutiny – Franz Kafka's work, for example, is as preoccupied with the issue of being as the problem of knowledge.

4. C. Kaplan, 'Review of *Rereading Modernism: New Directions in Feminist Criticism*, ed. Lisa Rado', *Modernism/Modernity*, 2:2 (1995), p. 116.

5. Ibid., p. 117.

6. See H. Carr, *The Verse Revolutionaries: Ezra Pound, H.D. and the Imagists* (London: Jonathan Cape, 2009).

7. G. Bornstein, *Material Modernism: The Politics of the Page* (Cambridge: Cambridge University Press, 2001), p. 1; see also McGann, *Black Riders*.

8. See The Brontës, *Tales of Glass Town, Angria, and Gondal: Selected Early Writings*, ed. C. Alexander (Oxford: Oxford University Press, 2010).

9. C. Isherwood and E. Upward, *The Mortmere Stories* (London: Enitharmon, 1994), p. 40.

10. S. Slote, 'Imposture Book Through the Ages', in S. Slote and W. Van Mierlo (eds), *Genitricksling Joyce* (Amsterdam: Rudopi, 1999), pp. 97–114, on p. 99.

11. Ibid., p. 100; and J. Scherer, *Le 'Livre' de Mallarmé*, 2nd edn (Paris: Gallimard, 1977), *passim*.

12. Isherwood and Upward, *Mortmere*, p. 45.

13. Ibid., p. 42. The *London Mercury*'s editor, J. C. Squire, had damned Eliot's poem for its seeming incomprehensibility; see J. C. Squire, 'Poetry', *London Mercury* 8 (October 1923), pp. 655–7.

14. Bornstein draws on and adapts the terminology of McGann, *The Textual Condition*, pp. 48–68.

15. W. B. Yeats, *The Secret Rose, Stories by W. B. Yeats: A Variorum Edition*, ed. W. Gould, P. L. Marcus and M. J. Sidnell, 2nd edn (London: Macmillan, 1992), p. 274; editors' italics. See also the editors' detailed discussion of the publication history of this passage (pp. 274–5).

16. See W. B. Yeats, *Short Fiction*, ed. G. J. Watson (Harmondsworth: Penguin, 1995).

17. Yeats's attention to the physical appearance of his books cannot be over-emphasized; witness for example his involvement with Dun Emer and Cuala Presses, the publishers of the majority of Yeats's collections in their first form during the twentieth century. Dun Emer Industries, Cuala Industries after 1908, was managed by Yeats's sisters, Susan (Lily) and Elizabeth (Lolly) Yeats from 1904, but was increasingly subsidized by the press's editor, W. B. Yeats. Forty-eight of Cuala Press's seventy or so titles are by Yeats, and he exerted considerable influence over their physical appearance, even to the colour of end-papers (to Lolly's chagrin). Cuala allowed Yeats – as Peppercanister would allow Thomas Kinsella many years later – an opportunity to publish his work in a format with clear national credentials; but it also provided him with, as it were, a 'dress rehearsal' for work which would subsequently by revised and reshaped in subsequent trade collections for London and New York publishers. See W. M. Murphy, *Family Secrets: W. B. Yeats and His Relatives* (Syracuse, NY: Syracuse University Press, 1995), pp. 86–264.

18. W. B. Yeats, *Autobiographies*, ed. W. H. O'Donnell and D. N. Archibald (New York: Scribner, 1999), p. 410.

19. On the modernist 'little magazine', see M. S. Morrisson, *The Public Face of Modernism: Little Magazines, Audiences, and Reception, 1905–1920* (Madison, WI: University of Wisconsin Press, 2001); M. Bradbury and J. McFarlane, 'Movements, Magazines and Manifestos', in M. Bradbury and J. McFarlane (eds), *Modernism 1890–1930* (Harmondsworth: Penguin, 1976), pp. 192–205; and F. J. Hoffman, C. Allen and C. F. Ulrich, *The Little Magazine: A History and Bibliography* (Princeton, NJ: Princeton University Press, 1946).

20. On the publication history of *The Waste Land*, see L. Rainey, *Revisiting 'The Waste Land'* (New Haven, CT: Yale University Press, 2005), pp. 71–101.

21. T. Clyde, *Irish Literary Magazines: An Outline History and Descriptive Bibliography* (Dublin: Irish Academic Press, 2003), p. 35.

22. Morrisson, *The Public Face*, p. 3.

23. Ibid., p. 7. For an exemplary case study of the often overlooked engagement of modernism with popular culture, see D. E. Chinitz, *T. S. Eliot and the Cultural Divide* (Chicago, IL: University of Chicago Press, 2003).

24. Clyde, *Irish Literary Magazines*, p. 35.

25. Morrisson, *The Public Face*, p. 10.

26. P. Reynolds, 'Reading Publics, Theater Audiences, and the Little Magazines of the Abbey Theater', *New Hibernia Review*, 7:4 (2003), p. 66.

27. See H. Adams, 'Yeats and Antithetical Nationalism', in V. Newey and A. Thompson (eds), *Literature and Nationalism* (Liverpool: Liverpool University Press, 1991), pp. 163–81.

28. T. Eagleton, *Heathcliff and the Great Hunger: Studies in Irish Culture* (London: Verso, 1996), p. 240.

29. See J. Eglinton, 'The Weak Point in the Celtic Movement', *Dana*, 11 (March 1905), p. 322. Eglinton also objected along similar lines to the dramatization of legendary and mythic material: see J. Eglinton, 'What Should be the Subjects of a National Drama? (2)', *Daily Express* (Dublin), 8 October 1898, p. 3.

30. W. B. Yeats, 'Literature and the Living Voice', *Samhain*, 6 (December 1906), p. 8.

31. Ibid., p. 6.

32. W. B. Yeats, *Letters to the New Island*, ed. G. Bornstein and H. Witemeyer (New York: Macmillan, 1989), p. 11.

33. W. B. Yeats, *Early Essays*, ed. R. J. Finneran and G. Bornstein (New York: Scribner, 2007), p. 8.

34. W. B. Yeats, 'The Play, the Player, and the Scene', *Samhain*, 4 (December 1904), pp. 25, 29, 31.

35. W. B. Yeats, 'First Principles', *Samhain*, 7 (November 1908), p. 7.

36. Yeats, 'First Principles', p. 8.

37. Yeats, of course, whose editorial role is stated on the magazine-cum-programme's cover.

38. For Yeats's Nobel address, see Yeats, *Autobiographies*, pp. 410–18. For a stimulating account of the Abbey's travails, see A. Frazier, *Behind the Scenes: Yeats, Horniman, and the Struggle for the Abbey Theatre* (Berkeley, CA: University of California Press, 1990).

39. On the bibliographical coding of a range of Irish publications, see J. C. C. Mays, *Fredson Bowers and the Irish Wolfhound* (Clonmel: Coracle, 2002).

40. See W. B. Yeats, 'To A. H. Bullen', 4–5 October 1907, in *The Collected Letters of W. B. Yeats*, vol. 4 (1905–7), ed. J. Kelly and R. Schuchard (Oxford: Oxford University Press, 2005), pp. 743–5.

41. W. B. Yeats, 'To John Quinn', 27 April 1908, in *Letters of W. B. Yeats*, ed. A. Wade (London: Rupert Hart-Davis, 1954), p. 509. For critical reception of the 1908 *Collected Works*, see A. N. Jeffares (ed.), *W. B. Yeats: The Critical Heritage* (London: Routledge & Kegan Paul, 1977), pp. 164–72.

42. W. B. Yeats, *Explorations*, selected by Mrs W. B. Yeats (London: Macmillan, 1962).

43. A line of textual scholarship in modern literature which takes its bearings from W. W. Greg's celebrated essay, 'The Rationale of Copy-Text', *Studies in Bibliography*, 3 (1950–1), pp. 19–36. For a lucid overview of this influential tradition, see G. T. Tanselle,

Selected Studies in Bibliography (Charlottesville, VA: Virginia University Press, 1979), pp. 309–54.

44. W. B. Yeats, *The Irish Dramatic Movement*, ed. M. FitzGerald and R. J. Finneran (New York: Scribner, 2003).

45. W. B. Yeats, *Mythologies*, ed. W. Gould and D. Toomey (Basingstoke: Palgrave Macmillan, 2005).

46. On the topic of authorial expectations, and their relationship to authorial intentions, see P. L. Shillingsburg, *Scholarly Editing in the Computer Age: Theory and Practice*, 3rd edn (Ann Arbor, MI: University of Michigan Press, 1996), pp. 53–70.

47. T. Mishkin, *The Harlem and Irish Renaissances: Language, Identity, and Representation* (Gainesville, FL: University of Florida Press, 1998), p. 21.

48. W. B. Yeats, 'Notes and Opinions', *Samhain*, 5 (November 1905), p. 9; cf. Yeats, *Explorations*, p. 192.

49. W. H. Auden, *Collected Poems*, ed. E. Mendelson (London: Faber, 1991), p. 247.

10 McCleery, 'Changing Audiences'

1. I would like to thank the following for their assistance: Andrew Rosenheim and Chris Beith formerly of Penguin; Hannah Lowery of the University of Bristol Library, and Ian Gunn. The staff at the Harry Ransom Humanities Research Center, the University of Texas at Austin, the University of Reading Library, the National Library of Ireland, the National Library of Scotland, the UK National Archives, and Edinburgh Napier University Library were ever patient and helpful. A shorter version of this essay appeared as 'The 1969 Edition of *Ulysses*: The Making of a Penguin Classic', *James Joyce Quarterly*, 46:1 (2008), pp. 55–73.

2. See G. Lernout, *The French Joyce* (Ann Arbor, MI: University of Michigan Press, 1990), p. 24.

3. See L. Rainey, 'The Cultural Economy of Modernism', in M. Levenson (ed.), *The Cambridge Companion to Modernism* (Cambridge: Cambridge University Press, 1999), pp. 33–69.

4. See for example J. P. Wexler, *Who Paid for Modernism? Art, Money and the Fiction of Conrad, Joyce and Lawrence* (Fayetteville, NC: University of Arkansas Press, 1997). For the background to *Dubliners*, see C. Hutton, 'Yogibogeybox in Dawson Chambers: The Beginnings of Maunsel and Company', in C. Hutten (ed.), *The Irish Book in the Twentieth Century* (Dublin: Irish Academic Press, 2004), pp. 36–46.

5. D. H. Lawrence, *The Letters of D. H. Lawrence*, ed. J. T. Boulton, 7 vols (Cambridge: Cambridge University Press, 1993), vol. 7, p. 448.

6. E. L. Bishop, 'The "Garbled History" of the First-edition *Ulysses*', *Joyce Studies Annual*, 9 (1998), pp. 3–36, on p. 35.

7. C. Duff, *James Joyce and the Plain Reader* (1932; New York: Haskell House, 1971), p. 21

8. See C. Turner, *Marketing Modernism between the Two World Wars* (Amherst, MA: University of Massachusetts Press, 2003). The newspaper advertisement is usefully reproduced in S. E. Casper, J. D. Chaison and J. D. Groves (eds), *Perspectives on American Book History: Artifacts and Commentary* (Amherst, MA: University of Massachusetts Press, 2002), pp. 342–3.

9. W. P. Jones, *James Joyce and the Common Reader* (Norman, OK: University of Oklahoma Press, 1955, 1970), p. 3.

10. Leslie Fiedler, while tracing his personal reading history of *Ulysses*, recounts the combination of artistic rebellion and teenage prurience in his 1934 reading before, as an academic, becoming 'a willing accomplice in the unfortunate process which has turned Joyce's books from the underground reading of young rebels into a part of required academic culture'. L. A. Fiedler, 'To Whom does Joyce Belong? *Ulysses* as Parody, Pop and Porn', in H. Ehrlich (ed.), *Light Rays: James Joyce and Modernism* (New York: New Horizon Press, 1984), pp. 26–37, on p. 28.

11. J. Carey, *The Intellectuals and the Masses: Pride and Prejudice among the Literary Intelligentsia, 1880–1939* (London: Faber & Faber, 1992), p. 21.

12. Ibid., p. 20

13. P. Bourdieu, *Distinction: A Social Critique of the Judgement of Taste* (1979; English translation: London, 1984).

14. P. Bourdieu, *The Field of Cultural Production* (Cambridge: Polity, 1993), p. 70.

15. P. D. McDonald, *British Literary Culture and Publishing Practice, 1880–1914* (Cambridge: Cambridge University Press, 1997), p.18; see also Finkelstein and McCleery (eds), *An Introduction to Book History*.

16. See J. Kelly, *Our Joyce: From Outcast to Icon* (Austin, TX: University of Texas Press, 1998), p. 3.

17. The Bodley Head Papers, University of Reading Library [uncatalogued].

18. Paul Léon to Frank Morley, 27 October 1933, Joyce-Léon Papers, National Library of Ireland.

19. [UK] National Archives HO [Home Office]/144/20071/186.428/61.

20. National Library of Ireland, Joyce-Léon Papers.

21. N. Joicey, 'A Paperback Guide to Progress: Penguin Books 1935–c.1951', *Twentieth Century British History*, 4:1 (1993), p. 56

22. B. Crutchley, 'The Penguin Achievement', *Book Collector*, 1:4 (Winter 1952), p. 211.

23. Max Reinhardt to Eunice Frost, 16 December 1958; Anthony Godwin to Max Reinhardt, 12 January 1961: both in DM1819, Folder 1C, Penguin Archive, University of Bristol Library.

24. Oliver Caldecott to Max Reinhardt, 12 October 1967; Max Reinhardt to Oliver Caldecott, 16 October 1967: both in Editorial File, *Ulysses*, Penguin Archive, University of Bristol Library.

25. Max Reinhardt to Oliver Caldecott, 1 November 1967; Guido Waldman, Bodley Head, to Oliver Caldecott, 11 December 1967: both in Editorial File, *Ulysses*, Penguin Archive, University of Bristol Library. See also J. Sutherland, 'Fiction and the Erotic Cover', *Critical Quarterly*, 33:2 (1991), pp. 3–36 for specific case studies of the tensions between publishers' artwork and authorial integrity.

26. Oliver Caldecott to Max Reinhardt, 17 October 1967, Editorial File, *Ulysses*, Penguin Archive, University of Bristol Library.

27. Internal memo from Hans Schmoller, 26 February 1968, Editorial File, *Ulysses*, Penguin Archive, University of Bristol Library.

28. Richard Ellmann to Oliver Caldecott, 20 March 1968, Editorial File, *Ulysses*, Penguin Archive, University of Bristol Library.

29. For Ellman's endorsement of *Portrait*, see W. S. Brockman, '*A Portrait of the Artist as a Young Man* in the Public Domain', *PBSA*, 98:2 (2004), pp. 191–207, on p.197.

30. I. B. Nadel, 'The Incomplete Joyce', *Joyce Studies Annual*, 2 (1991), pp. 86–100.

31. Genette, *Paratexts*, p. 270

32. Fritz Senn to Penguin Books, n.d, Editorial File, *Ulysses*, Penguin Archive, University of Bristol Library.
33. F. Senn, 'The Joyce Industrial Evolution, According to one European Amateur', *Journal of Modern Literature*, 22:2 (1998–9), pp. 191–7.
34. P. Fuller, 'Final Liberation for James Joyce', *City Press*, 8 May 1969, p. 10.
35. See, for example, the *Observer Review*, 20 April 1969, and the *Yorkshire Post*, 23 April 1969.
36. *Scotsman*, 26 April 1969.
37. *The Times*, Saturday Review, 19 April 1969, p. 12.
38. Richard Ellmann to Oliver Caldecott, 20 March 1968, Editorial File, *Ulysses*, Penguin Archive, University of Bristol Library.
39. See P. Baines, *Penguin By Design: A Cover Story 1935–2005* (London: Allen Lane, 2005), p. 124 and *passim*. See also A. McCleery, 'The Paperback Evolution: Tauchnitz, Albatross and Penguin', in N. Matthews and N. Moody (eds), *Judging a Book by Its Cover* (Aldershot: Ashgate, 2007), pp. 3–18.

11 Van Kalmthout, 'The Sound of Literature'

1. This paper has been translated by Janey Tucker.
2. S. R. Fischer, *A History of Reading* (London: Reaktion, 2003), p. 317.
3. Ibid., p. 276; A. Manguel, *A History of Reading* (New York: Viking, 1996), pp. 113–4.
4. For examples of this custom in Great Britain see Altick, *The English Common Reader*, pp. 249–50, 324–5, 330; Rose, *The Intellectual Life of the British Working Classes*, pp. 84–5; St Clair, *The Reading Nation in the Romantic Period*, pp. 344, 394–7.
5. This assumption is based on the fact that Dutch educationalists were usually oriented on educational theory in the surrounding countries, in particular Germany and Great Britain. Moreover, the Dutch approach had much in common with that used in France in the second half of the nineteenth and early twentieth century. See A.-M. Chartier and J. Hébrard, *Discours sur la lecture (1880–2000)*, with E. Fraisse, M. Poullain and J.-C. Pompougnac (Paris: BPI-Centre Pompidou & Fayard, 2000), pp. 229–33, 323–8 and 344–5.
6. Continued research will result in a monograph on the history of secondary literary education in the Netherlands between 1880 and 1940, including current methods of teaching literary reading.
7. An interesting study in relation to this is J. Dane, *De vrucht van bijbelsche opvoeding: Populaire leescultuur en opvoeding in protestants-christelijke gezinnen, circa 1880–1940* (Hilversum: Verloren, 1996), which does not focus on reading aloud, but it discusses the contemporary Dutch practice of Christian familial reading in general and the way in which this practice related to education. An important study on nineteenth-century literary education in Dutch secondary schools is G.-J. Johannes, *Dit moet U niet onverschillig wezen! De vaderlandse literatuur in het Noord-Nederlands voortgezet onderwijs 1800–1900* (Nijmegen: Vantilt, 2007), which, however, neither deals with reading aloud in particular. For literary education in the nineteenth-century Anglophone world, see A. Ellis, *Books in Victorian Elementary Schools* (London: Library Association, 1971) and A. Richardson, *Literature, Education, and Romanticism: Reading as Social Practice, 1780–1832* (Cambridge: Cambridge University Press, 1994).
8. R. Darnton, *The Kiss of Lamourette: Reflections in Cultural History* (London: Faber & Faber, 1990), p. 169.

9. J. Leest, *Het voortgezet onderwijs in de moedertaal* (Groningen: Wolters, 1932), pp. 32, 74–5.

10. G. Kalff, 'Voor Potgieter', *De Gids*, 61 (1897), part 1, p. 555.

11. See, for example, J. G. M. Moormann, *De moedertaal: Een didactiek voor het middelbaar (en lager) onderwijs* (Nijmegen: Dekker en Van de Vegt, 1936), pp. 5–7.

12. C. H. den Hertog, 'De taalstudie der onderwijzers, [V–VI]', *Noord en Zuid*, 12 (1889), pp. 109–10.

13. *Handelingen en mededeelingen van de Maatschappij der Nederlandsche Letterkunde te Leiden, over het jaar 1914–1915*, 2 vols (Leiden: Brill, 1915), vol. 1, p. 62; see also N. van Wijk, 'De rompstand en zijn betekenis voor taal en muziek', *De Gids*, 79 (1915), pp. 458–94. The theory had already been introduced in the Netherlands by J. van Ginneken, 'De rompstanden', *Nieuwe Taalgids*, 7 (1913), pp. 1–15.

14. Sometimes recitation competitions were also held; see for example A. J. Schneiders, 'Over voordragen', *Levende Talen*, 24 (1936), pp. 141–5.

15. H. de Vos, *Moedertaalonderwijs in de Nederlanden: Een historisch-kritisch overzicht van de methoden bij de studie van de moedertaal in het middelbaar onderwijs sedert het begin van de negentiende eeuw*, 2 vols (Turnhout: Van Mierlo-Proost, 1939), p. 120.

16. Early evidence of this is provided by H. W. van der Meij, 'De kunst van lezen', *Noord en Zuid*, 13 (1890), p. 291: 'Previously, the ability to read clearly and well was a basic requirement of a good education ... These days, we call in specialists for the purpose and listen to them'.

17. B. Verhagen, *Prosodie: Ontleding der structuur van het vers ten dienste van het voordrachtsonderwijs* (Amsterdam: Duwaer and van Ginkel, 1918), revised for B. Verhagen, *Prosodie der voordrachtskunst* (Groningen: Noordhoff, 1924); B. Verhagen, *Het gesproken woord* (Amsterdam: Paris, 1937); A. Vogel, *Voordrachtskunst: Theoretische en praktische beschouwingen* (Arnhem: Van Loghem Slaterus, 1919).

18. N. Baldwin, *Edison: Inventing the Century* (New York: Hyperion, 1995), p. 90.

19. J. J. Salverda de Grave, 'De gramofoon in de Sorbonne', *De Gids*, 77 (1913), part 2, pp. 143–52.

20. For example E. Legouvé, *L'art de la lecture* (Paris: Hetzel, 1877), which was reissued dozens of times and used very widely in the Netherlands as well as in France, and the also very popular *La lecture en action* (Paris: Hetzel, 1881) by the same author. By contrast, a book specially tailored to the Dutch situation was A. M. Eldar, *Spreken en zingen, in verband gebracht met de Nederlandsche taal.* (Tiel: Mijs, 1886), which was reissued in a twenty-fifth edition in 1943 and appeared in its forty-fourth (and last) edition as late as 1997.

21. J. Karsemeijer, 'De verwaarloosde component van het onderwijs in het Nederlands', *Levende Talen*, 24 (1936), p. 405.

22. J. B., 'De kunst van lezen', with a postscript by d.B., *Noord en Zuid*, 3 (1880), p. 241.

23. Ibid.

24. See for example 'Ned. Sectievergadering', *Levende Talen*, 21 (1933), pp. 69–71, which contains guidelines for mother tongue teaching in the lower classes of general secondary and elementary teacher training schools. In the section entitled 'Reading and speaking', the recommended categories for reading education are as follows: 'Silent reading and reproduction of the content'; 'Technique of reading aloud (to practice breathing, articulation, overview of a series of words, rhythmic linking of the series, appreciation of punctuation'; 'Circumstantial reading (including aesthetic appreciation), and recitation'; and 'Reading dialogues; dramatisation', p. 70.

25. Stemvers, F. G. A., 'Het moedertaalonderwijs op de middelbare school II', *Levende Talen*, 21 (1933), pp. 181–96, on p. 185.

26. Cited in M. L. de Keijser, 'Het lezen op de R.N.S. (Lezing gehouden te Goes, op de vergadering der Vereeniging van Leeraren aan Kweek en Normaalscholen in Zeeland', *Noord en Zuid*, 27 (1904), pp. 481–97, on p. 481.

27. Cited in F. Buitenrust Hettema, 'Uit de praktijk, III: Leesonderwijs', *Taal en Letteren*, 9 (1899), pp. 123–5, on p. 124.

28. F. Buitenrust Hettema, 'Uit de praktijk', *Taal en Letteren, 8* (1898), pp. 15–20, on pp. 15, 17–18.

29. C. G. N. de Vooys, 'Bevordering van een meer verzorgd mondeling taalgebruik', *Nieuwe Taalgids*, 34 (1940), pp. 129–31, on pp. 130–1.

30. J. Karsemeijer and G. Kazemier, *Los van de letter: Proza en poëzie met aanwijzingen voor goede voordracht voor de laagste klassen van gymnasia, lycea, H. B. S. en kweekscholen* (Groningen: Wolters, 1940).

31. J. B. Schepers, *Bragi*, 3 vols (Amsterdam: Van Looy, 1900–1).

32. J. A. Nijland, 'Iets uit de praktijk van mijn onderwijs', *Taal en Letteren*, 14 (1904), pp. 28–32, on p. 30.

33. J. de Vries, P. J. Idenburg, J. Moormann and J. J. Gielen, 'Het onderwijs in het Nederlandsch', *Jaarboek van de Maatschappij der Nederlandsche Letterkunde te Leiden 1937–1938* (Leiden: Brill, 1938), p. 64.

34. Leest, *Het voortgezet onderwijs*, pp. 103–4.

35. Den Hertog, 'De taalstudie', pp. 106–7.

36. Van der Meij, 'De kunst van lezen', pp. 294–5.

37. Leest, *Het voortgezet onderwijs*, pp. 32–7.

38. G. van Veen, *Plaats en beteekenis van het 'stil lezen' in onze lagere schole* (Groningen: Wolters, 1929).

39. A. H. van der Hoeve, P. Kohnstamm and G. van Veen, *De lagere school en het stil-lezen: Een onderzoek inzake het zelfstandig verwerken van leesstof door leerlingen der hoogste klassen van lagere scholen in de gemeente Utrecht* (Groningen: Wolters, 1933); A. H. van der Hoeve, P. Kohnstamm and G. van Veen, *Stil-lees-stof als denk-materiaal en denk-maatstaf: Een onderzoek aangaande de vorming en toetsing van 'theoretische intelligentie'* (Groningen: Wolters, 1935); T. Boersma, 'Leren denken door stillezen in groepsverband', *Paedagogische Studiën*, 22 (1941), pp. 33–55; see also N. Deen, *Een halve eeuw onderwijsresearch in Nederland: Het Nutsseminarium voor Pedagogiek aan de Universiteit van Amsterdam, 1919–1969* (Groningen: Wolters-Noordhoff, 1971), pp. 111–17.

40. See for example P. A. Diels, 'Het stille lezen', *Paedagogische Studiën*, 10 (1929), pp. 324–33 and 400–2; P. A. Diels, 'De opkomst van het stil-lezen', *Paedagogische Studiën* 15 (1934), pp. 216–27; P. A. Diels, 'De triomf van het stil-lezen', *Paedagogische Studiën*, 19 (1938), pp. 105–10; G. van Veen, 'De beteekenis van het stil-lezen (Naar aanleiding van P. A. Diels' "Het stille lezen")', *Paedagogische Studiën*, 10 (1929), pp. 394–400; G. van Veen, 'Het stil-lezen'. *Paedagogische Studiën*, 14 (1933), pp. 8–19; M. J. Langeveld, 'Enige opmerkingen naar aanleiding van een polemiek over het stil-lezen en over het stil-leeswerk in het algemeen', *Weekblad voor Gymnasiaal en Middelbaar Onderwijs*, 24 (April 1935), pp. 956–9; M. Holtrop, 'Hardop lezen en het mondeling expressievermogen', *Paedagogische Studien*, 16 (1935), pp. 327–38; W. Kramer, '"De triomf van het stil-lezen" en de gevaren van dien', *Nieuwe Taalgids*, 32 (1938), pp. 273–80.

41. M. J. Langeveld, *Taal en denken: Een theoretiese en didaktiese bijdrage tot het onderwijs in de moedertaal op de middelbare school, inzonderheid tot dat der grammatika* (Groningen: Wolters, 1934).

42. For similar changes in examinations in France, see Chartier and Hébrard, *Discours*, p. 452.

43. H. Godthelp, *Actief lezen: Teksten met vragen: Lees-taalboekje voor de lagere klassen van alle inrichtingen voor voorbereidend hoger- en middelbaar onderwijs, van de kweekscholen en de MULO-scholen*, 2 vols ('s-Gravenhage: Van Goor, 1937); H. Godthelp, *Belevend lezen*, 2 vols ('s-Gravenhage: Van Goor, 1938); M. J. Langeveld and B. G. Palland, *Denkend lezen: Een stilleesboekje voor opleidingsscholen en de eerste leerjaren van voorbereidend hoger en middelbaar onderwijs* (Groningen: Wolters, 1935), which still appeared in revised editions until at least 1972). The preparatory textbook for this was M. J. Langeveld and B. G. Palland, *Op weg naar denkend lezen: Een stil-leesboekje voor de zesde klasse der volksschool en de vijfde en zesde klasse der opleidingsschool* (Groningen: Wolters, 1937), issued in at least fourteen editions and which was still appearing until at least 1970.

44. B. van Meurs, 'De stil-leesmethode', *Levende Talen*, 27 (1939), pp. 160–9, on pp. 160, 169. On the inability of silent reading experiments to win over teachers in the early decades of the twentieth century see M. M. Mathews, *Teaching to Read, Historically Considered* (Chicago, IL: University of Chicago Press, 1967), pp. 194–5.

45. F. G. A. Stemvers, 'De leerschool der verveling', *Levende Talen*, 27 (1939), pp. 99–109, on pp. 101–2.

46. J. E. van der Laan, 'Lesen ohne Geheimnis', *Nieuwe Taalgids*, 33 (1939), pp. 227–31, on pp. 228–30. He quotes the following example: 'The poet has clearly gone out for a walk early on a fine winter's morning (!). What shows that he was not alone? Might the second person (!) be his young wife?' The poem concerned was Herman Gorter's rapturous 'Toen bliezen de poortwachters op gouden horens'.

47. Van der Laan, 'Lesen', p. 227.

48. F. G. A. Stemvers, 'Review of: Karsemeijer, J., and G. Kazemier, *Los van de letter: Proza en poëzie met aanwijzingen voor goede voordracht voor de laagste klassen van gymnasia, lycea, H. B. S. en kweekscholen* (Groningen: Wolters, 1940)', *Levende Talen*, 28 (1940), p. 380.

49. This is based on the fact that a new legislation for secondary education was adopted in the Netherlands in 1963. It entered into force in 1968 and led to a renewal of methods for mother tongue teaching.

12 Murphy, 'Intermediality'

1. J. J. McGann, 'Marking Texts of Many Dimensions', in S. Schreibman, R. Siemens and J. Unsworth (eds), *A Companion to Digital Humanities* (Oxford: Blackwell, 2004), at http://www.digitalhumanities.org/companion/ [accessed 16 July 2010].

2. L. Scheidt, 'Professional-Lurker' (14 April 2007), available from: http://www.professional-lurker.com [accessed 16 July 2010].

3. J. D. Bolter and R. Grusin, *Remediation: Understanding New Media* (Cambridge, MA: Massachusetts Institute of Technology Press, 2000), p. 19.

4. M. Federman, 'What is the Meaning of "The Medium is the Message"' (2003), at http://individual.utoronto.ca/markfederman/article_mediumisthemessage.htm [accessed 16 July 2010].

5.   G. Landow, *Hypertext 3.0: Critical Theory and New Media in an Era of Globalization* (Baltimore, MD: Johns Hopkins University Press, 2006), p. 7.

6.   A. López-Varela Azcárate and S. Tötösy de Zepetnek, 'Towards Intermediality in Contemporary Cultural Practices and Education', *Culture, Language and Representation*, 6:1 (2008), pp. 65–82.

7.   J. Hilton and D. Wiley, 'What Happens to Book Sales if Digital Versions are Given Away?', *Journal of Electronic Publishing / Digital Book World* (2010), at http://www.digitalbookworld.com [accessed 16 July 2010].

8.   'W3Schools Online Web Tutorials', *W3 Schools Online*, at http://www.w3schools.com [accessed 16 July 2010].

9.   *The Text Encoding Initiative* (2010), at http://www.tei-c.org [accessed 16 July 2010].

10. M. Sperberg-McQueen and L. Bernard, 'TEI Pizza Chef', *The Text Encoding Initiative* (2010), at http://www.tei-c.org/pizza.html [accessed 16 July 2010].

11. See http://www.quartos.org [accessed 16 July 2010].

12. See http://www.nines.org [accessed 16 July 2010].

13. J. Bryant, *Unfolding Melville: Sexuality, Politics, and the Versions of Typee* (Ann Arbor, MI: Michigan University Press, 2008).

14. S. Schreibman, *The Versioning Machine* (2004), at http://v-machine.org [accessed 16 July 2010].

WORKS CITED

Aafjes, J. D., *Buig de stem!: Leesboek ter bevordering van den goeden leesstem* (Amsterdam: Versluys, 1912).

Abbott, A., *Catalogue of the Mercantile Library of Philadelphia, Annual Report* (1867), in 'A Village Library', *Harper's New Monthly Magazine*, 36:216 (May 1868), pp. 774–7.

Abbot, J. G., 'Proceedings', Massachusetts State Convention, MA, 4 May 1853.

Adams, H., 'Yeats and Antithetical Nationalism', in V. Newey and A. Thompson (eds), *Literature and Nationalism* (Liverpool: Liverpool University Press, 1991), pp. 163–81.

Adams, T., and N. Barker, 'A New Model for the Study of the Book', in *A Potencie of Life: Books in* Society, ed. N. Barker (London: British Library, 1993), pp. 5–43.

Alberti, L. B., *On Painting*, trans. J. R. Spencer (New Haven, CT, and London: Yale University Press, 1966).

Allen, G., *Harold Bloom: A Poetics of Conflict* (New York: Harvester Wheatsheaf, 1994).

—, 'Mary Shelley as Elegiac Poet: The Return and "The Choice"', *Romanticism*, 13:3 (2007), pp. 219–32.

—, 'Mary Shelley's Letter to Maria Gisborne', *La Questione Romantica*, 1 (2009), pp. 69–82.

—, *Mary Shelley* (London: Palgrave, 2008).

Allingham, H. P., and E. B. Williams (eds), *Letters to William Allingham* (London: Longman, 1911).

Allingham, W., *Nightingale Valley*, comp. 'Giraldus' (London: Bell & Daldry, 1860).

Altick, R., *The English Common Reader: A Social History of the Mass Reading Public, 1800–1900* (Chicago, IL: University of Chicago Press, 1957).

Andrew, M., *A Variorum Edition of the Works of Geoffrey Chaucer, II: The Canterbury Tales, The General Prologue, Part One B, Explanatory Notes* (Norman, OK: University of Oklahoma Press, 1992), pp. 538–41.

Appleford, A. 'The Dance of Death in London: John Carpenter, John Lydgate, and the *Daunce of Poulys*', *Journal of Medieval and Early Modern Studies*, 38 (2008), pp. 285–314.

Auden, W. H., *Collected Poems*, ed. E. Mendleson (London: Faber, 1991).

Auslander, P., *Liveness: Performance in a Mediatized Culture* (London: Routledge, 1999).

Baines, P., *Penguin by Design: A Cover Story 1935–2005* (London: Allen Lane, 2005).

Baldick, C., *The Modern Movement* (Oxford: Oxford University Press, 2004).

Baldwin, N., *Edison: Inventing the Century* (New York: Hyperion, 1995).

Barry, J., *The Works of James Barry*, ed. E. Fryer, 2 vols (London, 1809).

Baxandall, M., *Giotto and the Orators: Humanist Observers of Painting in Italy and the Discovery of Pictorial Composition, 1350–1450* (Oxford: Oxford-Warburg Studies, 1971).

Bennett, S., *Theatre Audiences: A Theory of Production and Reception* (London: Routledge, 1994).

Benson, L. D. (gen. ed.), *The Riverside Chaucer*, 3rd edn (Oxford: Oxford University Press, 1987).

Bettley, J., 'Clark, Charles (1806–1880)', *ODNB* (Oxford: Oxford University Press, 2004), at http://www.oxforddnb.com/view/article/5457 [accessed 20 May 2010].

Bishop, E. L., 'The "Garbled History" of the First-edition *Ulysses*', *Joyce Studies Annual*, 9 (1998), pp. 3–36.

Blunden, E., *Keats's Publisher: A Memoir of John Taylor* (London: Jonathan Cape, 1936).

Boersma, T., 'Leren denken door stillezen in groepsverband', *Paedagogische Studiën*, 22 (1941), pp. 33–55.

Boffey, J., *Manuscripts of English Courtly Love Lyrics in the Later Middle Ages* (Woodbridge, Suffolk: D. S. Brewer, 1985).

—, 'Middle English Lyrics and Manuscripts', in T. G. Duncan (ed.), *A Companion to the Middle English Lyric* (Woodbridge, Suffolk: D. S. Brewer, 2005), pp. 1–18.

—, '"Cy ensuent trios chanunceons": Groups and Sequences of Middle English Lyrics', in G.D. Caie and D. Renevey (eds), *Medieval Texts in Context* (Turnhout: Brepols, 2008), pp. 85–95.

Boffey, J., and J. J. Thompson, 'Anthologies and Miscellanies: Production and Choice of Text', in Griffiths and Pearsall (eds), *Book Production and Publishing in Britain*, pp. 279–315.

Bolter, J. D., and R. Grusin, *Remediation: Understanding New Media* (Cambridge, MA: Massachusets Institute of Technology Press, 2000).

Booth, M. R., *English Plays of the Nineteenth Century*, 5 vols (Oxford: Clarendon Press, 1969–76).

—, *Victorian Spectacular Theatre 1850–1910* (London: Routledge & Kegan Paul, 1981).

Bornstein, G., *Material Modernism: The Politics of the Page* (Cambridge: Cambridge University Press, 2001).

Bourdieu, P., *Distinction: A Social Critique of the Judgement of Taste* (1979; English translation: London, 1984).

—, *The Field of Cultural Production* (Cambridge: Polity, 1993).

Bradbury, M., and J. McFarlane, 'Movements, Magazines and Manifestos', in M. Bradbury and J. McFarlane (eds), *Modernism 1890–1930* (Harmondsworth: Penguin, 1976), pp. 192–205.

Braden, G., *The Classics and English Renaissance Poetry: Three Case Studies* (New Haven, CT: Yale University Press, 1978).

Bradshaw, M., 'Reading as Flight: Fragment Poems from Shelley's Notebooks', in Webb and Weinberg (eds), *The Unfamiliar Shelley*, pp. 21–40.

Bratton, J., *New Readings in Theatre History* (Cambridge: Cambridge University Press, 2003).

Brewer, J., *The Pleasures of the Imagination: English Culture in the Eighteenth Century* (London: HarperCollins, 1997).

Brockman, W. S., '*A Portrait of the Artist as a Young Man* in the Public Domain', *Papers of the Bibliographical Society of America*, 98:2 (2004), pp. 191–207.

Broome, R. (Federal Writer's Project), 'How Branson's Bulldog Courage Won', Stiles M. Scruggs, South Carolina Writer's Project. Washington DC: Manuscript Division, Library of Congress.

Browne, J. H., *The Great Metropolis, a Mirror of New York* (Hartford, CT: American Publishing Company, 1869.

Brownson, O., *The Spirit Rapper, An Autobiography* (Boston, MA: Little Brown, 1854).

Brignull, A., *Charles Clark: The Bard of Totham* (Loughborough: The Hedgehog Press, 1990).

British Library Manuscripts Catalogue, at http://www.bl.uk/catalogues/manuscripts/INDEX.asp [accessed 20 May 2010].

Brontës, The, *Tales of Glass Town, Angria, and Gondal: Selected Early Writings*, ed. C. Alexander (Oxford: Oxford University Press, 2010).

Buitenrust Hettema, F., 'Uit de praktijk', *Taal en Letteren* 8 (1898), pp. 15–20.

—, 'Uit de praktijk, III: Leesonderwijs', *Taal en Letteren*, 9 (1899), pp. 123–5.

Bryant, J., *Unfolding Melville: Sexuality, Politics, and the Versions of Typee* (Ann Arbor, MI: Michigan University Press, 2008).

Brydges, Sir E., *Human Fate* (Essex: Great Totham Press, 1846).

Cabell, M. C., *Sketches and Recollections of Lynchburg by the Oldest Inhabitant* (Richmond: C. H. Wynne, 1858).

Cain, T., and R. Connolly, *The Complete Works of Robert Herrick,* 2 vols (Oxford: Oxford University Press, forthcoming).

—, *Lords of Wine and Oile: Community and Conviviality in the Work of Robert Herrick* (Oxford: Oxford University Press, forthcoming).

Carey, J., *The Intellectuals and the Masses: Pride and Prejudice among the Literary Intelligentsia, 1880–1939* (London: Faber & Faber, 1992).

Carlson, M., 'Theatre Audiences and the Reading of Performance', in T. Postlewait and B. A. McConachie (eds), *Interpreting the Theatrical Past: Essays in the Historiography of Performance* (Iowa City, IA: University of Iowa Press, 1989), pp. 82–98.

Carr, H., *The Verse Revolutions: Ezra Pound, H. D. and the Imagists* (London: Jonathan Cape, 2009).

Carruthers, M., *The Book of Memory: A Study of Memory in Medieval Culture* (Cambridge: Cambridge University Press, 1990).

Casper, S. E., J. D. Chaison and J. D. Groves (eds), *Perspectives on American Book History: Artifacts and Commentary* (Amherst, MA: University of Massachusetts Press, 2002).

Chartier, R., 'Figures of the Author', in *The Order of Books: Readers, Authors, and Libraries in Europe Between the Fourteenth and Eighteenth Centuries*, trans. L. G. Cochrane (Stanford, CA: Stanford University Press, 1992).

Chartier, A.-M., and J. Hébrard, *Discours sur la lecture (1880–2000)*, with E. Fraisse, M. Poullain and J.-C. Pompougnac (Paris: BPI-Centre Pompidou & Fayard, 2000).

Chinitz, D. E., *T. S. Eliot and the Cultural Divide* (Chicago, IL: University of Chicago Press, 2003).

Clanchy, M. T., *From Memory to Written Record* (Oxford: Oxford University Press, 1993).

Clark, C. (alias 'Bookworm'), *Tiptree Races* (Maldon, Essex: P. H. Youngman, 1833).

—, *John Noakes and Mary Styles* (Essex: Great Totham Press, 1834).

—, Letter to Thomas Frognall Dibdin, 10 June 1837; San Marino: Huntington Rare Book and Manuscript Library DI 105.

—, 'A Doctor's Doings, or The Entrapped Heiress of Witham' (Essex: Great Totham Press, 1839).

—, Letter to John Russell Smith, 10 February 1843; Chelmsford, Essex Public Records Office D/DU 668/7.

—, 'Whimsical Book-Plate', *Notes and Queries*, 141 (10 July 1852), pp. 32–3.

Clyde, T., *Irish Literary Magazines: An Outline History and Descriptive Bibliography* (Dublin: Irish Academic Press, 2003).

Coiro, A. B., *Robert Herrick and the Epigram Book Tradition* (Baltimore, MD: Johns Hopkins University Press, 1988).

Coleman, J., *Public Reading and the Reading Public in Late Medieval England and France* (Cambridge: Cambridge University Press, 1996).

—, 'Aurality', in P. Strohm (ed.), *Middle English, Oxford Twenty-First Century Approaches to Literature* (Oxford: Oxford University Press, 2007), pp. 68–85.

Collier, H., 'Richard Hill – a London Compiler', in E. Mullally and J. J. Thompson (eds), *The Court and Cultural Diversity* (Woodbridge, Suffolk: D. S. Brewer, 1997).

Conger, S. M., F. S. Frank and G. O'Dea (eds), *Iconoclastic Departures: Mary Shelley after Frankenstein* (London: Associated University Presses, 1997).

Cook, F. C., *Sermons* (London: John Murray, 1863).

Coolahan, M.-L., '"We Live by Chance, and Slip into Events": Occasionality and the Manuscript Verse of Katherine Philips', *Eighteenth-Century Ireland/iris an dá chultúr*, 18 (2003), pp. 9–23.

Coppee, H., *English Language Considered as an Interpreter of English History, Designed as a Manual of Instruction* (Philadelphia, PA: Claxton, Remsen & Haffelfinger, 1873).

Corns, T., *Uncloistered Virtue: English Political Literature 1640–1660* (Oxford: Clarendon Press, 1992).

Crane, M. T., *Framing Authority: Sayings, Self and Society in Sixteenth-Century England* (Princeton, NJ: Princeton University Press, 1993).

Creaser, J., 'Herrick at Play', *Essays in Criticism*, 56 (2006), pp. 324–50.

—, '"Times Trans-shifting": Chronology and the Misshaping of Herrick', *English Literary Renaissance*, 39:1 (2009), pp. 163–93.

Cremona, V. A., P. Eversmann, H. van Maanen, W. Sauter and J. Tulloch (eds), *Theatrical Events Borders Dynamics Frames* (Amsterdam: Rodolpi, 2004).

Cresswell, L., *Stemmata Alstoniana: A Collection of Genealogical Tables relating to the ancient family of Alston* (privately printed, 1898).

Crook, N., 'In Defence of the 1831 *Frankenstein*', in M. Eberle-Sinatra (ed.), *Mary Shelley's Fictions: From Frankenstein to Falkner* (London: Macmillan, 2000), pp. 3–21.

Crutchley, B., 'The Penguin Achievement', *Book Collector*, 1:4 (1952), pp. 211–13.

Cutter, C. A., 'New Catalogue of Harvard College Library', *North American Review*, 108: 222 (January 1869), p. 99.

Da Vinci, L., *Leonardo on Painting*, ed. and trans. M. Kemp and M. Walker (New Haven, CT, and London, Yale University Press, 1989).

Dane, J., *De vrucht van bijbelsche opvoeding: Populaire leescultuur en opvoeding in protestants-christelijke gezinnen, circa 1880–1940* (Hilversum: Verloren, 1996).

Darnton, R., 'What is the History of Books?', in *The Book History Reader*, ed. Finkelstein and McCleery, pp. 9–27.

—, *The Kiss of Lamourette: Reflections in Cultural History* (London: Faber & Faber, 1990).

Davis, J., and V. Emeljanow, *Reflecting the Audience: London Theatregoing, 1840–1880* (Hatfield: University of Hertfordshire Press, 2001).

Davis, T. C., *The Economics of the British Stage 1800–1914* (Cambridge: Cambridge University Press, 2000).

De Bolla, P., N. Leask and D. Simpson (eds), *Land, Nation and Culture, 1740 – 1840: Thinking the Republic of Taste* (Basingstoke: Palgrave Macmillan, 2005).

De Keijser, M. L., 'Het lezen op de R.N.S. (Lezing gehouden te Goes, op de vergadering der Vereeniging van Leeraren aan Kweek-en Normaalscholen in Zeeland', *Noord en Zuid*, 27 (1904), pp. 481–97.

De Man, P., *Allegories of Reading: Figural Language in Rousseau, Nietzsche, and Proust* (New Haven, CT, and London: Yale University Press, 1979).

De Palacio, J., *Mary Shelley dans son oeuvre* (Paris: Éditions Klincksieck, 1969).

De Vooys, C. G. N., 'Bevordering van een meer verzorgd mondeling taalgebruik', *Nieuwe Taalgids*, 34 (1940), pp. 129–31.

De Vos, H., *Moedertaalonderwijs in de Nederlanden: Een historisch-kritisch overzicht van de methoden bij studie van de moedertaal in het middelbaar onderwijs sedert het begin van de negentiende eeuw*, 2 vols (Turnhout: Van Mierlo-Proost, 1939).

De Vries, J., P. J. Idenburg, J. Moormann and J. J. Gielen, 'Het onderwijs in het Nederlandsch', *Jaarboek van de Maatschappij der Nederlandsche Letterkunde te Leiden 1937–1938* (Leiden: Brill, 1938), pp. 33–80.

Deen, N., *Een halve eeuw onderwijsresearch in Nederland: Het Nutsseminarium voor Pedagogiek aan de Universiteit van Amsterdam, 1919–1969* (Groningen: Wolters-Noordhoff, 1971).

Den Hertog, C. H., 'De taalstudie der onderwijzers [V–VI]', *Noord en Zuid*, 12 (1889), pp. 97–115.

Derrida, J., 'Some Statements and Truisms about Neologisms, Newisms, Postisms, Parasitisms, and Other Small Seismisms', in D. Carroll (ed.), *The States of Theory* (New York, Columbia University Press, 1989), pp. 63–94.

Dickens, C., *Oliver Twist*, Great Illustrated Classics (New York: Dodd & Mead, 1941).

—, *David Copperfield*, Great Illustrated Classics (New York: Dodd & Mead, 1943).

—, *The Letters of Charles Dickens*, Pilgrim edition, ed. K. Tillotson and N. Burgis, 12 vols (Oxford: Oxford University Press, 1977).

—, *Pilgrim Letters*, ed. K. Tillotson and N. Burgis, (Oxford: Oxford University Press, 1978).

Diels, P. A., 'Het stille lezen', *Paedagogische Studiën*, 10 (1929), pp. 324–33, 400–2.

—, 'De opkomst van het stil-lezen', *Paedagogische Studiën*, 15 (1934), pp. 216–27.

—, 'De triomf van het stil-lezen', *Paedagogische Studiën*, 19 (1938), pp. 105–10.

Dobranski, S., *Readers and Authorship in Early Modern England* (Cambridge: Cambridge University Press, 2005)

Duff, C., *James Joyce and the Plain Reader* (1932; New York: Haskell House, 1971).

Eagleton, T., *Heathcliff and the Great Hunger: Studies in Irish Culture* (London: Verso, 1996).

Eckel, J., *The First Editions of Charles Dickens* (1913; London: Haskell House, 1932).

Eckhardt, J., *Manuscript Verse Collectors and the Politics of Anti-Courtly Love Poetry* (Oxford: Oxford University Press, 2009).

Edwards, A. S. G., 'Middle English Inscriptional Verse texts', in J. Scattergood and J. Boffey (eds), *Texts and Their Contexts, Papers from the Early Book Society* (Dublin: Four Courts Press, 1997), pp. 26–43.

Eisenstein, E., *The Printing Press as an Agent of Change: Communications and Cultural Transformations in Early Modern Europe*, 2 vols (Cambridge: Cambridge University Press, 1979).

Egerton 2433 MSS, British Library, London.

Eglinton, J., 'What Should be the Subjects of a National Drama? (2)', *Daily Express* (Dublin), 8 October 1898, p. 2.

—, 'The Weak Point in the Celtic Movement', *Dana*, 11 (March 1905), pp. 321–5.

Eldar, A. M., *Spreken en zingen, in verband gebracht met de Nederlandsche taal* (Tiel: Mijs, 1886).

Eliot, S., and J. Rose (eds), *A Companion to the History of the Book* (Malden, MA: Blackwell, 2007).

Eliot, T. S., 'What is Minor Poetry?', *Of Poets and Poetry* (London: Faber & Faber, 1957), pp. 39–52.

—, *The Complete Poems and Plays of T. S. Eliot* (London: Faber & Faber, 1969).

Ellis, A., *Books in Victorian Elementary Schools* (London: Library Association, 1971).

Evans, R., 'Chaucer's Life', in S. Ellis (ed.), *Chaucer, an Oxford Guide* (Oxford: Oxford University Press, 2005), pp. 9–25.

Eversmann, P., 'The Experience of the Theatrical Event', in Cremona et al. (eds), *Theatrical Events Borders Dynamics Frames*, pp. 139–174.

Exman, E., *The Brothers Harper* (New York: Harper & Row, 1965).

Federman, M., 'What is the Meaning of "The Medium is the Message"' (2003), at http://individual.utoronto.ca/markfederman/article_mediumisthemessage.htm [accessed 16 July 2010].

Fein, S. (ed.), *Studies in the Harley Manuscript, the Scribes, Contents, and Social Contexts of British Library MS Harley 2253* (Kalamazoo, MI: Medieval Institute Publications, 2000).

Feldman, P. and D. Scott-Kilvert (eds), *The Journals of Mary Shelley*, 2 vols (Oxford: Clarendon Press, 1987).

Fields, J. T., *Yesterdays with Authors* (Boston, MA: Houghton, Osgood, 1879).

Fielder, L. A., 'To Whom does Joyce Belong? *Ulysses* as Parody, Pop and Porn', in H. Ehrlich (ed.), *Light Rays: James Joyce and Modernism* (New York: New Horizon Press, 1984).

Finkelstein, D. and A. McCleery (eds), *The Book History Reader* (London: Routledge, 2005).

Fisch, A., A. K. Mellor and E. H. Schor (eds), *The Other Mary Shelley: Beyond Frankenstein* (New York and Oxford: Oxford University Press, 1993).

Fischer, S. R., *A History of Reading* (London: Reaktion, 2003).

Fish, S., 'Interpreting the *Variorum*', in Finkelstein and McCleery (eds), *The Book History Reader*, pp. 450–8.

Flint, K., *The Woman Reader 1837–1914* (Oxford: Clarendon Press, 1993).

Forman, H. B, *The Shelley Library* (London: Reeves & Turner, 1886).

Fowler, A., *Kinds of Literature* (Cambridge, MA: Harvard University Press, 1982).

Fox, A., *Oral and Literate Culture in England, 1500–1700* (Oxford: Clarendon Press, 2000).

Fraistat, N., 'Illegitimate Shelley: Radical Piracy and the Textual Edition as Cultural Performance', *PMLA*, 110 (May 1994), pp. 409–23.

—, 'Shelley Left and Right: The Rhetoric of the Early Textual Editions', in *Shelley's Poetry and Prose*, 2nd edn (New York: Norton, 2002), pp. 645–53.

Frazier, A., *Behind the Scenes: Yeats, Horniman, and the Struggle for the Abbey Theatre* (Berkeley, CA: University of California Press, 1990).

Freedley, E. T., *Philadelphia and its Manufacturers* (Philadelphia, PA: Edwin Young, 1859).

Fuller, P., 'Final liberation for James Joyce', *City Press*, 8 May 1969, p. 10.

Fuseli, H., *The Life and Writings of Henry Fuseli*, ed. J. Knowles, 3 vols (London: H. Colburn & R. Bentley, 1831).

Gaskell, P., *A New Introduction to Bibliography* (Oxford: Clarendon Press, 1972).

Genette, G., *The Architext: An Introduction* (Berkeley, CA: University of California Press, 1992).

—, *Palimpsests: Literature in the Second Degree* (Lincoln, NE: University of Nebraska Press, 1997).

—, *Paratexts: Thresholds of Interpretation*, trans. J. Lewin (Cambridge: Cambridge University Press, 1997).

Gillespie, A., 'Balliol MS 354: Histories of the Book at the End of the Middle Ages', *Poetica* (Tokyo), 60 (2003), pp. 47–63.

—, *Print Culture and the Medieval Author: Chaucer, Lydgate, and their Books, 1473–1557* (Oxford: Oxford University Press, 2006).

Godthelp, H., *Actief lezen: Teksten met vragen: Lees-taalboekje voor de lagere klassen van alle inrichtingen voor voorbereidend hoger- en middelbaar onderwijs, van de kweekscholen en de MULO-scholen*, 2 vols ('s–Gravenhage: Van Goor, 1937).

—, *Belevend lezen*, 2 vols ('s–Gravenhage: Van Goor, 1938).

Godwin, W., *History of the Commonwealth of England*, 4 vols (London: Henry Colburn, 1824–8).

Goslee, N. M., 'Dispersoning Emily: Drafting as plot in *Epipsychidion*', *Keats-Shelley Journal*, 42 (1993), pp. 104–19.

—, 'Shelleyan Inspiration and the Sister Arts', in Webb and Weinberg (eds), *The Unfamiliar Shelley*, pp. 159–79.

Greg. W. W., 'The Rationale of Copy-Text', *Studies in Bibliography*, 3 (1950–1), pp. 19–36.

Griffiths, J. and D. Pearsall (eds), *Book Production and Publishing in Britain, 1375–1475* (Cambridge: Cambridge University Press, 1989).

Hall, M. C., *Michelangelo and the Reinvention of the Human Body* (New York: Farrar, Straus & Giroux, 2005).

Haltunnen, K., *Painted Women and Confidence Men* (New Haven, CT: Yale University Press, 1982).

Handlingen en mededeelingen van de Maatschappij der Nederlandsche Letterkunde te Leiden, over het jaar 1914–1915, vol. 1 (Leiden: Brill, 1915).

Hanna, R., 'Analytical Survey 4, Middle English Manuscripts and the Study of Literature', *New Medieval Literatures*, 4 (2001), pp. 243–64.

—, *The English Manuscripts of Richard Rolle: A Descriptive Catalogue* (Exeter: Exeter University Press, 2010).

Harty, K. J., 'Chaucer in Performance', in S. Ellis (ed.), *Chaucer, an Oxford Guide* (Oxford: Oxford University Press, 2005), pp. 560–75.

Hassan, I., *The Dismemberment of Orpheus: Toward a Postmodern Literature*, 2nd edn (Madison, WI: University of Wisconsin Press, 1982).

Hayes, I. I., *An Arctic Boat Journey, in the autumn of 1854* (Boston, MA: James Osgood & Company, 1871).

Hazlitt, W., *Table Talk, or, Original Essays* (London: John Warren, 1821).

Hellinga, L. and J. B. Trapp (eds), *The Cambridge History of the Book in Britain, vol. 3, 1400–1557* (Cambridge: Cambridge University Press, 1998).

Helper, H. R., *The Impending Crisis of the South: How to Meet It* (New York: A. B. Burdick, 1860).

Herford Percy, C. H., and E. Simpson (eds), *Ben Jonson Vol. VIII: The Poems. The Prose Works* (Oxford: Clarendon Press, 1947).

Herrick, R., *Herperides: or, The Works both Humane & Divine of Robert Herrick Esq* (1648; Menston: Scolar Press Facsimiles, 1968).

—, *The Poetical Works of Robert Herrick*, ed. L. C. Martin (Oxford: Clarendon Press, 1956).

Heuser, W. (ed.), *Die Kildare-Gedichte: die Ältesten Mittelenglischen Denkmäler in Anglo-Irischen Überlieferung* (1904; Darmstadt, 1967).

Hilton, J., and D. Wiley, 'What Happens to Book Sales if Digital Versions are Given Away?', *The Journal of Electronic Publishing / Digital Book World* (2010), at http://www.digital-bookworld.com [accessed 16 July 2010].

Hobbs, M., *Early Seventeenth-Century Verse Miscellany Manuscripts* (London: Scolar, 1992).

Hobhouse, J. C., *Byron's Bulldog: The Letters of John Cam Hobhouse to Lord Byron*, ed. P. Graham (Columbus, OH: Ohio State University Press, 1984).

Hoffman, F. J., C. Allen and C. F. Ulrich, *The Little Magazine: A History and Bibliography* (Princeton, NJ: Princeton University Press, 1946).

Holbrook, J., *Ten Years Among the Mail Bags* (Philadelphia, PA: H. Cowperthwait & Company, 1855).

Holme, R., *The Academy of Armory* (London, 1688).

Holtrop, M., 'Hardop lezen en het mondeling expressievermogen', *Paedagogische Studien*, 16 (1935), pp. 327–38.

Horsten, J. L., *Stemmen van verre en dichtebij: Lektuur voor het katholiek onderwijs en voor zelfstudie, met korte inleidingen en van aantekeningen voorzien door*, 6 (Tilburg: R.K. Jongensweeshuis & Antwerpen: Veritas, 1914).

Hughes, L. K., and M. Lund, *The Victorian Serial* (Charlottesville, VA: University of Virginia Press, 1991).

Hunt, L., *The Correspondence of Leigh Hunt*, ed. T. Hunt, 2 vols (London: Smith, Elder, 1862).

Hutton, C., 'Yogibogeybox in Dawson Chambers: The Beginnings of Maunsel and Company', in C. Hutten (ed.), *The Irish Book in the Twentieth Century* (Dublin: Irish Academic Press, 2004), pp. 36–46.

Ingpen, R., *Shelley in England* (London: Kegan Paul, 1917).

Ingram, R., 'Robert Herrick and the Making of *Hesperides*', *Studies in English Literature 1500–1900*, 38:1 (1998), pp. 127–47.

Iser, W., 'Interaction between Text and Reader', in Finkelstein and McCleery (eds), *The Book History Reader*, pp. 391–6.

Isherwood, C., and E. Upward, *The Montmere Stories* (London: Enitharmon, 1994).

J. B., 'De kunst van lezen', with a postscript by d.B. [=T.H. de Beer], *Noord en Zuid*, 3 (1880), pp. 236–44.

Jeffares, A. N. (ed.), *W. B. Yeats: The Critical Heritage* (London: Routledge & Kegan Paul, 1977).

Johannes, G.-J., *Dit moet U niet onverschillig wezen! De vaderlandse literatuur in het Noord-Nederlands voortgezet onderwijs 1800–1900* (Nijmegen: Vantilt, 2007).

Joicey, N., 'A Paperback Guide to Progress: Penguin Books 1935–c. 1951', *Twentieth Century British History*, 4:1 (1993), pp. 25–56.

Jones, W. P., *James Joyce and the Common Reader* (1955; Norman, OK: University of Oklahoma Press, 1970).

Joost-Gaugier, C., *Raphael's Stanza della Segnatura: Meaning and Invention* (Cambridge: Cambridge University Press, 2002).

Kalff, G., 'Voor Potgieter', *De Gids*, 61 (1897), part 1, pp. 550–5.

Kaplan, C., 'Review of *Rereading Modernism: New Directions in Feminist Criticism*, ed. Lisa Raldo', *Modernism/Modernity*, 2:2 (1995), p. 116.

Karsemeijer, J., 'De verwaarloosde component van het onderwijs in het Nederlands', *Levende Talen*, 24 (1936), 402–7.

Karsemeijer, J., and G. Kazemier, *Los van de letter: Proza en poëzie met aanwijzingen voor goede voordracht voor de laagste klassen van gymnasia, lycea, H.B.S. en kweekscholen* (Groningen: Wolters, 1940).

Kelly, J., *Our Joyce: From Outcast to Icon* (Austin, TX: University of Texas Press, 1998).

Ker, N. R., *Facsimile of British Museum MS. Harley 2253, Early English Texts Society* o.s. 255 (London, 1965).

Kramer, W., '"De triomf van het stil-lezen" en de gevaren van dien', *Nieuwe Taalgids*, 32 (1938), pp. 273–80.

Landow, G., *Hypertext 3.0: Critical Theory and New Media in an Era of Globalization* (Baltimore, MD: Johns Hopkins University Press, 2006).

Langeveld, M. J., *Taal en denken: Een theoretiese en didaktiese bijdrage tot het onderwijs in de moedertaal op de middelbare school, inzonderheid tot dat der grammatika* (Groningen: Wolters, 1934).

—, 'Enige opmerkingen naar aanleiding van een polemiek over het stil-lezen en over het stil-leeswerk in het algemeen', *Weekblad voor Gymnasiaal en Middelbaar Onderwijs*, 24 April 1935, pp. 956–9.

Langeveld, M. J., and B. G. Palland, *Denkend lezen: Een stilleesboekje voor opleidingsscholen en de eerste leerjaren van voorbereidend hoger en middelbaar onderwijs* (Groningen: Wolters, 1935).

—, *Op weg naar denkend lezen: Een stil-leesboekje voor de zesde klasse der volksschool en de vijfde en zesde klasse der opleidingsschool* (Groningen: Wolters, 1937).

Lawrence, D.H., *The Letters of D. H. Lawrence*, ed. J. T. Boulton, 7 vols (Cambridge: Cambridge University Press, 1993).

Leader, Z., 'Parenting Frankenstein', *Revision and Romantic Authorship* (Oxford: Clarendon Press, 1996), pp. 167–205.

Leest, J., *Het voortgezet onderwijs in de moedertaal* (Groningen: Wolters, 1932).

Legouvé, E., *L'art de la lecture* (Paris: Hetzel, 1877).

—, *La Lecture en action* (Paris: Hetzel, 1881).

Lernout, G., *The French Joyce* (Ann Arbor, MI: University of Michigan Press, 1990).

'Letter to John Bull', *Putnam's Monthly* (February 1853), pp. 221–9.

Lodge, D., 'My Joyce', in *Write On: Occasional Essays, '65–'85* (London: Penguin, 1986), pp. 57–69.

López-Varela Azcárate, A., and S. Tötösy de Zepetnek, 'Towards Intermediality in Contemporary Cultural Practices and Education', *Culture, Language and Representation*, 6:1 (2008), pp. 65–82.

Lowenstein, J., *The Author's Due: Printing and the Prehistory of Copyright* (Chicago, IL: Chicago University Press, 2002).

Lucas, A. (ed.), *Anglo-Irish Poems of the Middle Ages* (Blackrock, Dublin: Columbia Press, 1995).

Lyons, M., 'New Readers in the Nineteenth Century', in G. Cavallo and R. Chartier (eds), *A History of Reading in the West* (Amherst, MA: University of Massachusetts Press, 1999), pp. 313–44.

McCleery, A., 'The Paperback Evolution: Tauchnitz, Albatross and Penguin', in N. Matthews and N. Moody (eds), *Judging a Book by Its Cover* (Aldershot: Ashgate, 2007), pp. 3–18.

—, 'The 1969 Edition of *Ulysses*: The Making of a Penguin Classic', *James Joyce Quarterly*, 46:1 (2008), pp. 55–73.

McDonald, P. D., *British Literary Culture and Publishing Practice, 1880–1914* (Cambridge: Cambridge University Press, 1997).

McDowell, N., 'Herrick and the Order of the Black Ribband: Literary Community in Civil War London and the Publication of *Hesperides* (1648)', in Cain and Connolly (eds), *Lords of Wine and Oile*, (Oxford, Oxford University Press, 2011).

McGann, J. J., *The Textual Condition* (Princeton, NJ: Princeton University Press, 1991).

—, *A Critique of Textual Criticism* (Charlottesville, VA, and London: University Press of Virginia, 1992).

—, *Black Riders: The Visible Language of Modernism* (Princeton, NJ: Princeton University Press, 1993).

—, 'Marking Texts of Many Dimensions', in S. Schreibman, R. Siemens and J. Unsworth (eds), *A Companion to Digital Humanities* (Oxford: Blackwell, 2004), at http://www.digitalhumanities.org/companion/ [accessed 16 July 2010].

McGill, M., *American Literature and the Culture of Reprinting, 1834–53* (Philadelphia, PA: University of Pennsylvania Press, 2003).

McHale, B., *Postmodernist Fiction* (London: Routledge, 1987).

McKenzie, D. F., 'The Sociology of a Text: Orality, Literacy and Print in Early New Zealand', in Finkelstein and McCleery (eds), *The Book History Reader*, pp. 205–31.

McPherson, E. M., The Political History of the United States During the Period of Reconstruction (Washington, DC: Solomons & Chapman, 1875).

Manguel, A., *A History of Reading* (New York: Viking, 1996).

Marotti, A., *John Donne: Coterie Poet* (Madison, WI: University of Wisconsin Press, 1986).

—, *Manuscript, Print and the English Renaissance Lyric* (Ithaca, NY: Cornell University Press, 1995).

Marotti A. and M. Bristol (eds), *Print, Manuscript and Performance: The Changing Relations of the Media in Early Modern England* (Columbus, OH: Ohio State University Press, 2000).

Marshall, W. H, *Byron, Shelley, Hunt and The Liberal* (Philadelphia: University of Pennsylvania Press, 1960).

Mathews, M. M., *Teaching to Read, Historically Considered* (Chicago, IL: University of Chicago Press, 1967).

Mayer, D., *Harlequin in His Element: The English Pantomime 1806–1836* (Cambridge, MA: Harvard University Press, 1969).

Mays, J. C. C., *Fredson Bowers and the Irish Wolfhound* (Clonmel: Coracle, 2002).

Mellor, A. K., *Mary Shelley: Her Life, Her Fiction, Her Monsters* (New York and London: Routledge, 1989).

Miall, D. S., E. Greenspan and J. Rose (eds), *Book History* (Philadelphia, PA: University of Pennsylvania Press, 2006), vol. 9.

Michelangelo, *Life, Letters, and Poetry*, ed. and trans. G. Bull and P. Porter (Oxford: Oxford University Press, 1987).

Mishkin, T., *The Harlem and Irish Renaissances: Language, Identity, and Representation* (Gainesville, FL: University of Florida Press, 1998).

Mooney, L. R., 'Scribes and Booklets of Trinity College, Cambridge, MSS R.3.19 and R.3.21', in A. J. Minnis (ed.), *Middle English Poetry: Texts and Traditions, Essays in Honour of Derek Pearsall* (Woodbridge, Suffolk: D.S. Brewer, 2001), pp. 241–66.

Moormann, J. G. M., *De moedertaal: Een didactiek voor het middelbaar (en lager) onderwijs* (Nijmegen: Dekker en Van de Vegt, 1936).

Morgan, N., and R. M. Thomson (eds), *The Cambridge History of the Book in Britain, vol. 2, 1100–1400* (Cambridge: Cambridge University Press, 2007).

Morrisson, M. S., *The Public Face of Modernism: Little Magazines, Audiences, and Reception, 1905–1920* (Madison, WI: University of Wisconsin Press, 2001).

Moss, A., 'Theories of Poetry: Latin Writers', in G. P. Norton (ed.), *The Cambridge History of Literary Criticism: Volume III The Renaissance* (Cambridge: Cambridge University Press, 1999), pp. 98–105.

Moss, S., *Dickens' Quarrel with America* (Troy, NY: Whitston, 1984).

Moxon, J., *Mechanick Exercises on the Whole Art of Printing*, ed. H. Davis and H. Carter (1683–4; London: Oxford University Press, 1962).

Murphy, W. M., *Family Secrets: W. B. Yeats and His Relatives* (Syracuse, NY: Syracuse University Press, 1995).

Murray, H. M. R. (ed.), *The Middle English Poem, Erthe upon Erthe, Printed from Twenty-Four Manuscripts, Early English Text Society* o.s. 141 (London: Kegan Paul Trench Truebner, 1911).

Myrone, M., *Henry Fuseli* (London: Tate Gallery Publications, 2001).

Nascher, I. L., *The Wretches of Povertyville: A Sociological Study of the Bowery* (Chicago, IL: J. J. Lawzit).

'Ned. Sectievergadering', *Levende Talen*, 21 (1933), pp. 69–71.

Nadel, I. B., 'The Incomplete Joyce', *Joyce Studies Annual*, 2 (1991), pp. 86–100.

Nichols, S., 'Philology and its Discontents', in W. D. Paden (ed.), *The Future of the Middle Ages: Medieval Literature in the 1990s* (Gainesville, FL: University Press of Florida, 1994), pp. 113–41.

Nijland, J. A., 'Iets uit de praktijk van mijn onderwijs', *Taal en Letteren*, 14 (1904), pp. 28–32.

O'Brien, J., *Harlequin Britain: Pantomime and Entertainment 1690–1760* (Baltimore, MD: Johns Hopkins University Press, 2004).

O'Callaghan, M., '"Those Lyrick Feasts, made at the *Sun*, the *Dog*, the Triple *Tunne*": Going Clubbing with Ben Jonson', in T. Cain and R. Connolly (eds), *Lords of Wine and Oile: Community and Conviviality in the Work of Robert Herrick* (Oxford: Oxford University Press, forthcoming).

O'Neill, M., '"Trying to Make it as Good as I Can", Mary Shelley's Editing of P. B. Shelley's Poetry and Prose', in B.T. Bennett and S. Curran (eds), *Mary Shelley in Her Times* (Baltimore, MD: Johns Hopkins University Press, 2000), pp. 185–7.

Ong, W. J., *Orality and Literacy: The Technologizing of the Word* (New York: Routledge, 2002).

Ostrowski, C., *Books, Maps, and Politics: A Cultural History of the Library of Congress, 1783–1861* (Amherst, MA: University of Massachusetts Press, 2004).

Parkes, M. B., *Their Hands Before Our Eyes, a Closer Look at Scribes* (Aldershot: Ashgate, 2008).

Partington, C. F., *The Printer's Complete Guide* (London: Sherwood, Gilbert & Piper, 1825).

Patten, R. L., *Dickens and his Publishers* (Oxford and London: Oxford University Press, 1978).

Pawley, C., *Reading on the Middle Border – The Culture of Print in Late-Nineteenth Century Osage, Iowa* (Amherst, MA: University of Massachusetts Press, 2001).

Peacock, T. L., 'Memoirs of Percy Bysshe Shelley', *Fraser's Magazine*, 57 (June 1858) pp. 643–59; 61 (January 1860), pp. 92–109.

—, *Letters of Thomas Love Peacock*, ed. N. Joukovsky, 2 vols (Oxford: Oxford University Press, 2001).

Pearson, D., *Books as History: The Importance of Books beyond their Text* (London: British Library, 2008).

Peters, J. S., *Theatre of the Book, 1480–1880: Print, Text, and Performance in Europe* (Oxford: Oxford University Press, 2000).

Plomer, H. A., 'Some Private Presses of the Nineteenth Century', *Library Transactions of the Bibliographical* Society, 4: s2–1 (1899), pp. 407–28.

Postlewait, T., 'Constructing Events in Theatre History: A Matter of Credibility', in Cremona et al. (eds), *Theatrical Events Borders Dynamics Frames*, pp. 33–52.

Pressly, W. L., *The Life and Art of James Barry* (New Haven, CT: Yale University Press, 1981).

Public Libraries (Washington, DC: US Library of Congress, 1876).

Pugh, S., 'Ovidian Exile in the *Hesperides*: Herrick's Politics of Intertextuality', *Review of English Studies*, 57 (2006), pp. 733–65.

Puttfarken, T., *Titian and Tragic Painting: Painting Aristotle's Poetics and the Rise of the Modern Artist* (New Haven, CT, and London: Yale University Press, 2005).

Raben, J., 'Shelley's "Invocation to Misery", An Expanded Text', *Journal of English and Germanic Philology*, 65 (1966), pp. 65–74.

—, 'Shelley's "Boat on the Serchio": The Evidence of the Manuscript', *Philological Quarterly*, 46 (1967), pp. 58–68.

Radway, J., 'A Feeling for Books: The Book of the Month Club, Literary Taste and Middle Class Desire', in Finklestein and McCleery (eds), *The Book History Reader*, pp. 469–81.

Rainey, L., *Revisiting 'The Waste Land'* (New Haven, CT: Yale University Press, 2005).

—, 'The Cultural Economy of Modernism', in *The Cambridge Companion to Modernism*, ed. M. Levenson (Cambridge: Cambridge University Press, 1999), pp. 33–69.

Raylor, T., *Cavaliers, Clubs and Literary Culture: Sir John Mennes, James Smith, and the Order of the Fancy* (Newark, NJ, University of Delaware Press, 1993).

Reiman, D. (ed.), *The Romantics Reviewed: Contemporary Reviews of British Romantic Writers*, Part C, *Shelley, Keats, and London Radical Writers*, 2 vols (New York and London: Garland, 1972).

—, *Romantic Texts and Contexts* (Colombia, MO: University of Missouri Press, 1987).

Reynolds, P., 'Reading Publics, Theatre Audiences, and the Little Magazines of the Abbey Theatre', *New Hibernia Review*, 7:4 (2003), pp. 63–84.

Reid, D. A., 'Popular Theatre in Victorian Birmingham', in D. Bradby, L. James and B. Sharratt (eds), *Performance and Politics in Popular Drama: Aspects of Popular Entertainment in Theatre, Film and Television 1800–1976. Papers given at a Conference at the University of Kent at Canterbury, September 1977* (Cambridge: Cambridge University Press, 1980), pp. 65–89.

Rhees, W. J., *Manual of Public Libraries, Institutions, and Societies in the United States and British Provinces of North America* (Philadelphia, PA, 1859).

Richardson, A., *Literature, Education, and Romanticism: Reading as Social Practice, 1780–1832* (Cambridge: Cambridge University Press, 1994).

Robinson, C. E., 'Percy Bysshe Shelley, Charles Ollier, and William Blackwood', in K. Everest (ed.), *Shelley Revalued* (Leicester: Leicester University Press, 1983), pp. 183–226.

Roosevelt, R. B., *Five Acres Too Much* (New York: O. Judd, 1885).

Rosand, D., '*Ut pictor poeta*: Meaning in Titian's *Poesie*', *New Literary History*, 3 (1971–2), pp. 527–46.

Rose, J., *The Intellectual Life of the British Working Classes* (New Haven, CT: Yale University Press, 2001).

—, 'Re-Reading the English Common Reader', in Finkelstein and McCleery (eds), *The Book History Reader*, pp. 324–40.

Rota, A., *Apart from the Text* (Middlesex: Private Libraries' Association, 1998).

Rusling, J. F., *The Great West and Pacific Coast* (New York: Sheldon & Company, 1877).

Salverda de Grave, J. J., 'De gramofoon in de Sorbonne', *De Gids*, 77 (1913), part 2, 143–52.

Salt, H. S., *A Shelley Primer*, Shelley Society Productions, 4th series, 4 (London: Reeves and Turner, 1887).

Sargent, M.G., 'What do the Numbers Mean? Observations on Some Patters of Middle English Manuscript Transmission', in Connolly and Mooney (eds), *Design and Distribution*, pp. 205–44.

Scase, W., 'Imagining Alternatives to the Book: the Transmission of Political Poetry in Late Medieval England', in S. Kelly and J. J. Thompson (eds) *Imagining the Book* (Turnhout: Brepols, 2005), pp. 237–50.

—, *Literature and Complaint in England, 1272–1553* (Oxford: Oxford University Press, 2007).

Schepers, J. B., *Bragi*, 3 vols (Amsterdam: Van Looy, 1900–1).

Scherer, J., *Le 'Livre' de Mallarmé*, 2nd edn (Paris: Gallimard, 1977).

Schlicke, P., *Charles Dickens and Popular Entertainment* (London: Allen & Unwin, 1985).

—, *The Oxford Companion to Charles Dickens* (Oxford: Oxford University Press, 1999).

Schreibman, S., *The Versioning Machine* (2004), at http://v-machine.org [accessed 16 July 2010].

Schneiders, A. J., 'Over voordragen', *Levende Talen*, 24 (1936), pp. 141–5.

Sellars, R., and G. Allen (eds.) *The Salt Companion to Harold Bloom* (Cambridge: Salt Press, 2007).

Senn, F., 'The Joyce Industrial Evolution, According to one European Amateur', *Journal of Modern Literature*, 22:2 (1998–9), pp. 191–7.

Shelley, M. W., 'Alfieri' in *Lives of the Most Eminent Literature and Scientific Men in Italy*, 2 vols (London: Longman, 1835).

—, *The Letters of Mary Wollstonecraft Shelley*, 3 vols, ed. B.T. Bennett (Baltimore, MD, and London: Johns Hopkins University Press, 1980–8).

—, *Frankenstein or The Modern Prometheus: The 1818 Text (with variants, an Introduction, and Notes)*, ed. J. Reiger (Chicago, IL: University of Chicago Press, 1984).

—, *The Frankenstein Notebooks. A Facsimile Edition of Mary Shelley's Manuscript Novel, 1816–17 (With Alterations in the Hand of Percy Bysshe Shelley) as it Survives in Draft and Fair Copy Deposited by Lord Abinger in the Bodleian Library, Oxford (Dep. c. 477/1 and Dep. c. 534/1–2)*, 2 vols, ed. C. E. Robinson, *Manuscripts of the Younger Romantics* (New York and London: Garland Publishing, Inc., 1996).

— (with Shelley, P. B.), *The Original 'Frankenstein'*, ed. C. E. Robinson (Oxford: University of Oxford; Bodleian Library, 2008).

Shelley, P. B., *The Poetical Works of Percy Bysshe Shelley ... with Notes and a Memoir by William Michael Rossetti*, 2 vols (London: Moxon, 1870).

—, *The Letters of Percy Bysshe Shelley*, ed., F. L. Jones, 2 vols (Oxford; Clarendon Press, 1964).

—, *Posthumous Poems of Shelley: Mary Shelley's Fair Copy Book*, ed. I. Massey (Montreal: McGill-Queen's University Press, 1969).

—, *The Poems of Shelley, Volume 1: 1804–1817*, ed. G. Matthews and K. Everest (London and New York: Longman, 1989).

—, *The Complete Poetry of Percy Bysshe Shelley*, ed. D. Reiman, N. Fraistat and N. Crook, 8 vols planned, 2 published to date (Baltimore, MD: Johns Hopkins University Press, 2000–).

Sherman, W. H., 'On the Threshold: Architecture, Paratext, and Early Print Culture', in S. A. Baron, E. N. Lindquist and E. F. Shevlin (eds), *Agent of Change: Print Culture after Elizabeth L. Eisenstein* (Amherst, MA: University of Massachusetts Press, 2007), pp. 67–82.

Shillingsburg, P. L., *Scholarly Editing in the Computer Age: Theory and Practice*, 3rd edn (Michigan, MI: University of Michigan Press, 1996), pp. 53–70.

Shrank, C., '"These Few Scribled Rules": Representing Scribal Intimacy in Early Modern Print', *Huntington Library Quarterly*, 67:2 (2004), pp. 295–316.

Simpson, J., *Reform and Cultural Revolution, 1350–1547* (Oxford: Oxford University Press, 2002).

Slote, S., 'Imposture Book Through the Ages', in S. Slote and W. Van Mierlo (eds), *Genitricksling Joyce* (Amsterdam: Rudopi, 1999), pp. 97–104.

Smith, J., *The Printer's Grammar* (London: T. Evans, 1787).

Smyth, A., *'Profit and Delight': Printed Miscellanies in England, 1640–1682* (Detroit, MI: Wayne State University Press, 2004).

Sperberg-McQueen, M., and L. Bernard, 'TEI Pizza Chef', *The Text Encoding Initiative* (2010), at http://www.tei-c.org/pizza.html [accessed 16 July 2010].

Squire, J. C., 'Poetry', *London Mercury*, 8 October 1923), p. 656.

St Clair, W., 'The Impact of *Frankenstein*', in B. T. Bennett and S. Curran (eds), *Mary Shelley in Her Times* (Baltimore, MD, and London: Johns Hopkins University Press, 2000), pp. 38–63.

—, *The Reading Nation in the Romantic Period* (Cambridge: Cambridge University Press, 2004).

Stemvers, F. G. A., 'Het moedertaalonderwijs op de middelbare school II', *Levende Talen*, 21 (1933), pp. 181–96.

—, 'De leerschool der verveling', *Levende Talen*, 27 (1939), pp. 99–109.

—, 'Review of: Karsemeijer, J., and G. Kazemier, Los van de letter: *Proza en poëzie met aanwijzingen voor goede voordracht voor de laagste klassen van gymnasia, lycea, H. B. S. en kweekscholen* (Groningen: Wolters, 1940)', *Levende Talen*, 28 (Gronigen: Wolters, 1940), pp. 380–2.

Stowe, H. B., *Sunny Memories of Foreign Lands* (Boston, MA: Phillips, Samson & Company, 1854).

Sterne, L., *The Life and Opinions of Tristram Shandy, Gentleman*, ed. M. New (London: Penguin, 2003).

Stern, M. B. (ed.), *Publishers for Mass Entertainment in Nineteenth Century America* (Boston, MA: G. K. Hall, 1980).

Stow, J., *A Survey of London*, ed. C.L. Kingsford, 2 vols (London, 1925).

Strohm, P., *Social Chaucer* (Cambridge, MA.: Harvard University Press, 1989).

Sullivan, J. A., 'Managing the Pantomime: Productions at the Theatre Royal Nottingham in the 1860s', *Theatre Notebook*, 60:2 (2006), pp. 98–116.

Sutherland, J., 'Fiction and the Erotic Cover', *Critical Quarterly*, 33:2 (1991), pp. 3–36.

Swann, M., *Curiosities and Texts: The Culture of Collecting in Early Modern England* (Philadelphia, PA: University of Pennsylvania Press, 2001).

Swanson, R. N., 'Pardons for Every Occasion', in R. N. Swanson, *Indulgences in Late Medieval England* (Cambridge: Cambridge University Press, 2007).

Sweet, E., *The Future Life* (Boston, MA, and New York: W. White, 1869).

Swinburne, A. C., *Essays and Studies* (London: Chatto & Windus, 1875).

Tanselle, G. T., *Selected Studies in Bibliography* (Charlottesville, VA: Virginia University Press, 1979).

Taylor, A., 'Fragmentation, Corruption, and Minstrel Narration: the Question of the Middle English Romances', *Yearbook of English Studies*, 22 (1992), pp. 38–62.

Taylor, C. H., *The Early Collected Editions of Shelley's Poems* (New Haven, CT: Yale University Press, 1958).

Taylor, M., *British Pantomime Performance* (Bristol and Chicago, IL: Intellect Books, 2007).

Tebbel, J., *A History of Book Publishing in the United States* (New York: R. R. Bowker, 1972).

Thompson, J. J., 'Popular Reading Tastes in Middle English Religious and Didactic Literature', in J. Simons (ed.), *From Medieval to Medievalism* (Basingstoke: Macmillan, 1992), pp. 82–100.

—, 'Mapping Points West of West Midlands Manuscripts and Texts: Irishness(es) and Middle English Literary Culture', in *Essays in Manuscript Geography: Vernacular Manuscripts of the English West Midlands from the Conquest to the Sixteenth Century*, ed. W. Scase (Turnhout: Brepols 2007), pp. 113–28.

—, 'The Middle English Prose *Brut* and the Possibilities of Cultural Mapping', in M. Connolly and L.R. Mooney (eds), *Design and Distribution of Late Medieval Manuscripts in England* (Woodbridge, Suffolk: D. S.Brewer, 2008), pp. 245–60.

Tilley, C., et al. (eds), *Handbook of Material Culture* (London: Sage, 2006).

Tillotson, K., and J. Butt, *Dickens at Work* (London: Methuen, 1957).

Truxton Club, The Readers Circle, Minutes of 2 February 1886, 23 November and 7 and 22 December 1891, Cortland Historical Society.

Turner, C., *Marketing Modernism between the Two World Wars* (Amherst, MA: University of Massachusetts Press, 2003).

Tusser, T., *Hundreth Good Points of Husbandrie* (Essex: Great Totham Press, 1834).

Van der Hoeve, A. H., P. Kohnstamm and G. van Veen, *De lagere school en het stil-lezen: Een onderzoek inzake het zelfstandig verwerken van leesstof door leerlingen der hoogste klassen van lagere scholen in de gemeente Utrecht* (Groningen: Wolters, 1933).

—, *Stil-lees-stof als denk-materiaal en denk-maatstaf: Een onderzoek aangaande de vorming en toetsing van 'theoretische intelligentie'* (Groningen: Wolters, 1935).

Van der Laan, J. E., 'Lesen ohne Geheimnis', *Nieuwe Taalgids*, 33 (1939), pp. 227–31.

Van der Meij, H. W., 'De kunst van lezen', *Noord en Zuid*, 13 (1890), pp. 289–300.

Van Ginneken, J., 'De rompstand en zijn betekenis voor taal en muziek', *De Gids*, 79 (1915), part 3, pp. 458–94.

Van Meurs, B., 'De stil-leesmethode', *Levende Talen*, 27 (1939), pp. 160–9.

Van Veen, G., 'De beteekenis van het stil-lezen (Naar aanleiding van P. A. Diels' "Het stille lezen")', *Paedagogische Studiën*, 10 (1929), pp. 394–400.

—, *Plaats en beteekenis van het 'stil lezen' in onze lagere scholen* (Groningen: Wolters, 1929).

—, 'Het stil-lezen'. *Paedagogische Studiën*, 14 (1933), pp. 8–19.

Van Wijk, 'De rompstand en zijn betekenis voor taal en muziek', *De Gids*, 79 (1915), pp. 458–94.

Vargo, L., 'Close Your Eyes and Think of Shelley: Versioning Mary Shelley's Triumph of Life', in T. Clark and J. E. Hogle (eds), *Evaluating Shelley* (Edinburgh: Edinburgh University Press, 1996).

Vasari, G., *Lives of the Most Eminent Painters, Sculptors and Architects*, trans. G. du C. de Vere, 2 vols (London, 1996).

Venn, J. (comp.), *Biographical History of Gonville and Caius College 1349–1897 Volume 1: Admissions 1349–1713* (Cambridge: Cambridge University Press, 1897), p. 312.

Venn, J. and Venn, J. A. (comp. and eds), *Alumni Cantabrigiensis Part 1*, 3 vols (Cambridge: Cambridge University Press, 1922–4).

Verhagen, B., *Prosodie: Ontleding der structuur van het vers ten dienste van het voordrachtsonderwijs* (Amsterdam: Duwaer & Van Ginkel, 1918).

—, *Prosodie der voordrachtskunst* (Gronigen: Noordhoff, 1924).

—, *Het gesproken woord* (Amsterdam: Paris, 1937).

Vogel, A., *Voordrachtskunst: Theoretische en praktische beschouwingen* (Arnhem: Van Loghem Slaterus, 1919).

'W3Schools Online Web Tutorials', *W3 Schools Online*, at http://www.w3schools.com.

Wall, W., *The Imprint of Gender* (Ithaca, NY: Cornell University Press, 1993).

Ward, A. N., and M. Ward (eds), *The Husband in Utah: Sights and Scenes among the Mormons* (New York: Derby & Jackson. 1857).

Warfield, C. A., *Miriam Montfort* (New York: D. Appleton, 1873).

Warren, F. and B. White (eds), *The Dance of Death, Early English Text Society* o.s. 181 (London: H. Milford 1931).

Webb, T., 'John Hunt', *ODNB*.

—, 'John Hunt to Edwin Atherstone: Seven Letters', *Keats-Shelley Journal*, 58 (2009), pp. 139–58.

Webb, T., and A. Weinberg (eds), *The Unfamiliar Shelley* (Aldershot: Ashgate, 2009).

Wednesday Club, Minutes of February 4 1892 and February 24 1892, Onadaga Historical Society, Syracuse, New York.

Wenzel, S. (ed.), *Preachers, Poets, and the Early English Lyric* (Guilford, NJ: Princeton University Press, 1986).

—, *Fasciculus Morum: A Fourteenth-Century Preacher's Handbook* (Philadelphia, PA: Pennsylvania State University Press, 1989).

Wexler, J. P., *Who Paid for Modernism? Art, Money and the Fiction of Conrad, Joyce and Lawrence* (Fayetteville, NC: University of Arkansas Press, 1997).

Willard, F., *The Living Age* (Spring 1852).

Wittmann, R., 'Was There a Reading Revolution at the End of the Eighteenth Century?', in Cavallo and Chartier (eds), *A History of Reading in the West*, pp. 284–312.

Wolfson, S., 'Editorial Privilege: Mary Shelley and Percy Shelley's Audiences', in Fisch et al. (eds), *The Other Mary Shelley*, pp. 39–72.

Woudhuysen, H. R., *Sir Philip Sidney and the Circulation of Manuscripts, 1558–1640* (Oxford: Clarendon Press, 1996).

Wroe, A., *Being Shelley* (London: Jonathan Cape, 2007).

Yeats, W. B., 'The Play, the Player, and the Scene', *Samhain*, 4 (December 1904), pp. 24–33.

—, 'Notes and Opinions', *Samhain*, 5 (November 1905), pp. 3–14.

—, 'Literature and the Living Voice', *Samhain*, 6 (December 1906), pp. 4–14

—, 'First Principles', *Samhain*, 7 (November 1908), pp. 6–12.

—, *Letters of W. B. Yeats*, ed. A. Wade (London: Rupert Hart-Davis, 1954).

—, *Explorations*, selected by Mrs W. B. Yeats (London: Macmillan, 1962).

—, *Letters to the New Island*, ed. G. Bornstein and H. Witemeyer (New York: Macmillan, 1989).

—, *The Secret Rose, Stories by W B. Yeats: A Variorum Edition*, ed. W. Gould, P. L. Marcus and M. J. Sidnell, 2nd edn (London: Macmillan, 1992).

—, *Short Fiction*, ed. G. J. Watson (Harmondsworth: Penguin, 1995).

—, *Autobiographies*, ed. W. H. O'Donnell and D. N. Archibald (New York: Scribner, 1999).

—, *The Irish Dramatic Movement*, ed. M. FitzGerald and R. J. Finneran (New York: Scribner, 2003).

—, *The Collected Letters of W. B. Yeats, Vol. 4: 1905–07*, ed. J. Kelly and R. Schuchard (Oxford: Oxford University Press, 2005).

—, *Mythologies*, ed. W. Gould and D. Toomey (Basingstoke: Palgrave Macmillan, 2005).

—, *Early Essays*, ed. R. J. Finneran and G. Bornstein (New York: Scribner, 2007).

Zboray, R. J., *A Fictive People: Antebellum Economic Development and the American Reading Public* (Oxford: Oxford University Press, 1993).

INDEX

Abbott, J. G., 94
Adam, J., 48
Adams, H., 124, 188n27
Adams, T. R., 14, 164n14
Adamson, C., 177n32
Æ (George Russell), 123
Alberti, L. B., 38, 41–4, 48, 50, 172n12
Alexander, C., 187n8
Alfieri, V., 65, 177n29
Allen, C., 187n19
Allen, G., ix, 7, 174n2, 175n30
Allingham, W., 61–2, 175n1
Altick, R. D., 5, 164n17, 191n4
Alston, E., 29
Alston, T., 28–30
Alston, W., 29
Anacreon, 35
Andrew, M., 165n12
Appleford, A., 167n38
Archimedes, 45
Archibald, D. N., 187n18
Aristophanes, 52, 53
Aristotle, 43, 44, 63
Atherstone, E., 68, 69, 178n48
Auslander, P., 109, 185n14
Auden, W. H., 130, 189n49

Bacon, Sir Francis, 45
Bacon, R., 45
Baines, P., 191n39
Baldick, C., 119–20, 186n1
Baldwin, N., 192n18
Banim, M., 125
Barker, N., 3, 164n14
Baron, S. A., 171n43
Barry, J., x, xiii, 7, 37–50, 172n2–3, 7, 173n25, 38, 41

Barzizza, G., 41
Baxandall, M., 42, 173n14
Beith, C., 189n1
Bembo, P., 47, 173n31
Bennett, B. T., 64, 174n3, 175n32, 176n24
Bennett, S., 116, 117, 184n2, 186n33–6
Benson, L. D., 165n6
Bentham, J., 67
Bernard, L., 195n10
Bibbiena, Cardinal, 47
Bishop, E. L., 132, 189n6
Blackwood, W., 177n38, 178n42
Bloom, H., ix, 175n30
Blunden, E., 177n38
Bodenham, J., 26
Boersma, T., 193n39
Boffey, J., 165n13, 166n20, 21
Bolla, P. de, 172n10
Bolter, J. D., 194n3
Bornstein, G., 120, 121, 187n7, 14, 188n32, 33
Bourdieu, P., 133–4, 190n13, 14
Bradby, D., 185n25
Bradbury, M., 187n19
Braden, G., 169n21
Bradshaw, M., 179n63
Bratton, J., 186n34
Brewer, J., 172n9
Brignull, A., 78, 180n7, 13, 15, 18–20
Bristol, M., 169n19
Brockman, W. S., 190n29
Brontës, the, 120, 187n8
Brooks, J., 178n42
Broome, R. E., 93, 182n17
Booth, M. R., 109, 185n10, 12
Brougham, J., 100

Browne, J. H., 96, 182n35–7
Browning, R., 178n43
Brownson, O., 95, 182n26
Bullen, A. H., 128, 188n40
Burgis, N., 183n68
Butt, J., 91, 182n11
Brunfylld, 82–3
Bryant, J., 77, 160, 195n13
Brydges, Sir Egerton, 78
Busa, R., 157
Bush, V., 157
Byron, xi, 53, 66, 67, 68, 175–6n9, 178n47, 178–9n50

Cabell, M. C., 96, 97, 182n38
Caie, G. D., 166n20
Cain, T., ix, 167n1, 168n2, 13, 171n45, 49
Caldecott, O., 139, 190n24–6, 28, 191n38
Calderon de la Barca, P., 62, 175n5
Calfe, P., 169n27
Campbell, J., 120
Carey, J., 103, 133, 190n11, 12
Carleton, W., 125
Carlson, M., 185n22, 186n31, 34
Carpenter, J., 19, 20, 167n38
Carr, H., 120, 187n6
Carroll, D., 164n16
Carruthers, M., 164n1
Carter, H., 168n3
Casper, S. E., 189n8
Castiglione, B., 47, 173n31
Cavallo, G., 181n8
Caxton, W., 87
Cennini, C., 41
Charles I, 31, 70
Charles II, 31
Chartier, A. -M., 191n5, 194n42
Chartier, R., 95, 165n9, 181n8
Chaucer, G., 10–14, 158, 165n6–7, 9, 12, 166n21
Chinitz, D. E., 188n23
Cicero, 48, 54, 58
Cicerone, 39
Clairmont, C., 64
Clare, J., 76
Clark, C., x, xi, xiii, 7, 75–88, 180n1, 4, 7–9, 13, 15, 17–20, 25
Clark, T., 179n63

Clyde, T., 123–4, 188n21, 24
Cochrane, L.G., 165n9
Coiro, A. B., 168n9, 172n58, 62
Colburn, H., 177n38
Coleman, J., 167n10
Collier, H., 167n37
Collins, W., 100
Collyer, W. B., 179n53
Conger, S. M., 174n1
Connolly, M., 166n17
Connolly, R., 7, 168n2
Cook, F. C., 176n10
Coolahan, M. -L., 168n10, 169n16
Cooper, J. F., 100
Copernicus, N., 45
Corns, T., 171n47, 172n64
Corrie, M., 167n34
Cowper, W., 75
Crane, M. T., 26, 169n20
Creaser, J., 24, 168n8, 169n13
Cremona, V. A., 184n1
Cresswell, L., 170n31
Crook, N., ix, 7–8, 174n9, 175n5
Crutchley, B., 190n22
Curran, S., 174n3, 176n24
Cutter, C. A., 100, 183n58

Dane, J., 191n7
Darnton, R., 3–4, 144, 164n15, 166n18, 191n8
Davis, H., 168.n3
Davis, A., x, 7
Davis, J., 185n20
Davis, T. C., 117, 185n12, 186n37
Decembrio, A., 38
De Keijser, M. L., 193n26
Deen, N., 193n39, 201
Den Hertog, C. H., 192n12, 193n35
Derby, J. C., 104, 106
Derrida, J., 5, 164n16
Descartes, R., 45
De Vooys, C. G. N., 193n29
De Vos, H., 192n 15
De Vries, J., 193n33
Diels, P. A., 193n40
Dickens, C., xi, 5, 89–106, 181n3–5n8, 182n11n20–1, 183n68–9n74, 184n78
Dibdin, T. F., 79, 82, 85, 87, 180n2

Dixon, H., 77, 79
Dixon, J. W., 62
Dobranksi, S., 26, 168n11, 169n23
Domenichi, L., 44
Ducharme, D., 170n30
Duff, C., 132, 189n7
Duncan, T. G., 165n13
Dunhill, T. S., 126
Dunn, J. S., 76

Eagleton, T., 124, 188n28
Eberle-Sinatra, M., 174n9
Eckel, J., 181n4
Eckhardt, J., 170n42
Eco, U., 185n22
Edison, T., 146, 192n18
Edwards, A. S. G., 165n14
Egerton, F. H., 80
Eglinton, J. (W. K. Magee), 124, 188n29
Ehrlich, H., 190n10
Eisenstein, E., 164n3, 171n43
Elam, K., 186n31
Eldar, A. M., 192n20
Eliot, T. S., 24, 53, 119, 122, 168n7, 186n3,
    187n13, 188n23
Eliot, S., 2, 163n5
Ellis, A., 191n7
Ellis, S., 165n7
Ellmann, R., 139, 141, 190n28
Emeljanow, V., 185n20
Equicola, M., 38
Ernst, M., 141
Evans, R., 165n9
Eversmann, P., 184n2, 186n31
Everest, K., 175n34 n5, 177n38
Exman, E., 102, 183n67

Federman, M., 194n4
Feldman, P., 177n26
Fein, S., 166n26, 167n34
Fiedler, L., 190n10
Fields, J., 105, 184n83
Finkelstein, D., 163n1, 164n18, 190n15
Finneran, R., 129, 188n33, 189n44
Fisch, A. A., 174n1, 176n23
Fischer, S. R., 143, 191n2
Fish, S., 2, 6, 163n6
FitzGerald, M., 129, 189n44

Fletcher, J. G., 120
Flint, K., 181n8
Forman, H. B., 74, 178n42
Fox, A., 172n61
Fowler, A., 172n58
Fraisse. E. de, 191n5
Frank, F. S., 174n1
Fraistat, N., ix, 64, 67, 70, 175n5, 176n23,
    177n35 n37
Frazier, A., 188n38
Freedley, E. T., 103
Friel, B., 131
Frost, E., 190n23
Fryer, E., 172n2
Fuller, T., 31, 171n46
Fuller, P., 140, 191
Fuseli, H., 7, 37, 39–40, 44, 50, 172n4 n5,
    173n20

Galileo, 45
Garnett, R., 61, 175n6
Gaskell, P., 6, 164n23, 168n3
Genette, G., 139, 163n2, 190n31
Gerson, J., 19
Gielen, J. J., 193n33
Gilbert, S., 138
Gillespie, A., 166n21, 167n37
Glisson, H., 29, 170n35
Godthelp, H., 194n43
Godwin, A., 137, 190n23
Godwin, W., x, 52, 53, 56, 70, 177n38,
    179n54
Goethe, J. W. von, 175n5
Gorter, H., 194n46
Gorving, D. H., 98
Goslee, N. M., 73, 179n64
Gould, W., 129, 187n15, 189n45
Graham, P., 179n50
Grant, U. S., 94
Greenspan, E., 182n30
Griffin, C., x, xi
Griffin, G., 125
Griffith, A., 124
Griffiths, J., 165n4, 166n21
Griswold, R., 102
Grusin, R., 194n3, 198
Gunn, I., 189n1
Gustavus Adolphus of Sweden, 29
Gyles, A., 121

Hall, M. C., 173n16
Haltunnen, K., 182n15
Hanna, R., 165n16, 167n36
Harmar, J., 171n44
Hart-Davis, R., 188n41
Hare, H. R., 91
Harper, F., 103
Harty, K. J., 165n7
Harvey, J., 80, 83
Hassan, I., 186 n3
Hayes, I. I., 89, 180n1, 181n2
Hazlitt, W., 69, 177n38, 179n51
Hébrard, J., 191n5, 194n42
Hellinga, L., 164n3
Helper, H. R., 95, 182n32
Henry I, 19
Henry III, 16
Henry V, 19
Herford Percy, C. H., 171n56
Herrick, R., 23–36
Hesse, H., 139
Hettema, F. B., 193n27
Heuser, T., 167n31
Heuser, W., 166n30
Hill, R., 19, 167n35
Hills, J., 30, 170n39
Hind, R., 169n28
Hilton, J., 195n7
Hobbs, M., 170n40
Hobhouse, J. C., 178n50
Hoccleve, T., 14
Hogle, J. E., 179n63
Holbrook, J., 95, 182n28
Holme, R., 171n51
Holtrop, M., 193n40
Hood, T., 76, 77
Horace, 28, 34, 171n56
Hughes, L. K., 91, 92, 97, 182 n11
Hunt, J., 67–70, 177 n39, 178n43, 48, 50
Hunt, L., 64, 66, 67, 179n51
Hunt, M., 64
Hunt, T., 31
Hunter, A. 139
Hutchinson, T., 74, 175n5
Hutton, C., 189n4
Hyde, D., 123, 126

Idenburg, P. J., 193n33
Inghirami, T., 47–9, 173n31

Ingram, R., 26, 169n22, 171n50
Ingpen, R., 177n41
Iser, W., 2, 163n6
Isherwood, C., 120, 121, 187n9

Jeffares, N. A., 188n41
Johannes, G.-J., 191n7
Johnson, G. W., 76, 180n7
Johnson, J., 39
Johnson, L., 125
Johnstone, E., 100
Joicey, N., 190n21
Jones, W. P., 132, 189n9
Jonson, B., 23, 168n13, 171n56
Joost-Gaugier, C., 47, 173n31
Joukovsky, N., 176n14
Joyce, J., x, 8, 121, 123, 131–41, 164n27,
    187n10, 190n10
Julius II, 47–50, 173n31
Justinian, 48

Kafka, F., 186n3
Kalff, G., 192n10
Kalmthout, T. van, xii, 7, 143
Kaplan, C., 119, 120, 187n4
Karsemeijer, J., 192n21, 193n30, 194n48
Kazemier, G., 193n30, 194n48
Keats, J., 177n38
Kelly, J., 134, 188n40, 190n16
Kelly, S., 166n19
Kemp, M., 172n1
Kenner, H., 133
Ker, N., 206
Kickham, C., 125
Kingsford, C. L., 167n38
Kinsella, T., 187n17
Knowles, J., 172n5
Kohnstamm, P., 193n39
Kramer, W., 193n40
Kuczynski, M., 166n26

Lamb, C., 177n38
Landor, W. S., 177n38
Landow, G., 157, 195n5
Lane, A., xi, 134–40
Langeveld, M. J., 152, 193n40, 194n41, 43
Lanier, N., 171n54
Lawrence, D. H., 132, 138, 189n5
Leader, Z., 53, 54, 174n14

Leask, N., 172n10
Leest, J., 151, 192n9, 193n34
Legouvé, E., 192n20
Lenihan, L., vii, x, 7, 37
Lernout, G., 131, 189n2
Léon, P., 155, 190n18
Leo X, 47
L'Estrange, T., 63, 176n14
Lindquist, E. N., 171n43
Lodge, D. 8, 164 n27
Long, Baron Farnborough, C., 80
López-Varela Azcárate, A., 195n6
Love, N., 167n36
Lovelace, R. L., 171n44
Lowenstein, J., 169n19
Lowery, H., 189n1
Lucas, A., 167n32
Lukács, G., 138
Lund, M., 182n11
Lydgate, J., 14, 19, 20, 21, 167n38
Lyons, M., 91, 181n9

Macauley, T., 100
Mallarmé, S., 120, 211
Manguel, A., 143, 191n3
Man, P. de, 48, 49, 173n33
Marotti, A., 169n16
Mark, T., 129, 130
Marryat, F., 93
Marshall, W. H., 178n47
Masters, J. W., 77
Martin, L. C., 168n12
Martyn, E., 123
Massey, I., 64, 176n21, 178n45
Matthew, N., 191n39
Matthews, G. M., 65, 175n5, 177n34
Mayer, D., 108, 109, 112, 113, 117, 184n7,
     185n9, 186n38
Mays, J. C. C., 188n39
McCleery, A., vii, x, 7, 131, 190n15, 191n39
McConachie, B. A., 185n22
McDonald, P. D., 190n15
McDowell, N., 168n13
McElrath, T. L., 103
McFarlane, J., 187n19
McGann, J. J., 1, 2, 6, 163n3–4 , 7, 187n7,
     14, 194n1
McGill, M., 90, 181n5
McHale, B., 186n3

McKenzie, D. F., xi, 6, 163n1, 164n23
McParland, R., xi, 5, 89
McPherson, E. M., 182n22
Medici, Duke Cosimo, 43
Mellor, A. K., 55, 58, 174n15, 175n27
Melville, H., 160
Merkel, C. K., xiii, 147
Miall, D. S., 95, 96, 182n34
Michelangelo, 40, 43, 44, 172n8
Mierlo, W. van, 187n10, 192n15
Millar, A., 39
Milligan, A., 123
Milton, J., 37
Minnis, A. J., 167n40
Mishkin, T., 129, 189n47
Monfort, S. de, 16
Moody, N., 191n39
Mooney, L. R., 166n17–18, 167n40
Moore, B., 138
Moore, G., 125
Moormann, J. G. M., 192n11, 193n33
Morgan, N., 165n4
Morley, F., 190n18
Morris, I., 138
Morrisson, M. S., 123, 124, 187n19,
     188n22, 25
Moss, A., 33, 171n56
Moss, S., 184n80
Moxon, J., 168n3
Moxon, E., 63, 71, 74, 179n57
Mullally, E., 167n37
Murphy, O., xi, 8, 155
Murphy, W. M., 187n17
Murray, E. B., 179n68
Murray, H. M. R., 16, 167n35
Myrone, M., 172n4

Nadel, I. B., 139, 190n30
Nansogg, M., 28, 170n28
Nascher, I. L., 97, 183n39
Newey, V., 197
Newton, Sir Issac, 45
Nichols, S., 166n17
Nijland, A., 149, 150, 193n32
Norris, J., 29
Norton, J., 29

O'Brien, J., 108, 117, 184n6, 185n15, 186n39
O'Callaghan, M., 168n13
O'Connell, M., x, xi, 75
O'Dea, G., 174n1
O'Donnell, W. H., 187n18
O'Halloran, M., 167n1
Oldmeadow, E. J., 126
Ollier, C., 67, 177n38, 178n42
O'Neill, M., 64, 68, 176n24, 178n46, 179n68
Ong, W. J., 164n1
'O. T. D.', 61, 63
Ostrowski, C., 183n52
Ovid, 32

Paden, W. D., 166n17
Palacio, J. de, 64, 176n21
Palland, B. G., 194n43
Parkes, M. B., 165n16
Partington, C. F., 177n30
Patten, R., 101, 102, 181n4, 183n59
Pawley, C., 99, 183n51
Peacock, T. L., 176n14
Pearsall, D., 165n4, 166n21, 167n40
Pearson, D., 6, 164n23
Peters, J. S., 108, 109, 184n4, 185n15
Peterson, T. B., 102–4
Pirsig, R., 139
Plato, 43, 52, 63
Plomer, H., 78, 180n14, 209
Pond, J., 78
Pond, M. A., 76
Pontormo, 44
Pompougnac, J. C., 191n5
Pound, E., 53, 120, 122, 123
Poullain, M., 191n5
Postlewait, T., 184n1, 185n22
Pressly, W. L., 49, 173n38
Pugh, S., 35, 168n9, 170n29, 172n64
Puttfarken, T., 44, 173n21
Putnam, G. P., 102, 104, 106

Quinn, J., 128, 188n41

Raben, J., 64, 176n20
Radway, J., 5, 164n18
Rainey, L., 132, 133, 188n20, 189n3

Raphael, 37, 43, 44, 47–50, 173n31
Raylor, T., 168n13
Reid, D. A., 113, 115, 185n25
Reiger, J., 54, 174n16
Reiman, D. H., ix, 53, 175n31, 33, 5, 176n15
Reinhardt, M., 136, 137, 190n23
Reynolds, J., x, 37, 40
Reynolds, P., 124, 188n25
Richardson, A., 191n7
Richards, I. A., 121
Rieu, E. V., 141
Robinson, C. E., 52–4, 174n4, 16, 17, 177n38, 178n42
Roosevelt, R. B., 95
Roosevelt, T., 95
Rosand, D., 42, 173n14
Rose, J., 2, 5, 93, 163n5, 8, 164n19, 181n3, 5, 182n18, 30, 191n4
Rosenheim, A., 189n1
Ross, M., 123
Rossetti, W. M., 63–6, 72, 176n15, 6
Rota, A., 6, 164n23
Rubens, 37
Ruggle, G., 30
Rusling, J. F., 94–5, 182n25

Salt, H. S., 61, 175n4
Sadlier, M., 102
Salverda de Grave, J. J., 192n19
Sargent, M. G., 166n18
Scase, W., 166n19, 166n29
Scattergood, J., 165n14, 166n26
Scheidt, L., 194n2
Schepers, J. B., 193n31
Scherer, J., 187n11
Schlicke, P., 181n4
Schmoller, H., 138, 190n27
Schneiders, A. J., 192n14
Schriebman, S., 194n1, 195n14
Schuchard, R., 188n40
Schor, E. H., 174n1
Scott-Kilvert, D., 177n26
Scott, Sir Walter, 57–9, 100, 175n32
Seagull, J. L., 139
Seneca, 48
Senn, F., 140, 191n32, 33
Shakespeare, W., 37, 99, 100, 117, 146, 160

Shapcott, T., 168 n11
Sharrat, B., 185n25
Shelley, Lady Jane, 61
Shelley, M. W., ix, 7, 51–9, 61–74,
  174n1–4n9–10n15n17,
  175n27n32, 176n20–4, 177n25–
  6n28n30n36n38n40, 178n44n48,
  179n52, n54–8
Shelley, P. B., 53–9, 61–74, 174n4n15,
  17, 175n31–2n34n4–5n8–9,
  176n14n16n18–21n 23–4,
  177n27–8n38n41, 178n42–5n47–9,
  179n54n57n62–5n68
Sherman, W. H., 171n43
Shevlin, E. F., 171n43
Shillingsburg, P. L., 189n46
Shrank, C., 171n52
Siemens, R., 194n1
Sigerson, G., 126
Simons, J., 165n15
Simpson, D., 172n10
Simpson, J., 165n5
Simpson, E., 171n56
Slote, S., 120, 187n10
Smith, A., 100
Smith, H., 67
Smith, J. R., 76, 77, 78, 79, 83, 85, 86, 88,
  180n8n17n19n24
Smith, W., 181n4
Smyth, A., 169n24
Sperberg-McQueen, M., 160, 195n10
Squire, J. C., 187n13
St Clair, W., 5, 51, 52, 164n21, 174n3,
  179n67, 191n4
Stemvers, F. G. A., 193n25, 194n45, 194n48
Sterne, L., 39, 172n6
Stern, M. B., 184n85
Steward, Sir Simeon, 27, 29, 168n11
Strohm, P., 165 n9–10, 200
Stowe, H. B., 94, 182n24
Stubbin, S., 170n36,
Stow, J., 19, 167n38
Sullivan, J. A., xi, 7, 107, 184, 185n12
Sutherland, J., 190n25
Somerville, E., 123
Swann, M., 34, 172 n58–9
Swanson, R. N., 167n32
Sweet, E., 96, 182n33

Swinburne, C. A., 61, 66, 177n31
Synge, J. M., 125

Tabor, J., 29, 170n35
Tanselle, G. T., 188n43
Taylor, A., 165n15
Taylor, Jr, C. H., 64
Taylor, J., 177n38, 198
Taylor, M., 115, 184n2, 186n31–2
Tebbel, J., 103, 104, 105, 183n71, 76,
  184n79n89n87
Tennyson, Alfred, Lord, 117
Thackeray, W. M., 100, 105
Thales, 45
Thompson, A., 188n27
Thompson, J. J., vii, xii, 7, 9, 164, 165n15,
  166n17n19n21n29, 167n37
Thorney, R., 19
Thomson, R. M., 165n4
Tibullus, 32
Tilley, C., 163n9
Tillotson, K., 91, 182n11, 183n68
Titian, 37, 43, 173n14, 173n21
Toomey, D., 189n45
Tötösy de Zepetnek, S., 157, 195n6
Trapp, J. B., 164n3
Trilling, L., 138
Tucker, J., 191n1
Turner, C., 189n8
Tusser, T., 76, 82
Tynan, K., 123

Ubersfeld, A., 186n31
Ulrich, C. F., 187n19
Unsworth, J., 194n1
Upward, E., 120, 121, 187n9, 12

Van Ginneken, J., 193n13
Van der Hoeve, A. H., 193n39
Van der Laan, J. E., 194n46–7
Van der Meij, H. W., 192n16, 193n36
Van Meurs, B., 194n44
Van Veen, G., 193n38–40
Van Wijk, N., 192 n13
Vasari, G., 43–4, 173n19
Venn, J., 170n28n33n35
Venn, J. A., 170n28n33
Vere, G. du C. de, 173n19

Verhagen, B., 192n17
Vinci, L. da, 38, 42, 172n1
Viterbo, E. da, 38, 42, 172n1
Vogel, A., 192n17
Volterra, D. da, 44

Wade, A., 188n41
Waldman, G., 55, 190n25
Walker, M., 172n1
Wall, W., 25, 169n15n18
Ward, A., 93
Warnock, G. J., 138
Warren, F., 167n39
Warfield, C. A. (Ware), 95
Washburne, E. B., 94
Webb, T., ix, 177n39, 178n48n50,
    179n63n68
Weekes, J., 27, 169n28
Weinberg, A. 179 n63
Wenzel, S., 167n33–4
Wexler, J. P., 189n4
Whaley, T., 30, 170n38
White, B., 167n38
Whitehead, J., 29
Wiley, D., 195n7
Wilkins, W. G., 181n4

Willard, F. E., 92–3, 182n16
William the Conqueror, 19
Williams, E. B., 175n6
Williams, J., 31, 171n46
Williams, W. C., 138
Wingfield, J., 29
Wise, T., 178n43
Witemeyer, H., 188n32
Wittmann, R., 91, 181n10
Wollstonecraft, M., x, 55, 56, 175n32,
    176n24
Wolfson, S., 64, 70, 176n23
Woolf, V., 121
Woolsey, J. M., 141
Woudhuysen, H. R., 169n13
Wroe, A., 179n63

Yeats, E. (Lolly), 187n17
Yeats, G., 128–9, 129, 130
Yeats, J. B., 122
Yeats, S. (Lily), 187n17
Yeats, W. B., 7, 119–30, 186, 187n15–18,
    188n27n30n32–8n40–2, 189n44–5n48
Youngman, P. H., 76, 79, 85, 180n9

Zboray, R. J., 184n90

www.ingramcontent.com/pod-product-compliance
Ingram Content Group UK Ltd.
Pitfield, Milton Keynes, MK11 3LW, UK
UKHW020354010325
455677UK00021B/459